The Good, the Bad and the Unacceptable

The Good, the Bad and the Unacceptable

The Hard News about the British Press

RAYMOND SNODDY

faber and faber

LONDON · BOSTON

First published in 1992
by Faber and Faber Limited
3 Queen Square London WC1N 3AU

Phototypeset by Intype, London
Printed in England by Clays Ltd, St Ives Plc

A CIP record for this book is available from the British
Library
ISBN 0-571-16153-7

To Diana, Julia and Oliver

Contents

Acknowledgements

The people who deserve most thanks for helping to ensure this book came to be written are the entire team of the original *Hard News* programme and the miscreants of Fleet Street who kept them so busy. Special thanks are due to Bernard Clark, the man who came up with the idea of the programme, editor Paul Woolwich and deputy editor Lorraine Heggessey, and also to researcher and assistant producer Eamon Hardy, who nosed out for me newspaper glories and scandals from the past in the archives of the Newspaper Library at Colindale.

I am also grateful to the UK's five most famous newspaper proprietors – Conrad Black, the late Robert Maxwell, Rupert Murdoch, Viscount Rothermere and Lord Stevens – who were all generous with their time. Others who were enormously helpful with interviews and advice include Lord McGregor, Sir Frank Rogers, Andrew Knight, Max Hastings, Andreas Whittam Smith, David Montgomery, Brian MacArthur, Arthur Brittenden, Richard Harwood, Sheila Black, Ken Morgan, Dr Sally Taylor, Brian Park, Vyvyan Harmsworth, Professor Hugh Stephenson, Professor Jean-Claude Seargent, Peter Bottomley, Tom Evans, David Chipp, Margaret Jay, Michael Garcia, Jane Reed and Keith Parker. I will particularly remember the time spent with Roy Maddison, editor of the *Whitehaven News*, should I ever need reminding of what honest journalism in the public interest is really about.

I am grateful to Matthew Evans, chairman of Faber and Faber, who sought me out; to Susanne McDadd and Julian Loose, my editors at Faber and Faber, who know very well how to get completed books out of dissembling journalists; and to my agent Arthur Goodhart, who went far beyond the call of duty in helping to turn a glimmer of an idea into reality. I am also very glad that I had the services of the eagle eyes of Bob

Davenport, who edited the text and whose skills saved me from considerable embarrassment.

For any remaining errors and misjudgements the responsibility is, of course, mine.

Finally, my thanks to Diana, Julia and Oliver for their forbearance. They now know only too well what it means when a daily newspaper journalist starts writing a book in his 'spare time'.

Foreword

At a dinner given in honour of the US ambassador specializing in communications policy on 18 October 1991, conversation touched on the topical issues of sexual harassment and the newly awarded TV franchises and then turned to the press. It was time to legislate, to do something to protect the privacy of the individual from the prying eyes of an irresponsible press, insisted a City of London financier. Another guest, Leonard Marks, an American lawyer and former ambassador, was equally forthright: the only law that the UK needed on the press was a single bill, drawing on the US constitution, to stipulate that no government shall do anything to abridge the freedom of the press or the right to free expression.

The difference and tension between those two opinions express well what this book is about. Has the press in Britain gone so far that only legislation can curb its arrogance and mitigate the hurt caused to individuals by insensitive and incompetent reporting? Or is there, as many Americans tend to believe, a more fundamental truth involved: the cost of a press that is sometimes irresponsible and wrong is still a small price to pay for liberty?

The debate is far from being an academic one. Kenneth Baker, the Home Secretary, assured me during that same week in October that the government would be reluctant to introduce legislation to curb the press; but at the same time he was greatly concerned about how the case of Sir Allan Green – who resigned as Director of Public Prosecutions after being stopped by the police for alleged kerb-crawling – had been handled by the press. The point was not how Sir Allan himself had been treated but how his family had been hounded and harassed in the days after the incident when, in the wake of a ruined career, they had gone on holiday to Majorca. Something might have to be done, the Home Secretary suggested, to protect the privacy of families and those not directly involved.

The press in the UK is on probation as never before. A succession of ministers have, like Kenneth Baker, made it very clear that Lord McGregor's Press Complaints Commission represents probably the last chance for self-regulation of the press, and that if it does not work then legislation will almost certainly follow. David Mellor, now chief secretary to the Treasury, put the warning in colourful language when he was a Home Office minister. 'Some sections of the press are drinking at the Last Chance Saloon.' Senior Labour politicians such as Roy Hattersley are just as unambiguous.

This book explores issues of press standards and freedoms not just in the contemporary press but also through the eyes of heroes and villains of the past. It is not a history of the press, but it recognizes that such important matters as the abolition of pre-publication press censorship in 1695 and the removal between 1853 and 1861 of heavy duties on advertising and paper and of the compulsory stamp duty are of continuing relevance. And any book which even mentions press freedom must take its cue from John Milton's *Areopagitica* (1644): 'Promiscuous reading is necessary to the constituting of human nature. The attempt to keep out evil doctrine by licensing is like the exploit of that gallant man who thought to keep out the crows by shutting the park gate ... Give me the liberty to know, to utter and to argue according to conscience, above all liberties.'

I would like to be able to say that I wrote this book because I woke up one morning worrying about the freedom of the press and how the activities of some newspapers were threatening to undermine it in the UK – and that I then went on to muse about whether current standards of journalism really were in a free fall compared with other eras in press history, or whether the public, or at least influential sections of it, were merely becoming more sensitive, more demanding. The truth is however, that the treadmill to which the national daily newspaper journalist voluntarily chains himself is not naturally conducive to contemplation or reflection. The time frame is set. The clock is running and the telephone is already ringing. The most pressing need is to meet each day's deadline without making a catastrophic error or being made to look totally stupid by the opposition. Instead the origins of this book lie, like most human ventures, in chance and coincidence.

One afternoon in September 1988 a television producer called Bernard Clark called with an invitation to lunch. Not another independent trying to get publicity for an obscure programme on Channel 4, was my immediate thought. But he was insistent and a few days later I was in the back room of Bertorelli's in Charlotte Street facing a persuasive if rather scruffy figure who simply said: 'I'm doing a new programme on the press. I'd like you to present it.' No 'maybes' or 'would you like to be considered for . . .' Bernard Clark had made up his mind and the fact that I was a newspaper reporter with only scraps of television experience did not enter into it. I later discovered that Clark had been in the audience during a debate I chaired at the Edinburgh International Television Festival some weeks previously, and had made his decision there and then. There were no screen tests for me, which is probably just as well.

On 6 April 1989 the first edition of *Hard News* went on the air. Under the headline 'Toytown Tales Time' a reviewer of one of the early programmes, John Russell of the *Sunday Express*, described me as coming across 'like a domestic appliance salesman who is halfway through an assertion course'. Less certainly, Russell went on to suggest that the only interesting thing about the programme was the presenter's surname. 'Why don't they find someone called Raymond Bigears and make them a double act?' the *Sunday Express* added.

Hard News won a Royal Television Society award for its journalism and a Freedom of Information award from the Campaign for Freedom of Information. That it survived at all – never mind managing to break new ground in television coverage of the press – is a tribute to the tenacity and courage of founding editor Paul Woolwich, who went on to become editor of *This Week*. The programme proved, if proof be needed, how sensitive the press is to the merest hint that anything they do might be less than totally perfect. Woolwich faced what seemed a never-ending barrage of criticism, with editors and even an occasional proprietor screaming down the phone. Then there were complaints to the Broadcasting Complaints Commission – all won, except on matters of detail – and threats of injunctions. A libel writ is still outstanding from Mirror Group Newspapers.

This is not the book of the programme, although the stories told in the first chapter of the treatment two men received at the hands of national newspapers were covered in the first edition of *Hard News* and in the forty-eighth, the last I presented. But my abiding memory from that period is of the unwillingness of most newspapers to engage in any debate about standards and where the line should be drawn between the public's legitimate right to know and the destroying of private lives, and this is I think a central weakness. It certainly sets the British press apart from newspapers in the US, where on the whole the word 'ethics' can be uttered without hoots of derision.

The point of the book is ultimately a very simple one. It is that all journalists, broadsheet no less than tabloid, have got to make the time to get off the treadmill of deadlines to think a little more about what they do, the effect it can have on their fellow citizens and the impact their work is having on the reputation of the press. It is already nearly too late to avoid new government-imposed press restrictions.

1

'My whole world had fallen apart' The state of the press in the late 1980s

TOM Evans and Peter Bottomley have never met and they have little obvious in common. Evans is a British Rail ticket-collector at the south-London station of Herne Hill. Bottomley is a former Transport Minister, Conservative MP for Eltham and husband of Virginia Bottomley, the Health Minister. Dissimilar though they are, however, they have shared one traumatic experience: both have been the subject of hurtful and damaging headlines in tabloid Sunday newspapers.

Tom Evans received a 'page lead' (the main headline) in the *Sunday Mirror*, Robert Maxwell's mass-market Sunday paper, on 31 July 1988 in the most tragic of circumstances, after his Greek wife, Irene, and two of their three daughters died in a forest fire on the Greek holiday island of Cephalonia. A colour portrait of the Evans family shared the front page with a 'splash' claiming that film star Liz Taylor was facing a delicate spine operation that could leave her a cripple. Inside the hard-hitting paper, which competes directly with the *News of the World* and likes unusual human-interest stories, was the Evans piece, accompanied by two further photographs.

From the *Sunday Mirror*'s point of view this was not just a routine story of an overwhelming personal tragedy: an unusual twist had attracted the newspaper's attention. The headline on the Evans story read 'Blaze Tragedy Father's Ordeal'. But it was the 'strap' – the smaller subsidiary headline on top of the main headline – that gave the true flavour of the story: 'Greedy Greek undertakers force grieving husband to dig wife's grave.' This morbid claim is one that Evans has always denied and it is still the cause of bad feeling between him and his Greek relatives, who believed him responsible for what appeared in the paper.

Peter Bottomley, an MP in a marginal constituency, suffered a different kind of loss – a loss of reputation. On 21 May 1989 he found himself the front-page lead in the *Mail on Sunday* under one of the most compelling headlines a Sunday tabloid can serve up: 'Minister in Sex Case Row.' It was just the sort of racy political story that had helped Lord Rothermere's *Mail on Sunday* to overtake the *Sunday Express* and dominate the middle of the market. But this one wasn't true. The first paragraph of the story claimed that Peter Bottomley had been formally interviewed in the House of Commons by the head of the Obscene Publications Squad. He hadn't. Yet the story went on to give the clear impression that a government minister had somehow been involved in a sex scandal involving children. Again, this was not true.

These two examples are perhaps not quite in the same class as the more notorious of recent press excesses, such as the hounding of television presenter Russell Harty as he lay dying from the liver disease hepatitis B in June 1988, the reports which ended in the *Sun* paying £1 million in an out-of-court settlement to pop singer Elton John in December that year, and the murders and mutilations that never were in the Strangeways prison riot of April 1989. Yet the similarities in the experiences of Tom Evans and Peter Bottomley say a lot about the state of the British press, its news values and its working methods. Both articles were almost certainly written without personal malice or vindictiveness. In the case of Tom Evans, the story sprang from the continual need to find something interesting and unusual to put in each Sunday's paper. It was a story that would be sold on a single emotional and xenophobic image: a man forced to dig his wife's grave because of uncaring and uncivilized foreigners. With Peter Bottomley there was the even greater thrill of perhaps undermining a government minister, and the tantalizing possibility of a more exciting follow-up: 'Minister Resigns Over Sex Row.'

Both stories demonstrate how much damage and hurt can be caused when news values take precedence over human values: when the hunt for a story or pressure from their news editors takes journalists, deliberately or sometimes almost casually, beyond what is accurate, justifiable or even in their own best interests.

Subsequent events showed how the distance between ticket-collector and minister in terms of power, influence, knowledge and wealth greatly affected their options for redress. After failing to get satisfaction from the *Sunday Mirror*, Tom Evans complained to the Press Council, which was then the newspaper industry's complaints body. It took nearly a year for the Press Council to find in his favour and censure the *Sunday Mirror* in its adjudication.

When the *Mail on Sunday* story appeared, Peter Bottomley was able to phone journalists he knew personally and warn them that the claims were untrue. He then immediately issued a writ against the newspaper. Five months later a settlement was announced in the High Court. Lawyers for Associated Newspapers, publishers of the *Mail on Sunday*, accepted that the suggestion that Bottomley had been guilty of misconduct was false and baseless and agreed to pay 'a sum in damages appropriate to the seriousness of the libel and to vindicate Mr Bottomley's reputation'. No numbers were mentioned in court, but the amount is thought to be around £250,000.

How did these two stories come about, and how did their victims deal with them?

Peter Bottomley has always had a constructive relationship with journalists. As Transport Minister he has often enlisted their help to publicize road-safety campaigns and in the battle against drunken drivers. In the past, when journalists rang up to check a story and he told them it was untrue, his word had always been accepted.

According to Bottomley, the *Mail on Sunday* affair began in the most routine way with a case brought to his constituency surgery in 1987. A constituent who worked as a social worker in a children's home complained that he was being unfairly expelled from membership of the Transport and General Workers' Union. Bottomley was the perfect Conservative MP to approach on such an issue. Not only was he a long-standing member of the union, he was also president of the Conservative Trade Unionists and a fellow of the Institute of Personnel Management. He knew that you could not simply be thrown out of a union: the proper procedures had to be followed. He wrote immediately to TGWU Secretary Ron Todd and an investigation was promised. A year later he received a copy of the union appeal findings. Procedures had not been followed; the constituent was reinstated and his full union rights were restored. One small local dispute had been satisfactorily resolved with the help of a conscientious constituency MP.

That, as far as Peter Bottomley was aware, was all there was to it – except that he had started getting strange phone calls from journalists asking whether he was involved in child abuse. Although he does not know for certain who was responsible, he believes that false rumours were deliberately spread about him, probably by political opponents or by someone who may have resented his intervention in the union case. There had been completely unsubstantiated rumours that the social worker had been involved in child abuse in the children's home where he worked. Bottomley found himself

3

associated with these stories because he had helped oppose the social worker's expulsion from his union.

He noticed that the outbreaks of rumour and the calls from journalists seemed in some way to be linked to the progress of the hearings involving the social worker. One call, according to Bottomley, 'was from an *Evening Standard* journalist, one from someone who knows me on the *Sunday Telegraph* asking if I was a paedophile. I said no, and they seemed to accept that.'

Earlier calls included one from Jeremy Hands of Independent Radio News, who had apparently been given a story that Britain's Transport Minister was involved in drug-smuggling. Peter Bottomley denied the allegation, but three months later *Private Eye* ran a story claiming, he said, that 'half the country's media had been holed up in a hotel in Basingstoke waiting for me to turn up with the money to collect the drugs – a hoax.'

Matters became more sinister when on Monday 15 May 1989, seventeen months after Bottomley's original interview with his constituent, two Scotland Yard police officers appeared at his office at the Department of Transport asking for a private word. Did he know that damaging stories were being spread about him in his constituency? He did – would the officers like to see the original case notes? They were on their way to lunch and declined. The discussion lasted about two minutes and, as with the strange phone calls from journalists and the warnings from local councillors that someone was trying to set him up, Peter Bottomley thought no more of it – until Friday of that week.

While he was launching an initiative on motorcycle safety, a *Mail on Sunday* journalist rang and asked if he could come to see him immediately. When the journalist arrived, he asked what Bottomley knew about the social worker. He was offered copies of the minister's case notes and the letter to Ron Todd.

According to Peter Bottomley, the discussion lasted only three or four minutes. But, much to the minister's surprise, as the journalist was about to leave he asked about the visit earlier in the week by Scotland Yard detectives. 'I wouldn't discuss it with him,' Bottomley recalls.

Next in line, during the same lunch-time, was the *Sunday Mirror*. This time Bottomley taped his conversation with a journalist who said she had for some weeks been working on an investigation on the social worker involved and was particularly interested in Bottomley's attempts to help him. The MP told the reporter his questions contained defamatory innuendoes and refused to comment on any of them: he simply told the reporter

that he had met the social worker involved once, on 15 De[
about a union matter, and that had been the extent of his invol

Peter Bottomley, now seriously concerned, tried to get in touch
the journalists' editors. There was no reply from the *Sunday Mi*
Bottomley, who reads books about the press and knows a great deal ab(
workings, arranged through lawyers that he would be informed in advan(
the paper was planning to print anything about him so that the paper's
printing schedule would not be disrupted by late-night injunctions. (A judge
can issue a temporary injunction at any hour of the day or night to prevent
publication of an article until there can be a full hearing if he thinks the
article could be defamatory or injure someone's rights.) The *Sunday Mirror*
did not print the Bottomley story.

Sir David English, editor-in-chief of the *Daily Mail* and the *Mail on
Sunday*, did return Peter Bottomley's call. The minister told him, 'I don't
expect you to know what every one of your journalists is doing all the time,
but I think you are about to launch yourself into a mightily defamatory story
and I want you to know very clearly that I will sue.' The minister believed
he had an understanding with Sir David that nothing defamatory would be
printed about him unless it was true. He thought that was the end of the
affair.

On Saturday, Bottomley went off to watch the Cup Final at Wembley
before going on to visit a constituency friend in hospital.

'At 8.30 p.m. I called home after coming away from the bedside of my
friend and the world had fallen apart. Everyone was ringing. People were
starting to besiege my house.'

He drove straight to Blackfriars, to the back door of what was then the
Mail on Sunday office. He asked the man at the door if there was any
chance of having a paper and got his 50p ready. The man looked at the
minister, looked under his desk at the front page of the paper, looked again
and handed Bottomley a copy. He refused to take the 50p.

'There was my face and the headline which effectively destroyed everything I'd done in thirteen or fourteen years as a member of Parliament and
was potentially wrecking my family life, destroying my reputation. My whole
world had fallen apart. It was worse than being in the middle of bombs
during a riot in central America. I felt worse than the time when I was
looking at the fans who died in the Heysal stadium,' Peter Bottomley recalls.
'I have been involved with various nasty things in my life as an observer,
and occasionally as a participant. In two or three seconds I could see
everything that mattered to me going – my voluntary organizations con-

cerned with family welfare and child welfare, my family, my job, my chances of future jobs – everything just torn up and thrown away.'

He wasn't involved in a sex scandal and he hadn't been formally interviewed by the head of the Obscene Publications Squad. Without those claims the rest of the story wasn't a story and would have been completely incomprehensible to the average reader, Bottomley believes.

The Transport Minister acted immediately to try to limit the damage caused by a report which he knew could cost him his seat, however large and fulsome any eventual retraction. First he phoned John Cole, political editor of BBC Television, to tell him the story was not true and that if anyone referred to it on air – even in a review of the Sunday papers – he would take legal action. He also called to warn IRN, which provides a national news service to Britain's commercial radio stations, and talked to Chris Moncrieff, the chief political correspondent of the Press Association, the organization that distributes UK news to newspapers and broadcasting organizations throughout the country.

Only two other national newspapers – the *News of the World* and the *Sunday Telegraph* – carried versions of the stories in later editions, and the *Telegraph* story was 'cleaned up'.

That Sunday, Scotland Yard put out a statement saying the *Mail* was inaccurate in reporting that Peter Bottomley had been formally interviewed. 'The *Mail on Sunday* should then have rung me up', Bottomley believes, 'and said, "We are sorry. Whether or not we should have ever published the story, we have now been told with the authority of Scotland Yard that we were wrong. We apologize. What can we do to put it right?" I would have said if they had issued a statement on Sunday lunch-time saying "Very sorry . . . we apologize" I would have forgotten about it. I might have asked that £10,000 be given to the campaign against drinking and driving or some other good cause, but that statement would have undone the damage straight away.'

But there was no apology or correction. In fact, the first indication Bottomley had that the *Mail on Sunday* was not going to contest the case and argue in court that its story was true came months later, on 10 September, when the paper unexpectedly published a front-page apology. By then, he believes, the damage had long since been done. Constituents told Virginia Bottomley that her husband was obviously a pervert. A member of his staff was asked what was it like working for a rapist. Other constituents – both Labour and Conservative supporters and those with no political affiliation

– told the MP that in such a marginal constituency the effect of the story could be 'to have him out'.

Lord Rothermere, owner of the *Mail on Sunday*, is unreservedly critical of the Bottomley story. 'I thought it was disgraceful. I complained bitterly to Stewart Steven [the paper's editor, who had been away on the weekend in question], who was very upset by it. It was a totally disgraceful front page. It was something completely out of character for the *Mail on Sunday*. It was puerile. It was playing on the name Bottomley – your name is Bottomley therefore you are interested in bottoms. It was really disgraceful. And it cost us a lot of money,' the *Mail on Sunday*'s proprietor conceded.

Peter Bottomley did indeed get some money. But because there was an out-of-court settlement there was only a brief statement in court apologizing both for the sex story and for a previous *Mail on Sunday* story falsely alleging that he had been given preferential treatment to protect his home from a local road by-pass scheme. The settlement received virtually no press coverage, and Bottomley fears that some of the mud will stick so far as the 20 per cent of his constituents who probably read the story are concerned, quite apart from the many more who heard of it by word of mouth. 'The damage can't be undone. My constituents will still have a lingering doubt. I am vulnerable,' he says, although he concedes that the *Mail on Sunday* has now done everything it can to put things right.

Peter Bottomley believes there are clear lessons for the press from his case. It is the legitimate job of the press to vacuum up every rumour, tip and guess – including rumours about someone like himself – and he accepts that it may be necessary for the press to have the freedom to get things wrong sometimes. But before stories are printed, every effort should be made to try to ensure they are true and, when newspapers do get things wrong, errors should be put right as quickly as possible – preferably accompanied by an apology.

From a newspaper's point of view, however, apologizing is not always a simple matter. It can take time for a complaint to be investigated to see whether a story is indeed wrong, and during that process lawyers will not want anything to appear – such as an apology – that could affect the outcome of a libel suit. Peter Bottomley has received substantial damages for his appearance on the front page of the *Mail on Sunday*, but to this day he has never received a personal apology from any of those involved – not even after the completion of the case.

Given his experience at the hands of the press, it is not surprising that Peter Bottomley has very clear views on press rights and responsibilities.

What is unexpected, considering what happened to him, is the line that he takes. When John Browne, the Winchester MP, introduced a private member's bill in 1989 to bring in a privacy law to curb the press, Bottomley was the only MP who voted against it, apart from the two tellers, and he hasn't changed his position since, despite what happened to him.

'I don't believe in using the law to limit the press. First of all the law won't make every member of the press behave well, and I never want to get to the position that a journalist has to have a licence from someone like me, in government, to do their job. The press must have the right to be wrong,' insists Bottomley. Indeed, he believes that journalists make as significant a contribution to public life as politicians do.

Peter Bottomley was able to take on a large newspaper organization and, to a considerable extent, win. Things were rather different for Tom Evans. His brush with the press began when he agreed to an interview with Lisa Baudains, a reporter from the Fleet Street News Agency. The interview took place in the canteen at the Queen Mary Hospital, Roehampton, where his surviving daughter, Angela was recovering from the accident that killed her mother and sisters. The reporter was following up a story on the tragedy in the local paper, the *South London Press*.

Tom Evans says his main motive in talking to the news-agency reporter was to thank those who had helped him, including the Greek authorities. That intention was certainly not reflected in the *Sunday Mirror*'s story about 'tragic Tom' who lost his wife and two children and was then forced to dig his wife's grave. Heartless Greek undertakers had refused to carry out the burial because he didn't have the £250 fee, so Evans, the story said, had helped to dig the grave in return for a 50 per cent discount. 'I begged them not to make me do it but they wouldn't listen,' the *Sunday Mirror* quoted Tom as saying. 'I couldn't believe I was being forced to dig my wife's grave.' The paper went on to report Evans as claiming that his family had been sent to their deaths by Greek police who directed them along a track which led to the fire.

This, then, was a story that had almost everything – tragedy, heartless foreigners and a compelling universal human image that made for riveting reading: a man forced by lack of money to dig his wife's grave. The Fleet Street News Agency, an organization that lives or dies by selling articles to the nationals, was paid £1,000 for the story and the pictures.

After the article appeared, on 9 August 1988, Tom Evans wrote to the *Sunday Mirror*'s editor, Eve Pollard, denying that he had said or implied that Greek undertakers refused to carry out the burial because he didn't have the fee or that he had ever said he couldn't believe he was being forced to dig his wife's grave. He also denied making any claim that the family had been sent to their deaths by the Greek police.

Evans insists there was never any question of not being able to pay for the burials – the arrangements had all been handled by his Greek relatives, although in Greece it is apparently not unusual for relatives to help to dig graves in return for a reduction in price. He says he was asked – and voluntarily agreed – to help the undertakers to move a large boulder so that the grave could be completed, and had indeed been overcome by the heat and the realization of what he was doing. The Greek police, he says, had guided his wife and children away from the fires, but his wife had made a fatal decision to take a short cut.

Rather naïvely, perhaps, he said his main aim in talking about his experience had been to give his sincere thanks to the Greek authorities on the island of Cephalonia and to Inspector Charles McIlwright of the Brixton police, who had set up a trust fund for his surviving daughter.

Evan's letter to the *Sunday Mirror* was acknowledged and an investigation was promised. On 27 October a detailed response came from the paper's then deputy editor, Bill Haggerty, arguing that there had been no material misrepresentation. There was also an offer to publish in the paper a 'letter of thanks' to those who had helped Tom Evans.

Apart from writing a letter of complaint to the editor, Evans had no idea what to do about the story. He had contacted a solicitor specializing in libel and had been told he had a case. But, unlike Peter Bottomley, a law suit was not an option for Tom Evans – he simply did not have that kind of money. In Britain there is no form of legal aid to help mount libel cases, and solicitors may require a £10,000 deposit before they will even begin work on what is often a lengthy, costly and risky process. This means that in Britain only the relatively well off can consider using the law to protect their reputations.

Then one day, while collecting tickets at Herne Hill station, Evans had a conversation with one of his regular travellers, *Financial Times* journalist Lisa Wood. After he had told her about the incident, she helped him lodge a formal complaint with the Press Council and prepare his case. 'I had never even heard of the Press Council until she told me about it,' says Evans who at the time was a regular reader of the *Daily Mirror* and the *Sun* – 'mainly for the sport'.

In his complaint to the Council, Tom Evans argued that people like him – 'an ordinary working man' – should be protected from reporters at times of acute distress. 'I do not know how such protection can be afforded – perhaps only by newspapers being forced to reconsider their own policies in this area. It is in their own interests to do so because if complaints such as mine are upheld, and upheld publicly, perhaps more ordinary people will think twice before speaking to a reporter,' he said.

Admittedly there are often two sides to a dispute between a reporter and the subject of an article. They are looking for different results from the contact, and selective memories about what was said or promised are common. For instance, there is still a dispute over whether or not Tom Evans's father asked the Fleet Street News Agency to pay the family for the interview and the family photographs. After the complaint was made to the *Sunday Mirror*, the agency sent Tom Evans a cheque for £100 – a cheque that he never cashed. Lisa Baudains also insists that Evans did say many of the things he later disputed.

Her account to the Press Council illustrates how stories can change and harden as they progress through the editorial chain from initial interview to final publication. It also suggests that the young reporter was not responsible for the main misrepresentation that occurred.

The Press Council was told that the first paragraph of Ms Baudain's original report began, 'A British man had the gruelling task of digging his own wife's grave when she was burnt to death with two of their children.' The night news editor of the agency had later taken over writing the story and had added words that Tom Evans had never used, such as 'I begged them not to make me do it but they wouldn't listen.' This he justified on the grounds that it was acceptable to alter and amplify quotes in order to make their meaning clear to the reader. Likewise the words 'I couldn't believe I was being forced to dig my wife's grave' were never actually spoken but were used to convey what were assumed to be Tom Evans's feelings.

Nearly a year after the publication of the original story, the Press Council upheld Evans's complaint against the *Sunday Mirror*. The article had, it said, contained significant inaccuracies that had caused distress, and an offer to publish a letter was an inadequate remedy.

Tom Evans was happy at the eventual outcome, mainly because he now had an official piece of paper to show his Greek relatives. But bad feelings remain with some of his late wife's family: 'Older people tend to believe that what appears in the papers is true,' he says. At least as far as accounts of tragedies in the tabloids are concerned, this is not an assumption Tom Evans will make again. He reads the *Daily Telegraph* now.

The cases of Tom Evans and Peter Bottomley occurred during a period when press standards have come under unprecedented scrutiny. There have been vociferous complaints about individual journalistic excesses. Journalists tend to come lower even than politicians in polls of public confidence, rivalling estate agents and used-car salesmen for bottom place, and the trend has been getting worse. It was no surprise when an extensive Gallup poll conducted across six European Community countries in 1991 showed confidence in the press lower than in other social institutions such as the armed forces, the legal system, the police and the education services. Much more worrying for the British press, those expressing confidence had dropped from 29 per cent in 1981 to only 14 per cent in 1991, whereas over the same period, confidence in the press in the other European countries had risen from an average of 32 per cent to 35 per cent. Among many journalists there is a growing realization that something has to be done to raise both standards and the standing of journalists in public esteem.

Criticism of the press is nothing new. Almost from its earliest days there have been allegations of inaccurate, irresponsible, scurrilous and sensationalist reporting. Of course, these accusations often come from those in positions of power or with something to hide, but the history of the press is littered with scandals, forgeries, blatant political bias and, at least until the early years of the nineteenth century, the payment and acceptance of political bribes. It is also peopled by journalists who have made a contribution to society: who have exposed injustices; championed individuals, causes or freedom of speech; changed laws – and sometimes ended up in jail for their pains.

During the last fifty years, concern about everything from concentration of press ownership to the invasion of privacy has led to a series of Royal Commissions and inquiries. These have tried to define where the balance should lie between freedom for the press and protection for the individual against unwarranted intrusion and, with very little success, have tried to achieve that balance. That this concern was debated with a new intensity in the late 1980s can be shown by any available measure of unease – the number of complaints to the Press Council, the large sums of money awarded against the press in libel settlements, pressure in Parliament for legislation, and warnings from journalists themselves about the state of their craft.

If the complaints came only from politicians then they would deserve to be treated with scepticism. There is a long history of politicians trying to manipulate the press and becoming hostile when they fail. As David Lloyd George, the First World War Prime Minister, put it: 'The press? What you can't square you squash, what you can't squash you square.' But when even some of the most illustrious tabloid journalists of the last generation issue dire warnings about the state of popular journalism, then it is clearly time to listen.

In 1988, at a memorial service for Lord Jacobson, a former editorial director of IPC Newspapers, the current 'Dark Ages' of contemporary tabloid journalism received a devastating indictment from Lord Cudlipp, a former editor of the *Sunday Pictorial* and editorial director of the *Daily Mirror* – both very lively tabloid newspapers in his day. Information about foreign affairs had become relegated 'to a three-inch yapping editorial insulting foreigners'. Investigative journalism in the public interest had lost its integrity and now nothing, 'however personal, was any longer secret or sacred, and the basic human right to privacy was banished in the interests of publishing profit'. In the contemporary tabloid press, significant national and international events were 'nudged aside by a panting seven day and night news service for voyeurs, the massage parlour relaxations of polo players and the exclusive definitive autobiographies of kiss-and-tell nymphets aged eighteen and a half'.

In April of the same year, a serious debate on the issue of standards and quality was opened by a different area of the media – television – when John Birt, the then deputy director-general of the BBC, who was appointed director-general designate in July 1991, delivered the Fleming Memorial lecture at the Royal Institution. The ethical foundation of British journalism was not firm, he declared, and craft standards were slipping. Until the media put their own house in order, there was no chance of winning the argument for a freer flow of information and an end to the often obsessive secrecy of the British government. He argued that

> Some of our popular papers regularly contain stories which invade the privacy of individuals, but for no reason of public interest; which show insufficient concern for standards of good taste and of decency; which indulge on occasion in outright invention. When Macaulay declared 160 years ago that 'the gallery in which the reporters sit has become a fourth estate of the realm', newspapers were emerging from two centuries of repressive laws, financial corruption and political bribery. In today's fourth estate of the realm, reality too often mocks the grandeur of the term.

Some in turn mocked Mr Birt for his efforts – particularly his suggestion that the BBC should introduce such foreign inventions as 'fact-checkers' when the intrusion of the cameras and problems of political balance provoked far greater controversy for television than did the question of factual accuracy. The fact-checkers – people on American magazines who verify every fact and ring up those quoted in articles to see whether the comments attributed to them are accurate – never did show up at the BBC.

Yet John Birt has had wise things to say about the realm of journalism on at least one previous occasion. In 1975 he and Peter Jay, the journalist and former British ambassador to Washington, wrote articles for *The Times* warning of the 'bias against understanding' in much television journalism – a bias that came from concentrating on pictures and human interest in news coverage to the exclusion of context or explanation of what the pictures meant. One of his suggestions for reform that was treated sceptically at the time of the 1988 lecture was the appointment of ombudsmen on national newspapers to represent the interests of readers and the public. This has already come about, although principally in response to fear of legislation against the press as the alternative.

In his lecture, John Birt reminded his audience that the phrase 'freedom of the press' was chanted by the mob which carried courageous publishers in triumph through the streets of London in the eighteenth century after juries had acquitted them of seditious libel against George III and his ministers. 'Which of us could aspire to that honour now?' he asked.

Three years earlier, in 1985, Tom Baistow, a veteran commentator on the newspaper industry, once foreign editor of the *News Chronicle* and a former deputy editor of the *New Statesman*, launched a savage attack on the state of the newspaper industry in his book *Fourth Rate Estate*. He ridiculed the idea that the press was still willing or even able to perform its traditional function as watchdog on behalf of the public. 'The watchdogs have become press barons' poodles, yapping in support of their masters' views and commercial interests, barking against any threat to their undemocratic power,' Baistow wrote. He did, however, concede that there were honourable exceptions, such as *Observer* editor Donald Trelford's exposure of the Mugabe government's brutal campaign against 'dissidents' in Matabeleland – against the direct interests of his proprietor, Tiny Rowland, whose Lonrho group has extensive business interests in Africa. Peter Preston, at the *Guardian*, also had great freedom, because the liberal daily is controlled by the Scott Trust rather than by an individual proprietor, as did Geoffrey Owen at the *Financial Times*, because its owners, Pearson, have a tradition of not interfering in editorial policy.

Since Tom Baistow wrote his condemnation, the revolution in industrial relations in what used to be Fleet Street has at least opened up the possibility of new voices joining the national press – new voices which are not controlled by immensely rich proprietors and which can aspire to courageous, independent reporting.

In a remarkable period of little more than two months at the beginning of 1986, the national newspaper industry was transformed.

The first public signs of the Fleet Street 'revolution' came on 3 January, when Robert Maxwell, the publisher of Mirror Group Newspapers, announced agreement that 2,100 jobs out of 6,000 would go in London and Manchester. More importantly, Maxwell claimed that management control had been reasserted in an industry where power over manning levels and working practices had been effectively under the control of the printing unions. The negotiations had taken place against the preparations by Eddie Shah for the launch on 4 March 1986 of a revolutionary new newspaper – *Today* – that not only would use all the latest computer technology and colour presses but would employ only the number of staff needed to operate them, rather than the traditional union manning levels.

Shah was a successful publisher of free newspapers in the north-west of England who had established a national name after defeating print-union pickets at Warrington in November 1983. He had successfully used his new fame to raise money to take on what he saw as the hopelessly inefficient and spineless national newspaper industry.

The commercial threat that Eddy Shah posed to other papers turned out to be more apparent than real. It was Rupert Murdoch's dramatic transfer of his four national newspapers – *The Times*, the *Sunday Times*, the *News of the World* and the *Sun* – to a secretly prepared plant at Wapping in the London Docklands over the last weekend of January 1986 that made the changes irreversible. Most of the unions were left outside the gates at Wapping. Journalists were able to enter their copy directly into computer terminals, and, after editing on screen, their articles were automatically turned into print by a computerized typesetter. The print unions had insisted that journalists' copy should be keyed in again by their members before printing, whether it was necessary or not.

In rapid succession, the other national newspaper groups opened negotiations on manning levels and working practices. Within a few days of Wapping, David Stevens, now Lord Stevens, chairman of United Newspapers, publishers of the *Daily Express*, the *Sunday Express* and the *Daily Star*, said that 2,500 jobs must go out of a total of 6,800. In February, staff at Associated Newspapers, publishers of the *Daily Mail* and the *Mail on Sunday*, were told the company's cost structure would have to be brought in line with competing newspapers because of Wapping and the launch of *Today*.

The irony was that the eventual launch of *Today* was largely an anticlimax. The colour was of poor quality, the technology was overburdened and production was slow, and, more seriously, the technology had been allowed to dominate the editorial vision. No one seemed to know what the target audience was or what the paper really stood for. But *Today*'s importance as a harbinger of change is secure, although the paper survived only because it was bought out by Tiny Rowland's Lonrho group later that year and then was sold in July 1987 to Rupert Murdoch's The News Corporation, which has continued to fund its losses in the hope of eventual profit.

At the upper end of the market the opportunity to launch new newspapers using the latest technology and economic manning levels has, so far, only rarely been turned into business reality. The *Independent* has established itself and has been a positive force for higher standards by expanding the market for serious journalism. The *Sunday Correspondent* adopted a similar approach but soon ran into financial problems and folded, and the *Independent on Sunday* was struggling throughout 1991 in the face of a deep advertising recession, losing money at one stage at the rate of £6 million a year, forcing the Sunday title to be integrated with the parent daily with the loss of fifty-six jobs. As one of the terms of a refinancing which raised more than £16 million, barriers limiting individual shareholders to a maximum stake of 15 per cent were lifted – leaving the *Independent* potentially open to take-over in future.

At the more popular end of the market, the failures have included the *News on Sunday*, the *Post* (Eddy Shah's second move into national newspapers) and, in London, the *Daily News*. By contrast, David Sullivan proved there was a market for his soft-porn and fantasy newspaper *Sunday Sport*, which he gradually extended across the week as a new national daily newspaper, creating a new basement to the lowest end of the market.

The reality is that, despite the revolution in technology and industrial relations, the big media barons are virtually as powerful as they ever were. The cost of entry to the national newspaper market may in theory have been reduced, but the fact that the overall market is not growing and the difficulty of enticing readers away from papers they habitually buy have made it an uphill struggle for anyone to try to challenge their dominance.

Tom Baistow argued in *Fourth Rate Estate*, and still believes, despite the Wapping changes, that if press watchdogs on behalf of society are ever to get their teeth back there have to be much stricter controls on the concentration of ownership of national newspapers.

Baistow would be prepared to do a Faustian deal with government – a Freedom of Information Act in return for a right of privacy and a right of reply. A Freedom of Information Act would give automatic access to all official information except for specific items such as defence secrets or commercially confidential information. Government and other bodies are at present notoriously reluctant to permit access to information of public concern. In March 1989, for example, the then Transport Minister, Michael Portillo, refused to identify seven passenger ferries which had failed to meet enhanced stability standards recommended by the Zeebrugge disaster inquiry. He argued that it would be a breach of commercial confidentiality. Only when the press correctly identified the seven ships was their identity officially made public by the government – an example of how important information, that should have been available to the public as of right, became known only through the tenacity of reporters. If there is continuing concern about the standards of some sections of the British press, there is equal concern about the unnecessary secrecy of British society and about legal or government pressure on press freedom – pressure that includes threats to introduce statutory controls on the press if the latest attempts to achieve control by self-regulation break down.

The public's view of the press – of its transgressions and the need for legislation – seems to be more balanced and sophisticated than that of many back-bench MPs. A detailed public-opinion poll carried out by MORI for the *News of the World* and presented to an International Press Institute conference of editors and senior journalists in London in October 1990 did indeed find widespread support for more supervision of what appears in the papers.

Less than half of those questioned – 46 per cent – agreed with the statement that 'The press generally behaves responsibly in Britain', with 49 per cent of the sample disagreeing and 5 per cent holding no opinion. There was, however, a strong preference for self-regulation, with 25 per cent saying this should be carried out by a committee of editors and 41 per cent favouring greater regulation by the Press Council. Only 29 per cent wanted tighter laws.

The poll showed that the public is censorious about a wide range of behaviour – everything from acts of vandalism to cruelty to animals and child abuse – and by large majorities is happy for newspapers to report on those responsible. By way of contrast, 71 per cent thought it wrong to report on adultery involving those not in the public eye.

According to the survey, the public is protective of the royal family, with 57 per cent believing that royalty should be photographed only on public occasions; is sympathetic to the privacy of public figures, with 73 per cent believing that the press intrudes too much into their lives; and, by a 56 per cent majority, is in favour of a Freedom of Information Act.

The creation at the beginning of 1991 of the Press Complaints Commission, as recommended by the Calcutt Committee into Privacy and Related Matters, seems to fit well with the apparent public desire for a press made more responsible through self-regulation rather than by direct government interference.

Yet there remain many unanswered questions. Have standards really declined or has the public – or at least a vociferous part of it – merely become more sensitive? Surely popular newspapers get a new mandate for what they do every day from the market-place – from the millions who buy them? And isn't there a danger that cleaned-up newspapers will be boring newspapers that no one will want to buy, so that they lose their power for doing good as well as ill? Above all else, should anything further be done about the experiences of victims such as Tom Evans or Peter Bottomley, or are occasional casualties of a free press part of the price to be paid for an open society?

2

'It really was ill-mannered and rough a lot of the time'
Press scandals through the ages

WHEN King George IV died in 1830, at the age of sixty, *The Times* marked the occasion with the expected show of formal respect. As a sign of mourning for the loss of the sovereign, the newspaper appeared with thick black borders. But later, on the day of the funeral, the paper published a less conventional appreciation of the dead king:

> There never was an individual less regretted by his fellow-creatures than this deceased king. What eye has wept for him? What heart has heaved one sob of unmercenary sorrow? . . . If George IV had a friend – a devoted friend in any rank of life – we protest that the name of him or her never reached us. An inveterate voluptuary, especially if he be an artificial person, is of all known beings the most selfish . . . Nothing more remains to be done or said about George IV, but to pay – as pay we must – for his profusion.

The Times's 'appreciation' of George IV – well based on fact, it seems – puts present-day complaints about newspaper coverage of the royal family into perspective. It would be unthinkable today for any mainstream paper to make such scurrilous comments about a British sovereign living or recently dead. The 1830 obituary shows that ideas of what is publicly acceptable can change, and that there is nothing absolute about newspapers' standards, either. Rather, the content of newspapers reflects society's values at any particular time, and, while newspapers may speed up and spread social change, they rarely succeed against the trend. Really successful newspapers, such as *The Times* throughout much of the nineteenth century, have been in tune with, or just a little ahead of, what their readers were thinking.

Yet the 400-year history of the press shows too how little new there is in the present controversies about newspaper behaviour. Every modern complaint or call for legislation can be matched by stories from the past. When you get down to the fundamentals of questionable journalism – sex, violence, sensationalism, bias, inaccuracy and forgery – it is remarkable how little has changed.

That this continuity of subject-matter transcends the vast distance newspapers have travelled in style, presentation and technology can be illustrated by two stories from the *News of the World*, still Britain's top-selling Sunday newspaper, selling nearly 5 million copies a week in 1991 despite the recession.

The first story tells of the fate of beautiful 17-year-old Emma Munton, who went to a chemist in Lambeth to get medicine for a child suffering from whooping cough. While she waited, it was alleged, Edward Morse, the chemist, offered her a glass of wine. It looked like port, and Emma drank it, even though it tasted rather bitter. The next thing the girl remembered was being dumped into a canal. Two coal-workers saw her going under for the second time, but managed to pull her out and save her life.

'On her having so far recovered as to being enabled to speak she stated that she had been pushed into the water, but by whom she was not aware. There is not the slightest doubt of her having been violated, and that with great violence,' the *News of the World* reported, under the headline 'Extraordinary Charge of Drugging and Violation'.

That story appeared in the first issue of the paper, on 1 October 1843. The *News of the World* had started as it meant to go on. You may need a magnifying glass to read the print, and there is no picture of young Emma in her underclothes, but the tale of the accusation against the chemist is a worthy precursor of the story of Mrs A and Mrs B some 147 years later. This was the case of the two women who claimed that their Crawley doctor, Jeremy Stupple, had had sex with them in his surgery.

The *News of the World* was involved in the Stupple story from an early stage. Mrs A contacted the *News of the World* with allegations about Dr Stupple, but the paper decided that publication of them 'was inappropriate at that stage'. Instead, it advised the two women to take their allegations to the General Medical Council; any *News of the World* story would be determined by the GMC proceedings. It is possible, though, that the *News of the World* had at least an option on their story – win or lose – before the GMC's hearing of the complaint against Dr Stupple.

The General Medical Council cleared the doctor of the accusations in September 1990, but that did not stop the *News of the World* squeezing the maximum out of the sordid life stories of Mrs A – Debbie Finlayson – and Mrs B – Karen Wheeler – after the hearing. 'Blonde Mrs B – one of the two women who falsely accused GP Jeremy Stupple of having sex with them – is a nymphomaniac who has notched up a string of affairs,' claimed the paper. The following week the paper broadened the story out to reveal that, 'the man-hungry housewives of Crawley just can't get enough sex', according to Debbie Finlayson – Mrs A.

Rupert Murdoch, chief executive of the News Corporation, which owns the *News of the World*, saw the Mrs A and Mrs B story as a considerable journalistic coup. 'The *News of the World* tied them up. Our rivals would have given their right arms for that story. It was disgusting actually . . . but I read it,' he said.

The language, style and presentation of these two *News of the World* stories are vastly different, but two common threads are obvious. Sex and crime sell newspapers and, while respectable members of society are often quick to condemn such papers as the *News of the World*, many are equally quick to read them voraciously.

As early as Tudor times, attempts were made to stamp out the printing of 'lewd and naughty matters' – apparently without any noticeable success. Blunt language that would seem a shade strong for present-day papers was common.

On 23 December 1643, *Mercurius Aulicus*, the royalist newspaper produced in Oxford during the English Civil War, combined earthy language with propaganda against the 'Rebels' – Cromwell's Roundheads. The weekly publication recounted, to pick one example, how 'a prisoner of the Royalists had been found committing buggery on a mare – and on Sunday of all days, when His Majestie's Forces were at Church'.

Almost forty years later, in 1682, a Tory newspaper called the *Loyal Protestant and True Domestick Intelligencer* – a paper with a passion for embarrassing Puritans – told the story of the Dissenter minister who 'laid with two Wenches ten Nights at a Guinny a Night: that he exercised one while the other raised his Inclinations.'

The previous year the same paper reported a court case about the relationship between a 'great Mastiffe', a mistress and her maid. The mistress, the *Loyal Protestant* reported, had been seen 'Beast-like upon all Four, with her Posteriours Bare, and the Dog effectively performing'. The lady explained in court that she had got drunk at a fair 'and suffered three or four men to enjoy her, by which Coition she got the Venerial Disease, and supposing with herself that Copulation would help her Malady, and not having the Convenience of a Man, she betook herself to this crime for Remedy'.

Given such stories, it is not surprising that newspapers and those who produce them have never lacked their critics. In the seventeenth century, Ben Jonson in his play *The Staple of News* denounced the newsmongers as 'dishonest swindlers'. In the late eighteenth century, a pamphlet called *News and Newswriters*, which argued for firm censorship, had this to say about newspapers and news values: 'A paper without murders and robberies, and rapes and incest, and bestiality and sodomy, and sacrilege, and incendiary letters and forgeries, and executions and duels, and suicides, is said to be devoid of news.'

The philosopher and economist John Stuart Mill, writing in the nineteenth century, was equally forthright. Journalism, he wrote, was 'the vilest and most degrading of all trades because more affectation and hypocrisy and more subservience to the baser feelings of others are necessary for carrying it on than for any other trade from that of brothel-keeper upwards'.

At least some journalistic activities have changed over the years, though. The widespread accepting of bribes, or 'subsidies', by journalists and newspapers for taking the correct political line came to an end in the nineteenth century, when the growth of circulations and the consequent rise in advertising revenues provided a less compromised source of funds and, at the same time, a more sophisticated readership came to expect a greater degree of independence.

Also abandoned was the equally traditional practice of offering victims the chance to buy a puff or pay a 'suppression fee' to kill a spiteful item or an unflattering profile. The *Morning Post*, the predecessor of the *Daily Telegraph*, was a noted practitioner of the art of profiting from suppression fees towards the end of the eighteenth century.

In 1792 the *Daily Advertiser* printed a sly reference to the fact that the Prince of Wales had secretly married a Roman Catholic widow, Mrs Fitzherbert. 'It is confidently reported, that a certain marriage has been solemnised by a Romish Priest who immediately quitted the Kingdom,' the paper said. The Prince of Wales paid up to prevent anything worse appearing.

It was in contemptuous response to a request to pay a suppression fee that the Duke of Wellington uttered the immortal words – used out of context ever since – 'Publish and be damned!'

Eighteenth-century newspapers were fond of spicing their accounts of politics with juicy divorce cases that came before the House of Lords. 'The discovery of an admiral's wife in a Charing Cross brothel in 1771 was as good copy as the Countess of Eglinton's adultery in 1788 and Lady Abergavenny's in 1729,' Jeremy Black recounts in *The English Press in the*

Eighteenth Century. Divorce continued to provide titillating copy until legal restraints were introduced in the 1926 Judicial Proceedings Act. From then on, newspapers could report only that part of the evidence in divorce cases which was quoted by the judge in open court as part of the judgement.

In Victorian times, as Thomas Boyle's book *Black Swine in the Sewers of Hampstead* makes clear, there may have been caution about the terminology, but there was no lack of newspaper enthusiasm for reporting adulterous liaisons when they reached the divorce courts.

In 1858 the case of Mrs Robinson and her apparent adultery – it was never clear whether Mrs Robinson's love-affair had been a fantasy – with a hydrotherapist called Dr Lane caused a social panic about declining moral standards and provoked criticism of newspaper coverage. Despite objections from Dr Lane's lawyer, the prosecution was allowed to read extracts from Mrs Robinson's intimate diaries in court. The diaries' accounts of passionate kisses, whispered words and confessions of the past were produced word for word in the papers: 'Oh God! I never hoped to see this hour, to to have any part of my love returned. Yet so it was. He was nervous, and confused, and eager as myself. At last we raised ourselves and walked on happy, fearful, almost silent.'

This was too much for the *Saturday Review*, a London weekly. Under a headline 'The Purity of the Press', the *Review* complained that the news coverage of the case was emblematic of a general deteriorating cultural standard: 'The whole of these loathsome productions were reprinted at full length in *The Times* and several other daily newspapers,' it lamented.

Coincidentally in that same year, 1858, there had been another dramatic example of newspaper interest in sexual matters. An Anglican curate was tried *in absentia* in St James's Hall before a large audience of peers, MPs and clergymen. He was accused of encouraging attractive young women to discuss the intimate details of their sex lives, in a darkened room with candles and an altar. The papers which reported the affair did, however, hold something back: they said the questions asked were 'so grossly indecent as to be unfit for publication'.

At around the same time, the *Saturday Review* opened up another enduring running theme of press criticism – about the space and emphasis given to crime and criminals. As the *Review* pointed out, newspaper reports that pretended to unmask hypocrisy were actually indulging 'the lowest appetites of human nature'. The reporting of crime and retribution had been a stock in trade of the press from its earliest days, but the *Saturday Review* was on

this occasion exercised about the coverage given to one particular crime –
that of the poisoner William Palmer, who was executed in 1856.

Palmer, a Staffordshire surgeon, had been charged with murdering a
fellow horse-racing enthusiast, John Parson Cook, although Palmer may
also have poisoned his wife, mother and brother. The press coverage of the
case was so extensive and unrestrained that the trial had to be moved from
Stafford to London to ensure fairness. Palmer was convicted, largely on
the evidence of an expert on poisons from Guy's Hospital, and was returned
to Stafford for execution.

On 14 June the crowd of spectators and reporters gathered. *The Times*
was given the best vantage point, but a special correspondent for the *Leader*,
a London weekly, described the hanging in particularly minute and lengthy
detail: 'And now the hangman grasps the rope – Palmer bends his head –
the noose is slipped over – his face grows yet more ghastly – his throat
throbs spasmodically – he moves his neck round, as a man with a tight
collar ...' The coverage of this case, the *Saturday Review* noted with pre-
science, meant that newspaper sensationalism had become a cultural force
to be reckoned with. Actually witnessing the execution, it argued, would
have had a far less traumatic and injurious effect than reading all about it
in the *Leader*.

Another common charge against the press has always been that sensationalist coverage of a relatively small number of dramatic crimes creates
a false impression in the public mind about the frequency and risk of serious
crime. The media were found guilty of this charge in 1990 by a Home
Office inquiry on the Fear of Crime chaired by Michael Grade, the chief
executive of Channel 4. There is also considerable evidence that the press,
whether through whipping up or merely reflecting public fears, can effectively create new crimes. This usually happens when newspapers describe
in dramatic terms – often applying an imported name – behaviour that has
been around for a long time. Mugging is a recent example of this. There
has always been theft from individuals in the street, often involving violence;
but when a term like 'mugging' is imported from the USA, the crime
suddenly seems different, more threatening.

But the concern caused by mugging in the inner-city areas of London
in the 1980s and early 1990s seems mild compared with the panic whipped
up by the press in 1862 over a sudden and frightening outbreak of what
The Times called 'a new variety of crime' – garrotting.

'This modern peril of the streets created something like a reign of terror,'
the paper said, in which 'whole sections of a peaceable city community were

on the verge of arming themselves against sudden attack.' The new breed of garrotters, according to the *Cornhill Magazine*, moved in from the rear and put a right arm round the victim's forehead. When the neck was exposed, it was encircled by the attacker's left arm and the victim was thus rendered helpless and easy to rob.

Some papers said the technique of 'putting the hug on' had been learned from guards in the convict hulks. *The Times* was quite convinced that foreigners had to be responsible, because of the 'un-British' nature of the attack – although it had to concede that 'the ruffians who have been arrested are of pure English breed'.

Not all newspapers fell for this sensational new breed of criminal though. The *Daily News* took a more measured line and warned that the wild and exaggerated talk was 'furnishing food for farce writers and arrangers of pantomimes'.

By the turn of century, another new type of insidious crime was emerging in newspapers: 'The Cyclist Terror', caused by road-racing on bicycles. The *Daily Graphic* was among those that warned of the danger of this new-fangled method of transport being abused by the irresponsible. 'It is high time', the paper argued, 'that steps were taken to put down the too prevalent but utterly indefensible practice which constitutes a serious danger alike to the public in general and to the too enthusiastic cyclist in particular.'

In 1898 the paper drew attention to the dangers of 'mercantile tricycles' – tricycles used to carry goods around the centre of London. The paper told how one young tricyclist, Thomas Duff, was given seven days in prison in default of paying a 10 shilling fine plus costs for riding in Moorgate at eight to ten miles an hour, ringing his bell and expecting people to get out of the way.

Such newspaper attitudes to a fairly gentle offence, and the constant difficulty of coping with new phenomena that they reveal, can still be seen today – in the early 1990s, the popular press turned every 'acid house' party into a drugs orgy even on occasions when police said there was no evidence of drug taking.

But more serious crime – especially murder – has been a circulation-builder throughout newspaper history, though even murder hasn't been the story it used to be since the abolition of capital punishment in Britain in 1965.

Until then, every moment of a murder trial was given a terrible intensity by the possibility that the case would end with the judge donning a black cap, the traditional precursor to pronouncing sentence of death. After the trial, the story would move on to the fight to save the condemned; and, if clemency was not granted, attempts were made to buy up rights to the last letter. Even reporting of all-night vigils with distraught relatives on the eve of executions became part of the journalistic ritual of covering murder. One 'journalist' actually made a reasonable living by posing as a long-lost friend of the condemned prisoner to obtain a prison visit and with it an interview. Abolition ended all that.

The change was dramatic, and was one reason why former top *Daily Express* reporter Alfred Draper decided to turn his back on Fleet Street in 1972. Sensational murder cases that used to keep reporters out of town for weeks were now seldom more than one-offs. The excitement had gone. 'The end of capital punishment may have been enlightened but it had knocked the drama out of murder,' Draper recalled in *Scoops and Swindles*, his 1988 memoirs of a Fleet Street journalist.

Draper was one of those involved in the highly competitive task of buying up the last letters of young men about to be hung for murder. Another ace reporter who chased such scoops was Harry Procter of the *Sunday Pictorial* (now the *Sunday Mirror*). He told all in a 1958 book, *Street of Disillusion*.

Procter, an opponent of the death penalty, covered many murders and executions, including the case of Christopher Craig and Derek Bentley. The two were found guilty of murdering a policeman during an attempted robbery. Although it was Craig who had actually shot the policeman, because he was only sixteen at the time of the offence he was sentenced to life imprisonment rather than to death. Bentley, who had never fired a shot but who was eighteen, was hanged, although he always denied he had done anything to encourage Craig to open fire.

Before the execution, Procter took Bentley's father to lunch and made him a commercial offer. 'If on the night before he was hanged, Derek Bentley wrote a death-cell letter, we would pay generously for permission to publish that letter exclusively the following Sunday. Mr Bentley accepted my proposal,' Harry Procter recalled with satisfaction. A letter was written, and Procter had his story for the *Sunday Pictorial*.

In recent years the news appeal of murders has been further eroded by the increased frequency of the crime – particularly of domestic killings. To get much attention now, murders have to show signs of great brutality or have an unusual twist.

If sensational reporting of sex and crime is an integral part of the history of the press, so too is political bias. Often this amounts to little more than partiality – unrelenting support for a particular party or set of political views. But on many occasions bias has led to scandalous and dishonest reporting.

During the eighteenth century there was, according to G. A. Cranfield in *The Press and Society*, 'one of the most violent propaganda campaigns in the history of journalism'. The attack was against the Jewish Naturalization Bill of 1753. The bill would have allowed individual Jews resident in Britain for at least three years to become British citizens without having to take the sacraments. Only a few rich people would have been affected, because a private act of Parliament was still needed for each individual wanting to become a British citizen, but the *London Evening Post*, which had opposed Britain's first modern Prime Minister, Robert Walpole, and took a similar attitude to his patriot, dissident Whig and Tory successors, launched a virulent campaign against the bill as a way of embarrassing the government. The paper accused the Jews of historic massacres and published crude anti-Semitic verses:

> Come, Abram's Sons, from ev'ry Quarter come,
> Britain now bids you call her land your own . . .
> Revenge (your fav'rite Passion) you may hoist
> And once more triumph o'er the Cross of Christ.

The *Post* also reprinted from a political weekly, *The Craftsman*, 'News from One Hundred Years Hence' – 1853 – when Britain, it was imagined, would be controlled by the Jews. 'Last night the Bill for naturalizing Christians was thrown out of the Sanhedrin by a very Great Majority . . .'

The government backed down, and the Jewish Naturalization Bill was dropped.

The political bias faced by the Labour Party in its early days was hardly less subtle. The party has always believed – with considerable justification – that a large part of the national press is biased against it. The preponderance of national newspapers supporting the Conservative Party stems from the personal preferences of powerful newspaper proprietors, from the fact that national newspapers are large industrial enterprises and those who run them tend to identify with the interests of business.

It is unlikely, however, that the Labour Leader Neil Kinnock will ever be able to complain of anything comparable to the treatment meted out to Britain's first Labour Prime Minister, Ramsay MacDonald. Even before he became Prime Minister, in 1924, MacDonald had already been exposed by Horatio Bottomley, an MP and proprietor of *John Bull*, one of the most notorious and jingoistic Sunday newspapers of the period. The paper printed MacDonald's birth certificate, revealing that the Labour leader was illegitimate – something he had not known himself until the paper revealed it.

The *Daily Mail* even discovered a scandal in MacDonald's method of transport. When he became Prime Minister, MacDonald, who was not rich, had no car. During the week in London he travelled by taxi, and at weekends he went on the Metropolitan line from Baker Street for the main part of the journey to Chequers, the Buckinghamshire country home of Prime Ministers. Unexpectedly, MacDonald turned up one day in a chauffeur-driven Daimler. The *Mail* investigated and found that the Daimler and a gift of shares had come from an old family friend, Sir Alexander Grant, chairman of the biscuit company McVitie and Price. Despite the fact that both shares and Daimler were made available to provide assistance only while he remained Prime Minister, MacDonald's reputation suffered.

The *Daily Mail* had made its political position perfectly clear in the run-up to the October 1922 general election, won by the Conservatives under Bonar Law: it warned its readers that Labour would put up beer prices, abolish private ownership and perhaps even confiscate womens' gold wedding rings for the gold.

In the 1924 general-election campaign, following the collapse of Ramsay MacDonald's brief minority Labour government, the *Daily Mail* and some other Conservative newspapers surpassed themselves. The affair of the Daimler proved to be a minor matter compared with what was to come: the Zinoviev Letter – a story which broke in the *Daily Mail* on 25 October 1924, in the week of the election. Under the headline 'Civil War plot by Socialists' Masters', the *Mail* disclosed a letter from Grigori Zinoviev, president of the Communist International, 'addressed by the Bolsheviks of Moscow to the Soviet Government's servants in Great Britain, the Communist Party, who in turn are the masters of Mr Ramsay MacDonald's Government which has signed a treaty with Moscow whereby the Soviet is to be guaranteed a "loan" of millions of British money'.

This 'very secret' letter, the paper said, revealed a great Bolshevik plot to paralyse the British army and navy and to plunge the country into civil war. Armed warfare would be preceded by a struggle designed to persuade British workers to abandon ideas of compromise and false hopes that capitalism could be got rid of peacefully.

A copy of the letter had arrived mysteriously at the *Daily Mail's* offices. The paper declared itself duty-bound to publish it, and even took it upon itself to circulate copies to other London newspapers. On election day the

Daily Mirror, then also a Conservative newspaper, carried over its masthead the headline 'Vote Conservative To-Day To Keep Reds Away.' Under the headline 'Vote British, Not "Bolshie" ' there were pictures of the 'leaders of Law, Order, Peace and Prosperity' – Lloyd George, Stanley Baldwin, Herbert Asquith and Austen Chamberlain. The voter was given an alternative – 'to vote for the Overthrow of Society and Pave the way to Bolshevism' – with pictures of alternative Soviet candidates to vote for – Kamenev, Trotsky, Rykoff and Zinoviev.

The letter, the attendant publicity and the claims of an apparent threat to British democracy may not have determined the outcome of the election but they certainly contributed to the Conservative majority. Stanley Baldwin returned to power with 419 seats, the Liberals were reduced to a rump of 40 and Labour suffered a net loss of 40 seats.

The Zinoviev letter was suspected at the time of being a forgery, and Ramsay MacDonald denounced it as a hoax. But it was not until 1967 that it was demonstrated, by *Sunday Times* journalists, that the letter had almost certainly been produced by Russian émigrés in Berlin. It had found its way to the British Foreign Office with copies to the *Daily Mail* and the Conservative Central Office.

Forgeries, like bias, have a rich history in newspapers. The pattern is usually the same. A secret document either arrives anonymously or is offered for sale; the story it reveals is dramatic – a great exclusive which has to be kept away from rivals. The temptation to publish becomes so great that inconsistencies are overlooked and common sense is overruled. Often a friendly expert can be found to authenticate a signature or the historical context. And when the document is damaging to political opponents of the paper involved, the temptation to print can be almost irresistible. Later, of course, the document's flaws are so obvious that everyone asks how those involved could ever have been so stupid. For the newspapers who fall for forgeries, the cost in libel damages and lost reputations can be considerable.

The most recent major victims were the *Daily Mail* and the *Sunday Times*. On 19 May 1977 the *Daily Mail* exposed 'the amazing truth about Britain's State-owned car makers British Leyland'. The company, it revealed, had a multi-million pound overseas 'slush fund' for paying bribes and undercover commissions. The paper had obtained a letter from Lord Ryder, chairman of the National Enterprise Board, which made it clear that both he and Mr Alex Park, the BL chief executive, were involved in the 'Special Accounting Arrangements'. These arrangements had also been 'nodded through' by

Labour's Industry Secretary, Eric Varley, and the Bank of England would, according to the letter, be offering advice.

That the political context played a part in events is apparent from the tone of the piece. 'It is ironic that a British nationalised industry, publicly run through the National Enterprise Board, operating in a business climate established by a Labour Cabinet, should now be in the thick of this latest scandal uncovered after weeks of research by the *Daily Mail*,' was how the reporter Stewart Steven (now editor of the *Mail on Sunday*) put it.

Two days later the *Mail* had to announce that the Ryder letter was a forgery, created by a British Leyland executive, Graham Barton. David English, the paper's editor, apologized unreservedly to Lord Ryder, Eric Varley and Alex Park for being misled into publishing a falsehood.

In April 1983 it was the turn of the *Sunday Times* to get egg all over its face. The paper thought it had the scoop of the century: 'World Exclusive: How the Diaries of the Führer were Found in an East German Hayloft'. The paper's promise to serialize the diaries, first bought by *Stern* magazine in Germany, was accompanied by an article by the historian Hugh Trevor-Roper, Lord Dacre, supporting their authenticity. Yet within two weeks the German Federal Archives at Koblenz announced that the paper, glue and bindings of the sixty volumes of diaries were all of post-war manufacture.

The embarrassment was partly caused by a late change of mind to publish the diaries in the *Sunday Times* rather than *The Times*. This was due to fears of a spoiler story appearing in another publication, but gave those responsible little time for reflection. Internal memos advising caution were sent by sceptical *Sunday Times* journalists, who remembered an earlier fiasco over supposed Mussolini diaries. These warnings were swept aside by the excitement and inevitability of it all. The News Corporation had paid $400,000 for the British and Commonwealth rights, there was a production schedule to be met and, anyway, hadn't a leading historian of the period verified the scoop of the century as genuine?

If those involved in the decision had been better versed in the history of *The Times*, they might have been a little more cautious. The finances of the daily were crippled for years and its reputation was severely damaged when in 1887 it published a letter, 'signed' by the Irish political leader Charles Stewart Parnell, which indicated that Parnell privately condoned the Phoenix Park murders in Dublin – the killing of Lord Cavendish, the Chief Secretary in Ireland, and his Under-Secretary T. H. Burke. The letter had been one of a series offered to *The Times* for £1,780 by Edward Caulfield Houston, a young Irish journalist who was secretary of the Irish Loyal and

Patriotic Union. They appeared to implicate Parnell and an agrarian reform organization, the Land League, in murder and outrage.

Letter number two – the letter chosen for publication – concerned anger in Ireland at Parnell's public denunciation of the Phoenix Park murders. Denunciation, he wrote, had been the best policy – and indeed the only course open. But all concerned could be told 'that though I regret the accident of Lord F. Cavendish's death I cannot refuse to admit that Burke got no more than his deserts'. Other letters attacked the 'inexcusable inaction' in Ireland. 'Our best men are in prison and nothing is being done. Let there be an end of this hesitency [*sic*]. Prompt action is called for,' said one letter, signed 'Charles S. Parnell'.

The letters seemed to prove what *The Times* had suspected all along: the respectable parliamentary face of Parnell's Home Rule Party was merely a cover for crime and violence. They would also bolster *The Times*'s case against Gladstone's first Home Rule Bill for Ireland, which had just been introduced into Parliament.

Despite the obvious political importance of the documents, the paper did not rush into publication. It advertised in its own columns for signatures of famous men, including Parnell, so that it could check the authenticity of the signature. A hand-writing expert duly obliged. But when the paper approached its most distinguished legal adviser, Sir Henry James, it received a nasty shock. Sir Henry had seen the letters before and had serious doubts about their authenticity; he also mentioned that an Irish journalist called Richard Pigott was in some way involved.

The lawyer's doubts delayed publication but did not halt it. *The Times*, knowing the ammunition it had in reserve, prepared a series on Parnellism and Crime with the intention of publishing Parnell's letters as the *coup de grâce*.

On 18 April 1887 the paper published letter number two in facsimile form. For the first time in the history of *The Times*, the headline extended over two columns. In an accompanying editorial, the editor, George Earle Buckle, wrote of the grave importance of the document being put before the paper's readers and commended it to the serious consideration of the House of Commons.

Parnell almost immediately denounced the letter as a fabrication, its subject-matter preposterous and its phraseology absurd.

The Government set up a Special Commission to examine not just the letters but also the broader issues of violence in Ireland raised in *The Times*'s articles. The authenticity of the Parnell letters was destroyed in the witness-box when Richard Pigott was all but uncovered as the forger. Early in his cross-examination at the judicial hearings he was asked to write down an apparently random list of words, including 'hesitancy'. He spelled this with a second 'e' rather than an 'a' – the mistake made by whoever wrote the Parnell letters.

Pigott went missing during an adjournment in his cross-examination, but, before fleeing to Paris, he confessed in writing that he had indeed forged the letters. Later he travelled to Madrid, where he shot himself.

It cost *The Times* £200,000 to present its case before the Commission and another £5,000 for a libel settlement with Parnell. *The Times*, with a long tradition of serious and often weighty journalism, had behaved honourably in its own eyes. It had indeed made considerable efforts to check the truth of its allegations, but it had been undone by preconceptions and the need to believe that such a good story was true.

Things can and do go wrong in the best-ordered newspapers. In May 1991 the *Financial Times* published a large article about the discovery of what seemed to be the earliest surviving text of the sayings of Jesus. The article was by Robin Lane Fox, an Oxford University lecturer in ancient history and the paper's distinguished gardening correspondent. Neither Lane Fox nor anyone else at the paper noticed, until afterwards, the significance of the unusual name of the supposed discoverer of these priceless scripts – Batson D. Sealing ('Bats On De Ceiling').

The early days of financial papers in the late nineteenth and early twentieth century were more murky than batty. New dailies such as the *Financial News* and the *Financial Times* exposed many financial scandals and attempts to defraud the public with worthless shares and dummy companies. But there was a darker side to their own activities – particularly those of the *Financial News*, which merged into the *FT* in 1945. One of the flightier businessmen of the period, Whitaker Wright, revealed how the scandal worked at the winding-up proceedings of his failed company the London & Globe Finance Corporation in 1902:

> 'It is well known in the City that all the financial daily press and those who publish the reports of transactions on the Stock Exchange and call attention to them, put in the official lists and transactions of the tape and everything of that kind, will not do it, will not assist companies in any shape or form unless they have consideration in some form or another,' Wright said.

His company had sold shares at an artificially low price to the press and then bought them back at a higher price.

An internal Stock Exchange investigation found that ten journalists had been involved in such deals, including Harry Marks, the editor of the *Financial News*, three *FN* journalists and one from the *FT*. Even Douglas MacRae, managing director of the *Financial Times*, had in July 1900 picked up 6,500 shares at a bargain price. Wright's company had taken in more shareholders' money than it could conceivably put to use, yet it floated on the Stock Exchange and even attempted to manipulate the shares of other companies before finally overextending itself. When it failed, in 1900, it brought down a raft of other companies in its wake. Wright was arrested in New York and was returned to the UK for trial. He was sentenced at the Old Bailey to seven years in prison; instead, he took a cyanide tablet.

David Kynaston's centenary history of the *Financial Times* records that, despite the damaging revelations, the next day's *Financial News* praised Wright for his courage as a financier; it even claimed that he had falsified balance sheets only 'to tide over appalling difficulties in the hope of saving the shareholders' money'. The *Financial Times* took a much sterner view: 'A pestilent influence has been removed from the City,' the paper said.

The Wright case does not seem to have been a isolated incident. Similar stories were told in court by another notorious financier of the day, Ernest Terah Hooley, who made millions by floating a series of companies on the Stock Exchange. The *Financial News* was extremely complimentary about Hooley's companies, such as Simpson's Lever Chain Company and the New Beeston Cycle Company. None the less, when Hooley filed for bankruptcy, in 1898, he spilled the beans about his financial relationships with journalists. Harry Marks, the *FN* editor, had received £31,110 in cash and shares from Hooley. Hooley claimed this was not to make sure that the *FN* would refrain from publishing unfavourable comments but simply because Marks was a friend. The paper's leader-writer, H. J. Jennings, was also a beneficiary. Although MacRae, of the *FT*, didn't take a penny, his wife accepted a one-third stake in a racehorse called Northallerton – a horse Hooley had bought for £2,000.

Even *The Times* was not exempt from financial scandal. The muck-raking journalist Henry Labouchere accused the financial editor of *The Times* of taking bribes to keep quiet about attempts to rob the public, and the financial editor, whose name was Sampson, left the paper as a result.

The British press has long since left crude bribery behind. But another kind of scandal has proved more enduring – one more insidious than notorious cases of bias, fraud or forgery and which has certainly contributed more to human misery. This is the treatment by the press of ordinary citizens who have suddenly become newsworthy, whether because of a tragedy, a marital disaster or some other unusual feature of their lives.

There was no shortage of such scandals in newspapers of the 1940s and 1950s, as can be seen in the autobiographies of reporters who worked in the days before television became pre-eminent. Most of these accounts are marked by boastfulness and complacency: countless anecdotes reveal how the opposition was scooped on some now long-forgotten story which caused a momentary stir in the pubs of Fleet Street when the first editions came off the presses. Some of these press memoirs take the form of 'confessions', although even then they are not notable for their regrets.

The confessions of Harry Procter, the top investigative reporter of the *Sunday Pictorial*, covered many serious crime stories but also many other sad stories – sad both for those involved and for the press. Procter was understandably proud of his skills and how he could win people's confidence, persuade them to talk and get his story:

> After all, I am a specialist – a specialist in people. I like to feel that I have always shown kindness and love to those in trouble – honest decent people I mean, not crooks and murderers. I have lived with tragedy continuously for twenty years, but I am certain there is not a man, woman or child in Europe who ever objected to the way I handled them in their grief. They may have objected to my published story, but never to my interview.

The last sentence goes to the heart of a sort of moral blindness that afflicts some journalists working in this area. The kindness and love Harry Procter spoke of were clearly too often deployed to exploit people, or at least to persuade them to say things they would later regret when they appeared in print.

When he had first come to Fleet Street, at the age of twenty-two, Harry Procter had stood silently in front of the Edgar Wallace memorial plaque in the Street of Adventure and had offered up a silent prayer that he might uphold the standards of journalism. He may not have realized it, but Harry had chosen a rather strange mentor, for Wallace's imagination had sometimes been more powerful than his journalism.

Wallace, then an *Evening News* reporter, went too far during a Northcliffe campaign against Soap Kings like Lord Leverhulme. The reporter accused the big soap manufacturers of not weighing their wares fairly, and invented an interview with a poor woman who complained that paying more for soap deprived her children of butter on their bread. Leverhulme sued. After a second embarrassing libel, involving naval-dockyard stokers, Wallace was fired. The Fleet Street plaque was earned by his fiction and his fame rather than his journalism.

Harry Procter's own stories were only too authentic. One of his great scoops, in February 1955, was the case of the woman who found out that she had accidentally married her brother. While in the downstairs of a dingy hotel the journalist pack haggled with a representative over the price of the woman's story, Harry got to the woman herself upstairs, scooped up her and her baby and made a dash for it in his Humber, pursued by outraged hacks.

When the 'Woman Who Married Her Brother' later remarried, Harry was there at the wedding reception, as an honoured guest but also, of course, for the story and the best pictures. His newsdesk wanted that something extra – a picture of the brother and former husband at the wedding. Harry was reluctant, but nevertheless set it up by making sure the man was on hand, even though he hadn't been invited.

Harry Procter was only too aware of the enormous power he wielded over other people's lives – the power for good and, sometimes, the power for something approaching evil. As he admitted,

> To be exposed in bold headlines is a terrible thing for a victim – far worse than a heavy prison sentence. By it lives are completely ruined – not only the life of the subject of the exposure but of his wife, his children, his parents his friends. Exposure of poverty, injustice, crime is a good thing: but if this weapon is used carelessly and ordinary innocent people become its victims then it is a terrible thing indeed.

A telling example of what he meant was the story of a 40-year-old guide mistress who some thought had developed too close a friendship with a 17-year-old scout. Harry investigated and got his story, and then asked the woman for a photograph for publication. 'She quietly refused this and said: "Because of all this I have resigned my commission as a guide mistress, have given up a job which gave me no reward other than satisfaction of useful social work. Do not publish a picture of me, for it may cost me my job and I have an aged mother to support." '

As she talked, a Hasselblad long-range camera – 'a heartless ruthless instrument' – was taking pictures of 'this bread-winning spinster' from 100 yards away. 'Too far', says Harry, 'for the photographer to be attacked with a knitting needle or struck on the head with a guide's whistle. To her amazement she saw her picture in that week's *Sunday Pictorial*. So did her friends, her neighbours, her employers.' The story was the front-page lead.

Harry Procter does not explain what happened next, or what the point had been in the first place: an ability to uncover the human drama in a story clearly need not extend to any any real sympathy for those involved.

In the post-war years, tabloid journalism was, in its own way, every bit as competitive as now, with reporters racing in fast cars to be first to a story in Reading or Basingstoke. If the item was sensational or bizarre enough there would be the buy-up – paying for an exclusive – and the person involved would be whisked off to a hotel to protect the paper's investment and ensure no other reporters got near. Tyres of rivals would be let down. On really big stories a paper like the *Daily Express* would send four cars – three of them to block the road while the lead car got away with the quarry.

Arthur Brittenden, later to become the last broadsheet editor of the *Daily Mail*, took part in such mêlées:

> There were a lot of buy-ups in those days. Nowadays it's pop stars and sportsmen. Then it was ordinary people projected into the news because of domestic dramas, disputes or court cases. The mums and dads of criminals were bought up and there were great scenes at people's houses where they were besieged by reporters. It really was ill-mannered and rough a lot of the time.

There was also a much-valued subspecies of the journalistic profession – the snatchmen. They were usually failed photographers, and their job was to accompany reporters on interviews with relatives in tragedy stories and snatch – steal – pictures of the dead from mantelpieces. The good snatch-man could get out with the pictures the paper wanted without the victim realizing they had gone. Some photographs were returned; others were not.

The tradition of trampling on the sensibilities of those in the news when thought necessary certainly did not die out in the 1950s. Wensley Clarkson, a *Sunday Mirror* journalist in the 1980s who published his 'confessions of a tabloid journalist', *Dog Eat Dog*, in 1990, was a worthy successor to Harry Procter. Clarkson was, if anything, more outrageous, more cynical; he was not always concerned about the precise truthfulness of what he was writing, to a degree that would probably have shocked Harry Procter.

There was the story of 'the odd couple' – a Birmingham couple who had married and had a child and then both changed sex. Clarkson persuaded them to talk. To get an exclusive interview and get the couple away from rivals, a hotel room was booked and the two were led to a waiting car with blankets over their heads to prevent anyone else getting pictures. Why did the couple allow a total stranger to turn their world upside down? 'The answer is I told them what a traumatic time they were going through and suggested their case could provide encouragement to thousands of others caught in what the tabloids have since labelled "gender crisis".'

Then there was the celebrity interview. Clarkson once went off to Barbados in pursuit of actor Oliver Reed, who was on holiday with a 16-year-old girl who would later become his wife. After considerable fortification with rum punches, Clarkson wandered uninvited into Reed's villa, looked through the keyhole of the actor's bedroom and shouted, 'Everyone wants to know why you've run off with this girl. Don't you think it's a bit irresponsible?' The trespasser from the *Sunday Mirror* then got his exclusive 'interview' as he was chased through the house by the furious actor.

Perhaps the flavour of the journalism of Wensley Clarkson is best caught by his story about 'The Madonna of the Mountains'. The madonna was a young girl in northern Portugal who was being revered as a saint because, it was claimed, she had taken neither food nor drink for six years after talking to Christ.

When Clarkson arrived in her village, he discovered the whole story was obviously nonsense: the madonna was well enough to be out and about, and the local people said, 'She eats.' But that didn't stop the man from the *Sunday Mirror*. With the help of a photograph and some second-hand quotes from the local newspaper, he put together a story about the dark-haired teenager sitting serenely in her snow-white bed and smiling the quiet smile of a saint. 'Is the girl who should be dead a living miracle? Is she a saint? I visited Maria at her modest home in the village of Tropeco . . .' the story read.

'And so it went on,' Clarkson confesses. 'I never interviewed her. I never saw her, but I still created a great read. It is amazing what you can achieve with a little luck and a little cunning.'

Unfortunately there is no sign that the long tradition of printing stories that are unfair, untrue or exaggerated to the edge of irresponsibility is about to die out. The *Star* has made notable contributions to this tradition in recent years. The paper 'found' the skeleton of the missing Lord Lucan and splashed on the front page the story of the birth of the 14-lb baby, the biggest born in Britain for twenty years. The skeleton wasn't that of Lord Lucan and the baby didn't exist.

The *Star*'s coverage of the crash of an Austrian airliner in the Thai jungle on 27 May 1991 was a classic of its type. The crash killed 223 people, including Don McIntosh a 43-year-old Home Office civil servant on secondment to the United Nations anti-drug programme. He was involved in talks on the drugs issue with governments in the region and in monitoring attempts to persuade poor Thai farmers to grow more conventional crops instead of poppies.

'Sacrificed' was the *Star*'s headline over a story of how ruthless drug barons killed 223 people to get one man. 'Mr McIntosh was heading for a secret meeting in the Austrian capital. But the drug godfathers had named the UN agent as their No. 1 enemy – and made sure he didn't make it to Vienna,' the *Star* said. The story was based entirely on speculation and the coincidence of Don McIntosh's presence on the flight. What was really sacrificed was the *Star*'s credibility – although it wasn't alone: *Today* and the *Sun* were equally at fault. The first paragraph of the *Today* story read, 'A British drugbuster was blown up with the doomed Lauda Air jet to protect a £30,000 million heroin trade.' The *Sun*'s headline was 'Target 223 Blown Up As Drug Barons Wipe Out This Brit'. Before the week was out the plane's black-box flight-recorder revealed that an engine suddenly going into reverse thrust had been the cause of the crash, and neither bombs nor wicked drug barons had been involved in any way.

It is entirely legitimate for papers to speculate and raise questions about the presence of someone like Don McIntosh on board a crashed aircraft. For a paper like the *Star* to present such speculation as fact is just one more newspaper scandal.

3

'We reported as fully and fairly as we could'
Some classic press campaigns

ALL the fabricated scandals and intrusive stories written to titillate are more than balanced by the work of generation after generation of journalists who are serious about the integrity of their job, whether they work for popular or broadsheet nationals, regional or local papers. In any final evaluation of newspapers there are no 'qualities' and no tabloids, no simple division between sheep and goats. There is only what is good and honest and what is malicious, lax and biased, irrespective of the format or the size of the headlines.

Across the enormous range of journalism produced every day, stories that are factual, informative, thought-provoking and entertaining outweigh those that are tawdry. The former include journalism that defends the innocent, campaigns for reform, challenges unnecessary secrecy and even sometimes changes politicians' minds. There is worthy journalism, for example, that helps to cement a community's sense of identity by recording the small events of its daily life as well as the tragedies and misdemeanours. There is mainstream journalism that has none the less speeded up the process of social change in areas as diverse as penal reform and women's rights. There is journalism that has sent brave reporters around the world, to jail and sometimes to their deaths for expressing unpopular opinions, for challenging dictators of left and right or merely for trying to keep open the flow of information from dangerous places.

One of those who died was Farzad Bazoft of the *Observer*, who was hanged in Iraq in March 1990 after being convicted of spying. He had travelled to a rocket-testing site south of Baghdad to investigate reports that a huge explosion had killed hundreds. The final message that came back from the British embassy, and one intended for publication, was heartbreaking. It read

I love you mother. I love you father and I love you Farhad, Anahita, Afshin.

I am sorry if I went to Al-hilla Mr President. I always liked Iraq and its people. Everybody makes a mistake and I made one too.

I thank everyone in England and Iraq who tried to help me. If I have done anything wrong to anyone please forgive me, anywhere in the world. I like to thank Iraqi officials for their hospitality during my six trips to Iraq.

There have been allegations that Farzad Bazoft really was a spy. The *Observer*, after detailed checks with international intelligence agencies, is as certain as it can be that Bazoft was what he said he was – a reporter, albeit one who was inexperienced and foolhardy and prepared to push too hard for a story for safety's sake.

Another who died was David Blundy of the *Independent on Sunday*, one of the most experienced and talented foreign correspondents of his generation. He was shot dead by a sniper's bullet in El Salvador when he went back to check a story one last time.

The latest generation of journalists to go to war stayed in Baghdad to report the allied bombing long after everyone else, including diplomats, had been withdrawn. The journalists stayed at their 'posts' until removed by the Iraqi government, and returned to them as soon as they were free to do so.

Even when wars are over, danger remains. In May 1991 two *Financial Times* journalists – David Thomas, head of the natural-resources team at the paper, and Alan Harper, a staff photographer – went to Kuwait to work on a large special supplement on the reconstruction of the country. Their journey took them along a road flanked by burning wells, and leaking oil had formed pools on the road. It is not clear whether the oil ignited spontaneously as they passed or whether the blaze was caused by a skid and a crash. Thomas, Harper and several oil-workers caught in the same blaze were burned to death.

Such accidental deaths are tragic enough, but, according to the New York-based Committee to Protect Journalists, a body supported by charitable foundations, thirty-two journalists were deliberately killed around the world in 1990 and ninety-nine journalists, in twenty-four countries, were in jail. At least seventeen journalists were killed in Yugoslavia in 1991.

There are memorials to a few famous journalists, but for most – even those with some of the best-known bylines – professional oblivion can come with depressing speed. The public's memory of scoops that were struggled for fades much more quickly than the cuttings, and there is no more sobering sight for a journalist on the way to work than to see a copy of that day's newspaper already sticking out of a rubbish bin. But the work of all

British journalists does at least survive in microfiche form, held in the National Newspaper Library in the north-London suburb of Colindale, providing raw material to be sifted by future historians.

Like memorials to unknown soldiers, the Colindale library should have a memorial to the unknown journalist who carried out a difficult job well. Perhaps such a memorial should bear the words of Samuel Johnson, who worked as a political journalist for several years: 'I never open up a newspaper without finding something I should have deemed it a loss not to have seen; never without deriving from it instruction and amusement.'

Journalists contribute enormously to changes in social values, albeit in ways that cannot easily be quantified. 'One of the striking things about the press of the post-war period is that it was the press that provided the less literate public with knowledge about the changes in the social position and status of women. It provided them with knowledge of such issues as birth control and abortion,' says Lord McGregor of Durris, a former professor of social institutions at London University and chairman of the Press Complaints Commission, the self-regulatory body for the press which replaced the Press Council on 1 January 1991. Victorian attitudes to sex, he believes, were not really killed off until the 1950s, and the press played a major role in altering attitudes and promoting much higher standards of appropriate sexual behaviour on the road to greater equality between men and women.

Notwithstanding this general social influence, some individual reporters, editors and papers ought to be remembered for their work on a particular story or issue.

One of those who is now almost entirely forgotten is John Tyas, the leading parliamentary reporter of his day for *The Times*. In the summer of 1819 he travelled to Manchester to report on a meeting called to demand parliamentary reform.

Tension had been rising that year. Lord Liverpool's Tory government had put down riots with severity and had prosecuted the press for seditious libel as demands grew for universal suffrage and an end to the corn laws that blocked imports of grain and kept the price of food high. On 16 August, more than 60,000 had gathered in St Peter's fields to hear the radical reformer Henry 'Orator' Hunt.

The Times's owner, John Walter II, had increasingly retired to a dignified life in the country, and since 1817 the paper had been under the editorship of Thomas Barnes.

According to Derek Hudson's life of Barnes, the proprietor of *The Times* had warned his editor of the danger of rushing into print with views that were critical of the government. In response, Barnes had promised to try to curb his 'scribbling propensity'. He had denounced the Manchester meeting in advance, because of fears of disturbances, but he sent Tyas to cover it all the same.

Before 16 August was over, Hunt and Tyas were in jail, eleven people were dead and many more were injured in the incident that became known as the Peterloo Massacre.

What happened that day was described with precision by John Tyas, who completed his report for *The Times* in prison before being released by magistrates the following afternoon. He watched as at

> about half past 11 the first group of Reformers arrived at the ground bearing two banners, each of which was surmounted by a cap of liberty. The first bore upon a white ground the inscription of 'Annual Parliaments, and Universal Suffrage', and on the reverse side 'No Corn Laws'. The other bore upon a blue ground the same inscription, with the addition of 'Vote by Ballot'. As more groups arrived from all over Manchester and surrounding towns their banners and flags were collected and displayed on a dung-cart. At noon between 300 and 400 police marched on to the ground but were largely ignored. Not the slightest insult was offered to them.

Hunt had been speaking for less than twenty minutes when the Yeoman Cavalry were seen advancing at a rapid trot and in some disorder. As they halted to recover their ranks, panic struck some of those at the outskirts of the meeting.

'After a moment's pause the cavalry drew their swords and brandished them fiercely in the air.' Calling for three cheers, Hunt told the vast crowd to stand firm: the arrival of the Yeomanry was just a trick to interrupt the meeting.

> He had scarcely said those words before the Manchester Yeoman cavalry rode into the mob, which gave way before them and directed their course to the cart from which Hunt was speaking. Not a brickbat was thrown at them – not a pistol was fired during this period; all was quiet and orderly, as if the cavalry had been friends of the multitude and had marched as such into the midst of them.

Tyas wrote with a quiet detachment and a precise feel for detail which bring the events to life to a reader deciphering the tiny print more than 170 years later.

With a bugler at the front followed by an officer, the Yeomanry detachment then circled the wagons being used as a platform. The officer, brandishing his sword, went up to Hunt with a warrant for his arrest and said the Orator was his prisoner. Hunt told the crowd to be calm and peaceful, then turned to the officer and said, 'I willingly surrender myself to any civil officer.' When Mr Nadin, the chief police officer of Manchester, came forward, Hunt and Johnson, another leading reformer, jumped down from the wagon and surrendered.

Tyas had managed to get on to the makeshift platform, because he had been ill, and this was probably why he was arrested with the speakers. He told what happened next:

> As soon as Hunt and Johnson had jumped from the waggon, a cry was made by the cavalry, 'Have at their flags.' In consequence, they immediately dashed not only at the flags which were in the waggon, but those which were posted among the crowd, cutting most indiscriminately to the right and to the left in order to get at them. This set the people running in all directions, and it was not till this act had been committed that any brickbats were hurled at the military. From that moment the Manchester Yeomanry cavalry lost all command of temper.

The editor of the *Manchester Observer* was nearly run through by two privates. Tyas watched as a man five yards away from him 'had his nose completely taken off by a blow of a sabre' while another lay prostrate on the ground. As the *Times*'s reporter was being taken away by the constables to a nearby house, he saw a woman unconscious on the ground with two large gouts of blood on her left breast. 'Just as we came to the house, the constables were conducting Hunt into it, and were treating him in a manner in which they were neither justified by law nor humanity, striking him with their staves on the head.'

In an accompanying editorial, *The Times* commented that serious questions could be asked about the wisdom of bringing together so many people 'half employed and half starved' into one spot to be 'puffed up by prodigious notions of their own strength and inflamed by artful pictures of their own grievances'. All such reservations, however, sank to nothing 'before the dreadful fact, that nearly a hundred of the King's unarmed subjects have been sabred by a body of cavalry in the streets of a town of which most of them were inhabitants, and in the presence of those Magistrates whose sworn duty it is to protect and preserve the life of the meanest Englishman'.

The Times also told its readers how they would find 'amongst the names of the prisoners, that of a gentleman of the name of Tyas'. The paper went on to describe him as a man of talent and education, the nephew of an individual of great respectability in Manchester and 'as far as we judge from his preceeding conduct towards this journal, about as much of a Jacobin, or a friend of Jacobins, as is Lord Liverpool [the Prime Minister] himself'.

The Times's reports and comments were reproduced in other papers all over the country and created a groundswell of sympathy for the victims of the massacre.

The work of *The Times*'s reporter, which led to his being barred from the House of Commons, is an eloquent example of the power of the eyewitness. It certainly seems to have upset the government. On 25 August the paper published an open letter to his constituents from Sir Francis Burdett, the MP for Westminster, calling a meeting of protest against the 'Manchester Massacre'. Barnes was summoned to the Home Office for questioning by what turned out to be 'a very full Cabinet Council' including Lord Liverpool, Lord Sidmouth (the Home Secretary), the Duke of Wellington and Lord Harrowby (the Chancellor of the Exchequer). The ministers were mainly interested in taking action against the MP for Westminster, and went out of their way to make it clear there was no wish 'to molest *The Times*'. The interview was, however, clearly seen as an attempt to warn Barnes that he must watch his step. It did not have that effect.

In the autumn, despite attempts at official obstruction, *The Times* gave extensive coverage to the inquests of the dead of Peterloo. From then on, Barnes and *The Times* were allied with the cause of reform and against the government's notorious Six Acts, which included curbs on press freedom and the punishment of seditious and blasphemous libels, which embraced any writings that challenged the status quo.

That September *The Times* made its position on press freedom clear:

> We beg leave to say, that it is not the question whether or not the freedom of the press be productive of unmixed benefit to mankind. The question is, whether its advantages do not overbalance its evils. The question is, whether it be destroyed, or its actual freedom sensibly curtailed, we may not exchange occasional turbulence and conflict for the calm of despotism and the repose of the grave.

Almost forty years later another *Times* reporter – William Howard Russell – was to become much more famous than Tyas and to have an even greater discernible effect on events. Russell was the first of the professional war correspondents – a description he hated. His reports from the Crimea were the single most important factor in the resignation of Lord Aberdeen's Cabinet in 1855 and its replacement by one led by Lord Palmerston.

In the run-up to the war and under the editorship of John Thadeus Delane, *The Times* was at the height of its confidence and aggressiveness. The paper revealed 'on the next morning but one after the Cabinet meeting' the decision to send an ultimatum to the Tsar of Russia. An earlier secret proposal to Britain by the Tsar, suggesting the partition of Turkey, had also found its way into the columns of *The Times*.

For making such information public, the paper was denounced in the House of Lords by Lord Derby, leader of the Tory party. It was accused of perfidy and lack of responsibility. After listening to the debate, Delane replied to the attack with an article that reads almost like a journalistic manifesto. 'The part we have the honour to take in public affairs is guided and supported by as high a sense of honour of our profession and the interests of the country as will be met with among those who pursue in public life the distinctions of personal power or the emoluments of office,' he commented. Delane added that he preferred 'to live with men who shape their conduct to a purer standard of sincerity and truth' than politicians such as Lord Derby. To disclose the terms of the ultimatum to Russia had been a public service.

Delane was responsible for sending Russell (who had earlier reported on the Irish potato famine) with the British troops to the Crimea. Although he had little more status other than 'a travelling gentleman', he was allowed to draw army rations and to pitch his tent with the troops.

Russell's vivid reporting conveyed to the British people the near criminal negligence and ineptitude of the military authorities and the heroism and sufferings of the British soldiers. This was how he described the condition of the British Army before Sebastopol during the winter of 1854–5:

> In the tents the water was sometimes a foot deep – our men had neither warm nor waterproof clothing – they were out for twelve hours at a time in the trenches – they were plunged into the inevitable miseries of a winter campaign – and not a soul seem to care for their comfort, or even their lives. The wretched beggar who wandered the streets of London in the rain led the life of a prince compared with the British soldiers who were fighting for their country, and who, we were complacently assured by the home authorities, were the best appointed army in Europe.

It is ironic that Russell, with the help only of a horse, was probably able to report more directly and with less censorship and manipulation than many more modern reporters equipped with computer terminals and satellite receivers. Delane had offered to submit reports for scrutiny, but the army, not realizing what was about to happen to it, declined.

Russell was there when the Light Brigade was given the fatally ambiguous order to attack and rode along the North Valley into the mouth of the Russian guns rather than attacking Russians removing British guns from nearby redoubts:

> They swept proudly past, glittering in the morning sun in all the pride and splendour of war. We could scarcely believe the evidence of our senses. Surely that handful of men were not going to charge an army in position? They advanced in two lines, quickening their pace as they closed towards the enemy. A more fearful spectacle was never witnessed than by those who, without the power to aid, beheld their heroic countrymen rushing into the arms of death.

The Times reporter also wrote of the 'admirable completeness' of the French arrangements for their troops – everything from hospitals for the sick to bread and biscuit bakeries and wagon trains for carrying stores and baggage – every necessity and every comfort, indeed, at hand, the moment their ships came in'. There was privation rather than comfort for the British troops, who suffered terribly from the cold with one regulation blanket apiece, no proper provision for the sick and a multitude of complaints about the provision of supplies. 'But the officers at Gallipoli were not to blame. The persons really culpable were those who sent them out without a proper staff and without the smallest foresight or consideration,' wrote Russell.

There were complaints from the military that Russell and *The Times* were routinely giving away information useful to the enemy about the disposition of troops and the state of the army. But *The Times* mercilessly chronicled the follies and the inefficiencies of those conducting the war. The government was quickly persuaded to set up a single war office to end the bickering of overlapping authorities and to relax the strict parade-ground rules on uniforms.

The paper also started to advance a more fundamental and potentially revolutionary argument: that noble birth alone was not a sufficient qualification to run the army or the navy, or, indeed, to hold any high government office.

Public anger about the mishandling of the war intensified, until a radical MP, J. A. Roebuck, called for an inquiry into the condition of the troops at Sebastapol. His motion was carried and the government, interpreting this as a vote of no confidence, resigned.

After the war, the Duke of Newcastle told Russell to his face, 'It was you who turned out the government.' Lord Clarendon complained that, 'Three pitched battles would not repair the mischief done by Mr Russell.'

If the government really was turned out of office, it was *The Times* as much as the individual reporter that was responsible. For all Russell's bravery and skills as an observer and writer, it was, after all, *The Times* that had chosen to send him to the Crimea, and it was *The Times* that had continued to print his reports despite the criticism from politicians.

Field Marshall Sir Evelyn Wood wrote later that, although Russell had incurred much enmity, 'few unprejudiced men who were in the Crimea will now attempt to call into question that by awakening the conscience of the British nation to the sufferings of its troops, he saved the remnant of those grand battalions we landed in September.'

Long after the war, Russell wrote to Prince Gortschakoff, who had commanded the Russian troops at Sebastopol, and asked if there had been anything of military value to him in the reports in *The Times*. The prince replied that he had never found anything in them that he had not known beforehand.

Russell went on to report other wars, including the American Civil War. While in the United States he met President Abraham Lincoln, who told him he didn't know of anything more powerful than *The Times*, except perhaps the Mississippi. In 1895 he was awarded a knighthood for his services to journalism, and when he died in 1907, at the age of eighty-six, *The Times*'s obituary declared that, in an inherently ephemeral occupation, Russell had written newspaper articles which 'would be remembered as long as Englishmen interest themselves in the records of English valour, English heroism, English disasters and English victories'.

Lord McGregor believes the journalism of the Crimea was crucial to the history of the period: 'The combination of techniques of reporting, the market created for them and the type of journalist who was doing it destroyed for ever the privacy of governments.'

Another journalist who altered government policy was William Thomas Stead. Stead didn't go to war and didn't get a knighthood, but was sentenced to three months in Holloway prison as a 'misdemeanant of the first division'. Although he held rather romantic and, in the end, exaggerated ideas about the role and power of journalists, Stead managed to provoke a reluctant government into action with a powerful newspaper campaign – or, as he preferred to call it, 'escapade'.

Stead was editor of the *Pall Mall Gazette*. With his full red beard and evangelical passion for reform, he looked like a model of Victorian rectitude.

His faith in his profession was boundless. At one stage he advocated 'government by journalism', on the grounds that politicians were account-able to the electorate only at elections, whereas newspapers were account-able to their readers every day. In an article in the *Contemporary Review* in 1886, Stead wrote, 'I am but a comparatively young journalist, but I have seen Cabinets upset, ministers driven into retirement, laws repealed, great social reforms initiated, Bills transformed, estimates remodelled, pro-grammes modified, Acts passed, generals nominated, governors appointed, armies sent hither and thither, wars proclaimed and wars averted, by the agency of newspapers.'

Certainly Stead – who was once called a cross between Don Quixote and Phineas T. Barnum, the circus owner – campaigned against everything from Turkish atrocities in Bulgaria to the state of the London slums. Gladstone took up the cause of the Bulgarians, and a Royal Commission on Housing was set up to investigate the slums.

Stead had a considerable taste for sensation and a willingness to use new-fangled American journalistic techniques such as bold black headlines and interviews. Sensationalism, Stead believed, was justifiable 'up to the point that it is necessary to arrest the eye of the public and compel them to admit the necessity of action'.

In his greatest 'escapade', Stead brought together his passion for reform, a powerful interest in sex in general and virgins in particular, and his taste for sensation. The vehicle was a series of articles on child prostitution that began in the *Pall Mall Gazette* on 6 July 1885 under the headline: 'The Maiden Tribute of Modern Babylon'. These articles shook Victorian London. The subject-matter was shocking enough, but Stead also pulled no punches with the exposition. The cross-headings included 'How Girls Are Bought and Ruined' and 'Violation of Virgins'. Some Pall Mall clubs temporarily stopped taking the paper, and the articles were described as worse than any Egyptian plague visiting the homes of England. Stead was nick-named 'Bed-Stead' and MPs called for criminal prosecution.

Stead had become involved after being approached by reformers who feared a second failure in their attempt to get through Parliament a bill which would raise the age of consent from thirteen to sixteen and outlaw the sale of young girls to brothels. Not only was the age of consent then only thirteen but girls under the age of eight could not give evidence because it was believed they could not understand the concept of the oath. As a result, child prostitution was rife. Lord Shaftesbury said of it that,

'Nothing more cruel, appalling or detestable could be found in the history of crime all over the world.'

In his profile of Stead in *Lords and Labourers of the Press* Linton Andrews tells how Stead first approached Howard Vincent, a former head of the Criminal Investigation Department of Scotland Yard, and was told about those who procured and corrupted young girls. 'As soon as the child is over thirteen,' he was told, 'she can be inveigled into a house of ill fame and thence violated without any hope of redress, because if she has consented to go into the house she is held to have consented to her own ruin, although she might at that time be, and probably was, absolutely ignorant of what vice means.'

Stead decided to 'buy' a young girl just over thirteen to demonstrate the need for an increase in the age of consent. Those he consulted about his plan included Archbishop Benson and Cardinal Manning. He was even helped in his plan by General Booth of the Salvation Army.

In return for £5, the mother of Eliza Armstrong handed over her daughter to a former brothel-keeper turned Salvationist, ostensibly for a life of vice. The girl was first certified to be a virgin by a midwife. Stead then spent some time with the girl, to demonstrate that he could have had sex with her, if that had been his intention. Later, a doctor confirmed that the girl had not been interfered with in any way. Present-day tabloids would probably get into terrible trouble if they went even nearly as far as the eminently respectable Stead.

The *Pall Mall Gazette* article began in a way that scarcely seems sensational: 'In ancient times, if we may believe the myths of Hellas, Athens after a disastrous campaign was compelled by her conqueror to send once every nine years a tribute to Crete of seven youths and seven maidens.' But with the showmanship of later revelatory journalism, he warned that the squeamish and prudish would be shocked by the report of his secret commission: it would be read 'with shuddering horror that will thrill throughout the world'. In an accompanying comment on the front page, Stead attacked the Church, the press, the law and Parliament as accessories to the crime of child prostitution because of their silence. The press, which happily reported verbatim all the details of the divorce courts, recoiled in pious horror, he said, 'from the duty of shedding a flood of light upon these dark places which indeed are full of habitations of cruelty'.

As the articles continued, the Home Secretary asked Stead to stop publishing them. Stead replied that he would stop just as soon as the Home Secretary promised to ensure the bill's passage. No such promise was forthcoming. 'I then told him', Stead wrote, 'I would go on with publication until the roused indignation of the public compelled the Ministry to do their duty.' And that was precisely what happened. Public meetings up and down the country endorsed Stead's stand, and Parliament passed the bill which raised the age of consent to sixteen and accepted the evidence of younger children.

The escapade increased the circulation of the *Pall Mall Gazette* from 8,360 to 12,250 – an indication of how small some newspaper circulations were in those days – although the paper lost some respectable advertising as a result of the articles.

As though to punish him for his temerity, Stead was prosecuted for abducting Eliza and was found guilty on a technicality: he had needed the agreement of the girls' father but had only had the consent of her mother. He served two months of his sentence, but it does not seem to have been too great a burden. His newspapers arrived at 7.15 a.m. and a messenger came at 10 a.m. to pick up any articles he had written.

Stead was always eccentric – for example, he liked to catch and cook mice and eat them on toast – and after resigning the editorship of the *Pall Mall Gazette*, in 1890, he became increasingly obsessed with spiritualism and conducted interviews beyond the grave. The spirits did not, however, warn him against joining the maiden voyage of the *Titanic*, in 1912, and Stead died as he had lived. 'After it struck the ice-berg Stead behaved with the unearthly courage which had so distinguished his journalism,' Piers Brendon writes in *The Life and Death of the Press Barons*. 'He helped women and children aboard the boats and refused to wear one of the scarce life-jackets. He was last glimpsed standing alone on the deck in a prayerful attitude of profound meditation. His final request was that the heroic bandsmen, who went on performing as the ship sank, should play "Nearer My God To Thee".'

Keith Murdoch, father of Rupert Murdoch, achieved the near impossible. He saved many lives, changed the policy of a British government, prompted the sacking of a general and contributed to the resignation of Winston Churchill – and all this with a dispatch that was never published, or at least not in his lifetime.

Murdoch's story demonstrates how a reporter's observations and words can count even if they are read by only a tiny number of people, albeit highly influential people.

For six years after graduating from high school in 1903, Keith Murdoch was an apprentice reporter on the *Melbourne Age*, a period that included a year in the paper's London office. As the First World War broke out in Europe in 1914, he became Melbourne correspondent of the *Sydney Sun*.

It was a disappointing time for him. He failed to win the one Australian place in the press corps which accompanied the Gallipoli landings against the Turks in 1915 and had to accept second prize – running the London cable office of an Australian newspaper group. He was given a small job to do in Cairo on the way to London – for a fee of £25, he was to investigate complaints about the inefficiency of the Australian forces' postal service.

Murdoch received the permission of General Sir Ian Hamilton, the officer in charge of the Dardanelles campaign, to visit campaign head-quarters on the Gallipoli peninsula to carry out his investigations. The army was determined to ensure that he really was investigating postal complaints and not reporting on the war, and he had to give an undertaking not to publish anything that had not been passed by the military censor. The visit turned out to be decisive for the future careers of both Murdoch and Sir Ian.

When he arrived in Gallipoli, Keith Murdoch was appalled and outraged by what he saw – nothing less than the pointless sacrifice of thousands of Australian and New Zealand soldiers by incompetent British commanders.

What could Murdoch do, given his semi-official role? He met a frustrated British war correspondent, Ellis Ashmead-Bartlett, who had been prevented from filing his reports by the military authorities. Murdoch agreed to carry an Ashmead-Bartlett dispatch to London. But news of its existence leaked out, and on the way the report was confiscated by the authorities. Nevertheless, when he arrived in London, Murdoch wrote an 8,000 word account of conditions in the Dardenelles, presumably based on his own and Ashmead-Bartlett's observations – an account intended for the Australian Prime Minister, Andrew Fisher.

Before it was sent, Murdoch had lunch with Geoffrey Dawson, the then editor of *The Times*. Because of the importance of his story, the young Australian was sent to meet the paper's proprietor, Lord Northcliffe, a political ally of Lloyd George.

Northcliffe told Murdoch that the time spent carrying that 'very terrible dispatch' to the Antipodes could be better spent and suggested taking immediate action by showing it to Lloyd George. Murdoch then met and was questioned by members of the war Cabinet. His report was copied and accorded the status of a Cabinet paper. It was declassified by the Australian government only in 1980.

'Flies are spreading dysentery, and we must be evacuating 1,000 sick and wounded men every day. When the autumn rains come and unbury our dead, now lying under a light soil in our trenches, sickness must increase,' Murdoch wrote in his dispatch, quoted by *The Times* in a profile in 1990. Every man knew, he warned, that previous operations had been grossly bungled by the general staff and that 'Hamilton had led a series of armies into a series of cul-de-sacs.' He added that 'the conceit and complacency of the red feather men are equalled only by their incapacity'.

The effect was immediate. Twenty-four hours later Hamilton was relieved of his command, and within days his successor, General Munro, recommended evacuation – a recommendation that was accepted by Lord Kitchener, the Secretary for War.

Ironically for a journalist, Keith Murdoch had almost as much effect as Russell with but a single dispatch – and one that was never published in his lifetime.

Journalists played a much more ambiguous role in the years before the Second World War.

One of the most powerful drawings by the left-wing cartoonist David Low in the run-up to war appeared on 3 January 1938. It featured the ballet of the 'Shiver Sisters' – J. L. Garvin, editor of the *Observer*, Geoffrey Dawson, editor of *The Times*, and Lord Rothermere, all dancing furiously in tutus made out of newspaper. They were dancing to the command of a diminutive Dr Goebbels, the German propaganda chief, and to a record of German foreign policy. The cartoon appeared in Lord Beaverbrook's *Evening Standard*. Beaverbrook, although no appeaser, was at the time insisting there would be no war 'this year or the next' and appeared to see optimism as simply good for business.

No one associated with the *Daily Mirror* was caricatured in the cartoon line-up of the Shiver Sisters' ballet. Unlike their 'betters' at *The Times*, both the *Mirror* and its sister paper the *Sunday Pictorial*, under the editorship of Hugh Cudlipp, gave early and unequivocal warnings to the British people and government of the dangers of appeasement and the risks involved in trying to do deals with Hitler.

In May 1937, Dawson of *The Times*, who believed that the peace of the world depended on Britain having good relations with Germany, wrote a notorious letter to his correspondent in Germany following Nazi criticism of the paper. 'It would interest me greatly to know precisely what it is in *The Times* that has produced this antagonism in Germany. I did my utmost, night after night, to keep out of this paper anything that might hurt their susceptibilities,' he wrote. And that October Dawson was arguing in a leader that, although there was a point where Britain might have to make a stand, 'a supreme effort for appeasement' was needed until that point was reached.

The complete contrast between the two papers could be seen less than a month later, when the *Mirror* condemned Fascist 'frightfulness' in Spain and criticized those in Britain who were trying to talk Hitler into a nicer mood. 'We shall be fools if we don't remember his "plan". It is all in his unreadable book,' the *Mirror* warned, foreseeing the conquest of eastern Europe and the destruction of France.

In 1989, on the fiftieth anniversary of the declaration of war, Hugh Cudlipp, now Lord Cudlipp, the last surviving national newspaper editor of the period, wrote of how the bulk of the British press had hoodwinked the public with a diet of lies, distortion and baseless optimism. It was only the tabloids who could reopen their files without a sense of shame. 'There is now no closed season in the national sport of castigating the more odious of the present day tabloids but the follies of the higher echelon newspapers of the Thirties were vastly more iniquitious. What was at stake was not moral mores but national security and our martial capacity to survive a six-year war.'

The *Mirror* leader-writer Richard Jennings composed mini-leaders as pithy as a Japanese haiku:

> The dictators mean war.
> Be strong.
> Re-arm.
> Seek allies.
> Appeasement will not save us; it is
> leading to disaster.

In September 1938 the *Mirror* attacked what it called the 'heil-Hitlerite organs of the British press' who portrayed the problems between Britain and Germany as merely about minority populations in Czechoslovakia. 'We believe', the *Mirror* said, 'that a firm resistance to threats may even now save us from a real war with weapons. But it is the last chance.' The *Mirror*'s consistent advice was to arm, arm, arm and to set up a form of National Service.

The paper also gave an important platform to Winston Churchill, then in the political wilderness, and forcefully argued for his return to the Cabinet.

In his political history of the *Mirror*, Maurice Edelman tells how in July 1939 Cecil King, then a director of the *Mirror*, and Cudlipp visited

Churchill and persuaded him to write what turned out to be an influential series of articles. The articles began with a warning to Germany that it could not overrun much of eastern and central Europe and then make peace with the Western Powers. 'Napoleon, sword in hand, sought victorious peace in every capital in Europe. He sought it in Berlin, in Vienna, in Madrid, in Rome and finally in Moscow. All he found was St Helena,' Churchill wrote.

Less than two weeks before the outbreak of war, the future Prime Minister warned in the *Mirror* that there was no question of buying peace or of further concessions in the face of threats of violence. 'We cannot pay Germany to leave off doing wrong,' Churchill said.

On 4 September 1939, the day after the outbreak of war, the *Mirror* appeared with a roaring-lion symbol on its front pages. On page 10 of that edition, the columnist Cassandra – William Connor – had prepared a page in the form of a poster: 'WANTED! For Murder . . . For Kidnapping . . . For Theft And For Arson – Adolf Hitler *alias* Adolf Schicklegruber . . .'

It was another, very different, conflict that brought out the best in what was then the *Manchester Guardian*, even if the paper's performance did rather more for its reputation in London and abroad than in the better-off suburbs of the Manchester area. In 1956 the *Guardian* unambiguously warned of the dangers of going to war over Nasser's nationalization of the Suez canal: it roundly condemned the attacks on Egypt when they were unleashed and, in the aftermath of the conflict, it patiently picked out evidence of collusion between the Israelis, the French and the British. (James Morris, the writer later to become Jan Morris, then a *Guardian* reporter, revealed that French aircraft flown by pilots in French uniform had played an important and possibly even decisive part in the Israeli attack in the Sinai.)

Although the *Manchester Guardian* was the outstanding opponent of Britain's Suez policy, the *Daily Mirror*, the *Economist* and the *Observer* were also among the critics of the government's actions.

On 30 October, when Sir Anthony Eden, the Prime Minister, issued an ultimatum to Egypt to accept the presence of Anglo-French forces in key places such as Port Said and Suez, Alastair Hetherington, at the age of thirty-six, was in the editor's chair at the *Guardian*'s headquarters in Cross Street, Manchester (he did not formally become editor until the next day). 'It took me only five minutes to make up my mind. The ultimatum was consistent with all that we already know of Eden's policy. He was seizing the opportunity to make war on Egypt. He wanted to dislodge Nasser,'

Hetherington recalls in his autobiography, *Guardian Years*. As the front page was prepared, the new editor went quietly off to write his leader.

'The Anglo-French ultimatum to Egypt is an act of folly, without justification in any terms but brief expediency. It pours petrol on a growing fire. There is no knowing what kind of explosion will follow,' Hetherington began. The ultimatum could lead to war not only with Egypt but with the whole Arab world, and countless other nations would consider Britain and France to be in the wrong, the paper argued.

Right from the beginning of the Suez Canal crisis, the *Manchester Guardian* had warned of the folly of considering force against Nasser:

> What Colonel Nasser has done may be awkward, commercially damaging to the West, and perhaps even part of a plan for creating a new Arab Empire based on the Nile. But it is not ground for armed action – unless he closes the canal, or seizes the British maintenance bases there, or turns against his neighbours. We must be ready for action, but we must not launch it without cause.

The *Manchester Guardian* was lucky: its coverage and editorials were being guided behind the scenes by information from one of its North American correspondents, Max Freedman. This correspondent, who had top-level sources in the US administration, was filing private messages saying not only that the British government was preparing military action to seize the Suez canal but that the Americans were urging caution.

According to the historian of the *Manchester Guardian*, David Ayerst, the paper's line on Suez had a marked effect – Labour was provoked into taking a strong line, many Conservatives were alerted to the direction Eden was planning and the Commonwealth learned that there was serious opposition to war in Britain.

The paper later discovered that Eden had called for preparations to take over control of the BBC to prevent the broadcasting overseas of the critical comments of Hugh Gaitskell, the Labour Party leader, and those of the *Manchester Guardian*, but memoirs suggest that the *Guardian*'s evidence of opposition to Suez within Britain was important in limiting the disruptive effect of the unpopular action within the Commonwealth.

Alastair Hetherington, writing twenty-five years after the event, had no regrets whatever about the decisions taken in haste in Cross Street:

> We reported as fully and fairly as we could. We gave as much space and prominence to opponents as to friends. We reflected, I believe, a more balanced perspective of world reaction than did most other newspapers. We used the

advocacy of our leader columns and occasionally special articles to try to bring home to readers – and to the country's leaders – the mistaken and dangerous course of British policy. We succeeded perhaps better than at the time we knew.

Above all else it was a success for honest journalism that did not hesitate to expose the follies of governments.

Harold Evans was an editor who succeeded to an extent he could never have imagined possible. In September 1972, as editor of the *Sunday Times*, he took on an apparently impossible task – trying to win proper compensation for the children born without arms or legs, or with only rudimentary limbs, after their mothers had taken the drug Thalidomide during pregnancy. It is a story of remarkable perseverance by a newspaper in a campaign against inflexible and unnecessarily slow and secret legal practices, and against the large multinational company Distillers, which marketed the drug and was apparently putting its responsibilities to shareholders before a moral duty to the children.

When Evans decided to try to do something about compensation for the children – there were about 450 of them in Britain – Thalidomide was already a very old story. Some compensation settlements had been made, but they averaged only £16,000. Most of the children were by then around eleven years old and had still not received a penny of compensation. Because the cases were still before the court, publication of any comment about the drug or the children was likely to be judged a contempt of court. 'This was why there had been silence in the press and Parliament for a decade,' Harold Evans wrote in *Good Times, Bad Times*. It was that legally imposed silence that Evans decided to challenge.

Quite apart from the legal barriers, Harold Evans believed that the 'episodic' way in which news is defined by newspapers and broadcasters contributed to the silence on Thalidomide. Journalism, the *Sunday Times*'s editor argued, still had not learned how to write about slow-moving processes as well as about dramatic events.

The paper was prevented from telling the full story of the history of the drug while the case was *sub judice*, because it would inevitably go to the heart of the issue of legal liability. But could the level of compensation be challenged to try to get better terms for the children?

With the help of its lawyer, James Evans, the *Sunday Times* found a way and launched the campaign in its issue of 24 September 1972. At its heart was a leading article, headlined 'Children on Our Conscience', which argued that, leaving aside legal liability, Distillers had a moral duty to provide better compensation for the children. There were also articles on the history of the Thalidomide litigation and a critical analysis of the terms offered for settlement and what they meant for the children.

The articles were followed up in a BBC interview with Harold Evans, but the only other reaction was a letter from the Attorney General's office suggesting that the articles could be in contempt of court. Later that week, however, the campaign was given a significant boost when Jack Ashley, the Labour MP, put his weight behind it.

A second week's material was published. When a draft article planned for the third week of the campaign was shown to Distillers, the company issued a writ to try to prevent publication. The draft article was banned by the High Court, which ruled that no pressure could be allowed once legal proceedings had begun.

Harold Evans says the turning-point in the fight came when the Labour opposition gave up a day of its parliamentary time for a full debate, and Distillers was heavily criticized. Prime Minister Edward Heath announced a government trust fund of £3 million for congenitally disabled children, with a further £3 million for the Thalidomide children once the legal proceedings were over. Within weeks a Royal Commission was set up under the chairmanship of Lord Pearson to look at the whole question of personal-injury damages.

The pressure on Distillers grew – from both its shareholders and its customers. In the end, in January 1973, the company agreed to pay £28.4m to compensate all the families – vastly more than the original amount offered.

Such an outcome would have been success enough for most newspapers. But Harold Evans and the *Sunday Times* went on with their legal battle to win the right to tell the full Thalidomide story.

Later in 1973 the Appeal Court rejected the High Court's view that a writ must always end all discussion. Lord Denning argued that, in addition to the interests of the parties involved in litigation, there were other interests – the public interest in matters of national concern and 'the freedom of the press to make fair comment'. But in July 1973 the Appeal Court judgement was itself overturned by the highest court in the land – the Law Lords.

Harold Evans and some of the journalists involved – Bruce Page, Phillip Knightly and Elaine Potter – then took their case to Europe to argue that they had been deprived of their rights to receive and impart information under the European Convention for the Protection of Human Rights, which

Britain had signed in 1953. In July 1977 the European Commission of Human Rights found Britain to be in breach of the convention, and, because the banned draft article was carried as an appendix to the judgement, the *Sunday Times* was at last free to publish.

Final victory came on 26 April 1979, when the international judges of the European Court of Human Rights ruled by a narrow majority that the rights of the *Sunday Times* journalists had been infringed by the House of Lords' upholding the original High Court injunction. The ruling in Europe led to a British Act of Parliament that meant that in future a case such as Thalidomide would become *sub judice* only when it was set down for trial rather than, as in the past, when a writ was issued.

For Harold Evans, the European Court's ruling went far beyond Thalidomide. 'It put its judgement in a way which appealed to me, not so much on the right of the press to publish as the right of an individual to information which may affect his life, liberty and happiness. That is a powerful weapon against many of the censorships that have grown up in my generation in Britain,' Evans wrote in *Good Times, Bad Times*.

The *Sunday Times*'s campaign was an absolute model of its kind. Not only did it achieve its principal target, winning better compensation for the Thalidomide children, it also rolled back at least some of the unnecessary secrecy that still surrounds many aspects of British society.

Newspaper virtue did not stop in the 1960s or 1970s, although it has become almost conventional wisdom that television – through programmes such as Granada's *World in Action* and *This Week* on Thames TV – has partly taken over the mantle of investigative journalism. To some extent this is hardly surprising. Television has often been able to devote up to a year of resources and patience to an investigation – something that most newspapers have generally been unable or reluctant to do.

The view that investigative newspaper journalism is in decline is one that distresses *Sunday Times* editor Andrew Neil. 'I grow increasingly weary of journalists whose heyday was in the 1960s or 1970s constantly bemoaning the lack of investigative journalism in the *Sunday Times*.' Neil can with some justice point to stories such as the exposure of how the French government funded the bombing of the Greenpeace ship *Rainbow Warrior* in 1985, the revelation of details of Israel's secret nuclear-bomb factory in 1986, the naming of the senior industrialists most responsible for polluting Britain's rivers in 1989 and, in 1991, the uncovering of corruption in local government in Liverpool which led to arrests.

With ITV franchises going in most cases to the highest bidder in 1991, the balance may be about to shift again towards investigative journalism in newspapers. On ITV at least, there is a severe danger of a shortage of money – so much will be going to the Treasury – and an obvious danger of current-affairs programmes which attract relatively low ratings being moved out of influential peak-time slots.

In an age when newspaper standards are under attack, it is important to remember that you can still pick up the papers and see important journalism. And not just in the broadsheets. The *Mail on Sunday*'s editor Stewart Steven ran a powerful and ultimately successful campaign to remove the injunctions issued by the courts to prevent anyone writing about, or even doing anything to help, the children taken screaming from their homes in the cases of alleged sex abuse in Rochdale. The injunctions issued by Sir Stephen Brown, president of the Family Division of the High Court, and Mr Justice Carter, forbade the children from talking to anyone who might help them and prevented newspapers making any inquiries on their behalf. Counsel's advice was that not even local councillors could do anything to help their constituents.

Newspapers are at their best when they are not sticking their noses into someone's private life but dealing with matters of life and death and justice. A good example is Robert Fisk, whom many consider the most distinguished foreign correspondent of his generation. In February 1991 he wrote from the Gulf on 'the bad taste of dying' – an attempt to describe the reality of modern warfare for those who have to endure it. 'In a ground war sound and reality no longer marry up. To a soldier in his first ground battle, reality is broken apart like a film whose soundtrack has wobbled out of sync. Shells burst in silence, explosions have no source,' he wrote.

Fisk's reporting of the Gulf War for the *Independent* was controversial both with politicians and with some fellow journalists. The *Independent*'s correspondent stayed clear of the 'pool' system which gave journalists a limited degree of access to military units and briefings in return for accepting restrictions on what could be reported. Instead, Fisk made his own way to the front and severely criticized those who, he believed, too easily accepted military restrictions.

On 6 February 1991 Fisk wrote of a new cosy and damaging relationship between reporters and military in the Gulf War. 'You are warriors too,' he quoted an American colonel as saying to journalists as he handed out small American flags that had been carried in the cockpits of the first US jets to bomb Baghdad. 'So thorough has been the preparation for this war, so dependent have journalists become upon information dispensed by the

Western military authorities in Saudi Arabia, so enamoured of their technology, that press and television reporters have found themselves trapped,' Fisk argued.

Robert Fisk and other 'unilaterals', as they came to be called, were criticized for their independence and for their unwillingness to be controlled by the military information machine or to identify too closely with 'Our Boys' against 'The Enemy' – Iraq. Hardly anyone – the main exception was John Keegan, defence editor of the *Telegraph* – predicted correctly that there would be a quick Allied victory.

The *Guardian* distinguished itself in the aftermath of the war. On 3 April 1991 the paper gave up virtually its entire front page to an article by its reporter Martin Woollacott, who had escaped from Saddam Hussein's troops into the mountains of Turkey after two weeks of covering the Kurdish rebellion in northern Iraq. His report was hardly objective in the conventional sense: its first paragraph read, 'A monstrous crime is being perpetuated in Kurdistan. As the Kurdish people's brief springtime of freedom ends, they are and will be subject not only to the effects of a war waged in their own cities and towns without restraint or morality but to the reimposition of Saddam Hussein's brutal regime and his revenge on those who have challenged him.'

Just as newspapers are by their very nature more interested in bad news than good, so the *Sun* is often remembered more for its very public transgressions than for the obvious good it does. When the *Sun* lifts its gaze from publishing trivia about the lives of minor television actors or indulging in mindless jingoism, it can be very good indeed. In major stories such as disasters the paper often leaves the broadsheets leaden-footed. But its enormous power is used to best effect when it tries to rescue individual citizens from the clutches of bureaucrats or campaigns to overturn obvious injustices.

In September 1991 the *Sun* got its teeth into the case of 81-year-old Rose Stamps and, a favourite target, British Telecom. Rose was being pursued by BT to pay off a telephone bill for £1,395.57 – a bill that had been run up by intruders at her old flat. Rose said she had asked BT to cut off the line. One day after the *Sun* ran the story, the paper was able to write, 'Bullying British Telecom was yesterday shamed by the *Sun* into scrapping pensioner Rose Stamps's £1,395.57 bill for calls she never made.'

Earlier in the year the paper had an even more satisfying victory, this time over the Ministry of Defence. The men from the ministry were refusing to pay special compensation to three soldiers who lost their legs when a discarded shell exploded while they were digging a trench during a military exercise in Canada in 1989. The *Sun* led a campaign for compensation and really got the MoD in its sights when the Armed Forces Minister, Archie Hamilton, suggested that the men could get an office job where they wouldn't need their legs. The campaign was even supported by Prince Philip, and in July 1991 Prime Minister John Major overruled his Defence Secretary, Tom King, and asked for talks on compensation to begin.

There is no obvious pattern to the production of high-quality journalism and no guarantee that it will survive for long where it does exist. As we have seen, it depends to an extraordinary degree on tenacious individuals. But good journalism rarely flourishes in isolation. It needs a favourable newspaper culture and context. Individual journalists need the backing of enlightened editors who stand up to the inevitable attacks and threats of legal action. Apart from overt pressures, journalists also face continuous attempts by lobbyists, public-relations firms and politicians to manipulate them to present a particular view of the world. The carrot is usually access to exclusive information; the door can slam shut if an 'unhelpful' article is published. The editors in turn need the support of proprietors who are not consumed by their own sense of self-importance, political certainty or overwhelming desire for profit.

Profit is important, though. A loss-making newspaper is seldom a self-confident newspaper, and the fact that its survival depends on subsidies, even if only from the rest of its group, can make a paper vulnerable to advertisers threatening to withdraw their business if a particular campaign is not toned down. Distillers, the largest single advertiser in the *Sunday Times*, withdrew its advertising because of the paper's Thalidomide campaign.

Yet, while it is interesting and uplifting to recall famous reporters, distinguished editors and successful campaigns, these do not represent the greatest achievement of newspaper journalism. That lies much more in the extent and range of interesting, accurate and useful information produced day after day to tight deadlines: information that helps to shape the world and people's view of their place in it.

4

'It's a queer old world, isn't it?'
False information and the press

ENORMOUS personal suffering can be caused by individual newspaper stories that are inaccurate or that intrude into people's privacy for no good reason. A few examples pass into the collective memory of the country, either because of the fame of those involved, the outrageousness of the behaviour alleged or the size of the libel damages eventually awarded. Such scandal stories damage the reputation of the press and perhaps play some part in coarsening the tone of public discourse, but in most cases they amount to little more than marks in the sand and are swept away by each day's new tide of print.

It is much more serious when significant sections of the press consistently misjudge an important social issue and either fail to provide enough reliable information for informed judgement or actively mislead their readers.

As Harold Evans has argued, the press is better at handling single events than it is at handling gradual social processes which have no obvious beginning or end. With a small number of honourable exceptions, such as the *Observer*, few newspapers showed sustained concern for the environment until the problem became so obvious and pressing that there was seen to be commercial and circulation advantage in the issue. Then newspapers began sprouting environmental correspondents and developed an instantaneous interest in green politics.

It has proved more difficult for some sections of the press to come to terms with the phenomenon of AIDS – Acquired Immune Deficiency Syndrome – and this may have had dangerous consequences for their readers. By any standards, AIDS is one of the major stories of both the 1980s and the 1990s. Around the world many thousands have already died, and as yet there is no cure once the 'full-blown' disease develops.

The HIV virus, which most scientists believe causes AIDS, can be transmitted by the exchange of bodily fluids – semen, vaginal fluid or blood. It can be passed on during sex, during transfusions of infected blood, when sharing needles to inject drugs and when semen from an infected man is used in the artificial insemination of a woman – although screening now prevents that happening. The most frightening aspect of the virus is the fact that someone can be HIV-positive for as long as eight years with no symptoms, before the onset of AIDS. Yet during that time he or she is capable of transmitting the virus to others.

All of this basic information and more is readily available to anyone who asks. There is even a leaflet *HIV & AIDS – A Guide For Journalists* produced by the Health Education Authority and the National Union of Journalists. Yet, to their lasting disgrace, many popular newspapers have consistently reported AIDS as a 'gay plague' and therefore a problem which has little to do with the community as a whole.

For years, Terry Sanderson has written a 'Media Watch' column for *Gay Times*. In a booklet on how Fleet Street treats gay issues, he described how AIDS had many of the essential elements of a tabloid story: 'a tragic fatal disease which is, for good measure, sexually transmitted; overtones of pseudo-religious morality; "innocent" victims as well as a culpable villain; and of course homosexuality. How the papers revelled in it. Thousands of column inches, hundred of lurid headlines and, day after day, an almost vindictive desire to avoid the truth.'

An example was the enthusiastic coverage of the death from AIDS of film star Rock Hudson in 1985. Many papers went into detail about the star's previously unrealized homosexuality, but the *Daily Star* went one stage further with 'Terror in Tinseltown', which played up the fear of the actresses who had been involved in film love scenes with Rock Hudson, even though there was no likelihood of AIDS being transmitted during such scenes. For its part, the *Sun* contributed a story quoting an American psychologist Paul Cameron as saying that all homosexuals should be exterminated to stop the spread of AIDS. It was time to stop pussy-footing around, he argued.

In his booklet, Terry Sanderson pleaded that, rather than the meting out of blame or persecution, the difficult issues involved needed honest discussion. 'No other disease has been blamed on an identifiable minority like this; no other disease is given a morality,' he argued.

The facts are on Sanderson's side. Although so far most cases of HIV infection and of AIDS in the UK have involved gay and bisexual men and injecting drug-users, that situation is changing. Elsewhere in the world the spread of the virus has been mainly through heterosexual sex. In Africa, where the first cases of the disease were identified in the mid-1970s, the numbers of men and women afflicted are roughly even.

Despite the grim history of press coverage of the issue, the articles that appeared within two days of each other in December 1990 were still remarkable. One was a leading article in the *Daily Star*; the other was a column in the *Sun*. Together, these pieces could have been read by upwards of 14 million people. The articles were written to complain about World AIDS Day and the fact that 'the mawkish minority' had dared to mark the occasion with television documentaries on the disease. While the words in the *Star* and the *Sun* were very slightly different, their theme was depressingly familiar – that AIDS is an affliction of 'promiscuous shirtlifters' and male entertainers, and only sanctimonious 'twerps' could ever imagine it would affect ordinary decent folk.

Under the headline 'AIDS isn't so Special', the *Star* was prepared to concede that AIDS is a horrible killer illness but then so too are cancer, heart diseases, multiple sclerosis and a host of others, and these affect a lot more people. Sufferers from such menaces and their loved ones, the paper argued, must be wondering why AIDS is singled out for such lavish attention. 'Is it because AIDS has ravaged the high-profile world of show business, killing many male entertainers? Could it be that the mortal terror of those with "sophisticated" lifestyles is being used to instil needless fear in ordinary folk? *It's a queer old world, isn't it?*' said the *Star* profoundly.

Over in the *Sun*, the paper's then television critic, Garry Bushell, was warning of the terrible epidemic threatening to engulf Britain – the plague of AIDS documentaries. 'Shirtlifters' might be dropping like ninepins, but where was the evidence that the disease would blitz normal, decent people? 'How long before the TV trendies realize no one believes the hysteria? People know who AIDS affects, and how,' Bushell argued, with a tone of righteous certainty.

The problem is that, in a rather frightening sense, Garry Bushell is right. A very large number of people do indeed appear to 'know' – or at least believe they know – that AIDS doesn't pose any serious threat to them. A Gallup survey to mark the World AIDS Day that the *Star* and *Sun* took such exception to found an alarming level of complacency about the disease, especially among women in the UK. Less than one in three people in the UK believes AIDS is a serious risk to British women, even though, in heterosexual intercourse, the probability of a woman contracting HIV from an infected man is much greater than that of a man contracting HIV from an infected woman.

The statistics do little to support the confidence of papers like the *Sun* that AIDS is a just a problem faced by homosexuals and others with 'sophisticated' lifestyles. In New York, AIDS is now the largest cause of death for those under thirty – of both sexes. And, according to the World Health Organization, 6 million people worldwide, including 2 million women, now have the HIV virus which usually leads to AIDS. By the end of 1990, 179 women in Britain were suffering from AIDS, an increase of 72 per cent in twelve months. According to the Department of Health, heterosexual intercourse was by far the fastest growing route by which women were being infected. Even more alarmingly, by the beginning of 1991 the number of heterosexual cases being seen at London clinics already equalled that of gay men four years earlier. A study published in the *Lancet* in June 1991 showed that one in 500 pregnant women in London was infected with the virus – four times the proportion in 1988.

By classifying AIDS as a 'gay plague', albeit one that can also affect intravenous drug-users and haemophiliacs, papers such as the *Sun* and the *Star* are at the very least confusing their readers and lulling them into a false sense of security. The coverage represents a dramatic failure by some editors and columnists to come to terms with one of the most significant and tragic stories of the final decades of the twentieth century. The dangerous mixture of prejudice and ignorance displayed in their pages may actually have cost some readers their lives.

In 1988 the Health Education Authority was mocked when it launched an anti-AIDS campaign aimed at heterosexuals. The *Daily Express* accused the HEA of spreading a 'false message of AIDS', while the *Mail* thought that a campaign directed at heterosexuals was 'a lie, a waste of funds and energy and a cruel diversion'. Later that year the *Daily Star* called for the creation of 'leper-like colonies' for AIDS sufferers, because 'the human race is under threat from promiscuous homosexuals', the spawning-ground for the disease, according to the *Star*.

The late George Gale, the *Mail's* 'voice of common sense', had forthright views on the government spending money on television advertising to persuade young adults to use condoms to prevent the transmission of the HIV virus.

'The best way to avoid AIDS is to refuse to permit anal intercourse, with or without condoms. The message to be learned – that the Department of Health should now be urgently propagating – is that active homosexuals are potential murderers and that the act of buggery kills.'

Not all newspapers are equally ill-informed in their AIDS coverage.

Margaret Jay, the former *Panorama* journalist who is director of the National AIDS Trust, the coordinating body for voluntary AIDS organizations, has found a clear distinction between the popular press and the broadsheets in the reporting of AIDS. The broadsheets have understood the seriousness of the issue and have on the whole been helpful, she says. The *Daily Mail* and the *Daily Express* were a little slower off the mark, but they got there – particularly when AIDS became a royal concern and the Princess of Wales began identifying herself in public with AIDS victims. 'I don't think it has got through to *Today*, the *Star* or the *Sun*. Probably the *Star* and the *Sun* are the worst,' Ms Jay believes. On this issue, at least in recent years, the *Daily Mirror* tended to take its lead on AIDS from its publisher, the late Robert Maxwell, who decided that such a major issue needed his personal intervention. He didn't quite manage to raise the £50 million he once hoped to find in order to tackle the disease, but he did personally donate £1.5 million.

The *Sun* has produced the most outrageous and irresponsible headline ever to be written on top of a story about AIDS: 'Straight Sex Cannot Give You AIDS – Official.' This appeared above a story quoting the Irish peer Lord Kilbracken as saying that the chances of getting AIDS from heterosexual sex were 'statistically invisible'. The story was based on Department of Health statistics showing that only a small number of heterosexuals had so far contracted full-blown AIDS as opposed to the HIV virus. An editorial trumpeted that people could forget the idea that ordinary heterosexual people could get AIDS – they couldn't. So the *Sun* had been right all along and everyone else had been part of a vast conspiracy to delude the public. 'The risk of catching AIDS if you are heterosexual is "statistically invisible". In other words "impossible". So now we know – anything else is just homosexual propaganda. And should be treated accordingly,' the *Sun* said.

Unfortunately that was not an isolated aberration. The next day the paper followed through with a piece by Dr Vernon Coleman, the paper's doctor, arguing, under the headline 'AIDS – The Hoax of the Century,' that the truth was simple: AIDS had never been a major threat to heterosexuals.

This was all too much for Lord Kilbracken, who was given space in the paper a week later to explain that he had never said you couldn't get AIDS from heterosexual sex.

The paper was heavily censured by the Press Council for a misleading report that seriously misquoted Lord Kilbracken and a headline that was a gross distortion of the statistical information supplied by the Department of Health. '... the *Sun* dealt with the refutation of its article and editorial in an entirely dismissive manner and the paper has never withdrawn from its declared untruth. The paper has persisted in its irresponsible declaration that AIDS cannot be contracted heterosexually,' said the Council. It called on the *Sun* to publish an appropriate correction and to apologize to its readers.

The *Sun* carried the Press Council adjudication at the bottom of page 28. At the end came the following apology: 'The *Sun* was wrong to state that it was impossible to catch AIDS from heterosexual sex. We apologize.' But more disgraceful than the brevity and stiff formality of this 'apology' was the fact that the paper reproduced some of its original material claiming to show that heterosexuals, with few exceptions, didn't get AIDS.

It is difficult to escape the conclusion that senior journalists at the *Sun* still hadn't grasped certain key points – that there is an important difference between those who are HIV-positive and those who have AIDS; that in most cases one turns into the other after a particularly dangerous time-lag; and that the HIV virus, unusual though it is, is not somehow targeted specifically against homosexuals.

The paper just wouldn't let go of the issue. When Garry Bushell claimed in his 'Soapbox' column that there was no heterosexual AIDS explosion and there never would be, Professor Michael Adler, professor of genito-urinary medicine at Middlesex Hospital, tried to explain in the paper why Bushell was wrong. In an admirably direct article, Professor Adler told how one of his patients, a 22-year-old secretary with one previous boyfriend, had become HIV-positive after a one-night stand; and how another patient, a 45-year-old woman with grown-up children, had become infected after intercourse with her bisexual husband. Studies from all over the world, Professor Adler insisted, showed that most men and women with AIDS were infected by straightforward, normal sex. 'The idea that AIDS is a gay plague is a myth created by people who don't want to believe that they are at risk. And it threatens to destroy us unless our thinking changes drastically,' he argued.

Was the *Sun* at last mending its ways? Was this, at last, a slightly more practical apology for all the dangerous nonsense the paper had written on the subject over the years? Not quite. Professor Adler had made a tactical error: one of his examples involved a bisexual, and that of course meant the marriage was not normal. In an editorial that challenged Professor Adler's view, the paper did, however, concede that people now accept that AIDS is no longer exclusively a disease of homosexuals, and that heterosexuals would be crazy not to take precautions. 'Yet why do some medical authorities deny that AIDS is predominantly a homosexual disease? *Concealing the truth merely increases the danger*,' argued the *Sun* – revealing the depths of its continuing confusion.

Margaret Jay grants that AIDS is a difficult issue for newspapers to cover. 'I equate the difficulty of covering AIDS properly with the difficulty of covering the Iran–Iraq war or Northern Ireland properly. The thing goes on and on and there is no simple solution.' Many of the victims prefer anonymity, so there is also a scarcity of the sympathetic human-interest stories that might help to dispel prejudice.

By raising initial awareness that there was a life-threatening new disease on the way, the press did play an important role in the early part of the campaign against AIDS – the government, rather belatedly, realized that there was a problem and began to spend large sums of money on highly symbolic, threatening and some thought rather counter-productive advertisements featuring icebergs and tombstones. But all that attention raised expectations of doom that could not be matched by the slow-moving disease. The inevitable happened – some journalists started denouncing AIDS as a hoax on the public.

Apart from a fair degree of homophobia, Margaret Jay believes some journalists have been operating their own personal denial syndrome on AIDS. 'A lot of journalists, if they really searched their hearts and looked into their own lives, would have reasons to be worried about this whole thing.' She hopes that more journalists will now play their part in taking the battle against AIDS forward to the next stage – from awareness to actually changing behaviour. The director of the National AIDS Trust says, 'I don't think it's the Black Death, but I seriously think it's a major problem.'

Whatever the true scale of the threat posed by the disease, it is certainly a problem that deserves more thoughtful coverage than articles about 'shirt-lifters'. Perhaps, as a first step in improving the flow of information on AIDS to the public, the Health Minister should scoop up a specialist on the disease and see the editors of errant newspapers one at a time for a concentrated briefing; then at least they could no longer have the excuse of ignorance on the subject.

A slow-moving story like AIDS may be difficult to cover, but the 'explosion of evil' that broke out in Strangeways Prison Manchester on 1 April 1990 presented difficulties of a more pressing kind. It was immediately apparent that this was the most violent revolt in the history of the British penal system, but journalists were unable to get definitive information on what was happening inside the prison as part of it was in the hands of inmates.

However, the headlines the next day could not have been more emphatic. The riot that broke out in the chapel during Sunday morning service at Strangeways had effectively left a major prison in the hands of more than 1,000 rioting inmates, with destruction on an unprecedented scale. But most serious of all, the press reported, the violence had turned in on itself and was directed not only at the authorities and the prison staff but also at the Rule-43 prisoners – the sex offenders, the 'nonces' of prison slang, the lowest form of prison life.

The numbers of dead, and the certainty with which the death toll was advanced, varied slightly from newspaper to newspaper. The *Daily Mirror* headline said '11 Die in Jail Riot'. The London *Evening Standard* plumped for twenty, but showed some caution by saying the men were 'feared' dead.

As the siege and the coverage continued, the death toll rose even higher, and on 3 April the *Sun* reached the peak with a front-page 'exclusive' that more than thirty prisoners might have been killed, although the story was attributed to jail warders and the '30 Die' headline had single quotation marks around it – the usual newspaper headline device for separating fact from claim and counter-claim.

The *Daily Mirror* also had quotation marks in the headline of its main front-page story – 'Prison Mob "Hang Cop" '. The cop involved was a convicted rapist, Sergeant Dennis Davies, and the truth was that he had not been hanged: he was actually serving his sentence safely in Armley Prison in Leeds. The *Mirror* apologized properly the next day.

The numbers of deaths being claimed were themselves horrendous. More horrendous still were the manner of those deaths, according to accounts by prisoners, prison officers and staff from the emergency services. Prisoners were hanged following kangaroo courts, or were castrated by fellow inmates. Others were thrown from the landings into the central well of the prison and were impaled on furniture. There were reports of throats being slit, forced injections of cocktails of drugs stolen from the prison pharmacy and batterings by iron bars, and even more grotesque stories of bodies being dismembered and disposed of down the drainage system. There were even claims of traces of blood and flesh being found on an industrial mincer in the prison kitchens.

Nothing remotely like this had happened before in the British prison system. When considered in conjunction with the poll-tax riots a month earlier, there was enough material here to launch numerous features on 'Violent Britain'.

Yet when the last prisoners gave themselves up, twenty-five days after the siege began, it was finally proved that the definitive newspaper stories had all been wrong. There were no bodies in the prison. No one had been hanged, castrated or impaled, although two people had died during the affair – a prisoner who had been beaten and a prison officer with a heart condition who had died in hospital some days after leaving the prison.

Does the Strangeways affair qualify as the worst example in recent years of sensationalism run riot, journalistic standards gone mad?

'I don't think any of us distinguished ourselves mightily on the Strangeways prison riot,' Max Hastings, editor of the *Daily Telegraph*, admits. He accuses the tabloids of seizing on the worst reports and rumours in an unquestioning way because they didn't want to question them. 'Most of us try to put a reasonably sensible contextual spin on a set of wild rumours, but everyone printed the most gruesome, the most appalling accounts, and because they came from warders or men in uniform they were believed,' he added.

Twelve days after the riot broke out, and before the siege was over, his paper published a powerful leading article wondering what the public made of such headlines as 'A Kangaroo Court . . . Then 20 Executed', which by then were already looking hopelessly exaggerated if not yet definitively proved to be untrue. A 'historic' editors' code of conduct, designed to curb press excesses, had been signed only five months earlier. What did such reporting say about that?

'Today, if anything, standards are lower than before,' the *Daily Telegraph* wrote. 'Offensive bullying of the Royal Family has plumbed new depths. Blatant exaggerations on sensitive public issues are published and stand uncorrected. Privacy is invaded as freely as ever.' The *Telegraph* called on the only people with the power to act – the newspaper proprietors – to do so; otherwise, said the paper, lapsing into prison slang, 'we shall all go down', freedom of expression would be diminished and in the long run the public would be the losers.

It was a fine, ringing declaration – and of course there is no arguing against the case that the newspapers collectively, along with most broadcasters, simply got Strangeways wrong. Undoubtedly, enormous heartache and suffering was caused. In the chaos in the prison system that followed the riot, with hundreds of prisoners being dispersed to prisons all over the country and therefore temporarily unaccounted for, many parents of Rule-

43 prisoners must have spent sleepless nights wondering whether their sons had been the victims of the kangaroo courts.

Yet Strangeways is not quite the unambiguous newspaper scandal it appears at first sight to be. It is also an eloquent testimony to the great difficulty reporters have in trying to piece together events if they cannot physically get to the main players involved – in this case, the prisoners – and when the official source of information – in this case, the Home Office – is, if not wilfully secretive, at the very least reticent to a fault. The Home Office's reluctance to go beyond neither confirming nor denying the dramatic stories being provided by others contributed significantly to the confusion.

The full complexity of what happened appeared in *Press at the Prison Gates*, the last inquiry into complaints against newspapers held by the Press Council before it was disbanded. The Council, never noted for its sense of humour, at least managed a little gallows humour on this occasion, opening with a verse from Oscar Wilde's *The Ballad of Reading Gaol*:

> The Governor was strong upon
>   The Regulations Act:
> The Doctor said that Death was but
>   A scientific fact:
> And twice a day the Chaplain called,
>   And left a little tract.

Reporters told the inquiry of enormous efforts made to check the pervasive and repeated stories of death and mutilation in the face of a wall of silence from official sources.

William Newman, managing director of the *Sun*, insisted that the paper's reporting had been conducted in the most thorough and professional manner possible. He stressed that there had been no invention, no duplicity, no intention to mislead. 'The fact is that we believed what we had been told from a multiplicity of sources and were so confident that we were being told the truth that we presented the deaths as facts,' he said.

An insight into how errors developed was provided by the account offered by a *Sun* journalist – 'Reporter A'. He described how a well-known, authoritative and senior member of the emergency services, who had asked not to be identified, said there were unconfirmed reports of twelve dead. Because the *Sun* reporters were worried at the lack of official confirmation, they called the source again. This time he said that he had heard the prison governor, Brendan O'Friel, who was later to describe the riot as 'an explosion of evil', talk of three confirmed deaths and up to twelve feared dead. 'We were right,' said Reporter A. 'Twelve feared dead. The Home Secretary, the Prison Officers Association and the prison governor were still saying, weeks later, that they could not rule out fatalities. The story filed on 1 April and published on 2 April was correct.' He added:

I can't answer for the headline 'Twelve Dead in Jail'. But without question, I would do the same again with the copy, in the same circumstances. The story was correct at the time and the situation was unique – especially and disastrously in the inefficient naivety and perhaps inexperience of so-called press officers who were completely unprepared and did not have a contingency plan to deal with media inquiries.

Michael Unger, editor of the *Manchester Evening News*, a regional evening paper published a few hundreds yards from Strangeways, also echoed the *Sun*'s and many other papers' complaints about how the Home Office handled the affair, and he rejected allegations of exaggeration and sensationalism.

The *Manchester Evening News* had probably the best local contacts of any of the papers with reporters outside Strangeways, and the difficulties papers faced can best be illustrated by the front pages of its different editions on 2 April. In the first edition, the main *MEN* headline said, '20 Dead'. By the second edition, a question mark had been added – '20 Dead?' There was further caution in later editions, when the headline changed to 'Mayhem' and any reference to specific numbers of dead was dropped. Under a dramatic picture of the prison rooftop protest, there was another subheading, but in later editions part of this was put in quotes – 'Sex offenders "castrated after drug-crazed inmates rampage".' As evidence that he did make considerable efforts to be fair and balanced, the paper's editor can point to the progressive caution displayed throughout the day.

To a very considerable degree, journalists were merely picking up and transmitting to a wider audience the genuine fears, guesses and beliefs of many of those professionally involved in the Strangeways siege: prison officers and their union representatives, police and ambulance workers and prisoners themselves. The Chairman of the Manchester Prison Officers' Association, Ivor Serle, was one of the few officials involved who was willing to go on the record, and he persistently spoke of a 'gut feeling' that bodies would be found inside the prison. His impressions seemed to be confirmed when on the second day the authorities delivered twenty body bags to the prison.

Perhaps the most compelling and respectable evidence of all came from solicitors in open court representing Strangeways prisoners who had been moved to other prisons. One was Robert Vining, who told Oldham magistrates that his client, a Strangeways inmate, had spoken of seeing three bodies hanging from balconies in the prison's central block, including that of a 17-year-old he knew. Other solicitors told similar stories, and some refused to believe until the very end that there were no bodies in the prison.

Ian Ferguson, a Church Army captain, told Lord Justice Woolf's inquiry into the riot that many prisoners had told him of men being hanged and beaten to death.

How could so many people have been so comprehensively wrong about the events in Strangeways? Was there an outbreak of mass hysteria in the immediate aftermath of the riot?

Some possible explanations emerged later. It seems there may indeed have been 'bodies' littering the prison on 1 April. A number of resuscitation dummies were strung up inside the prison and could have been mistaken for bodies at a distance. Some prisoners may have overdosed on drugs stolen from the prison pharmacy and been lying unconscious for a time, and a number of Rule-43 prisoners may have feigned death to try to avoid the all-too-real threat of violence in the prison. And, some suggested, prisoners may have deliberately spread false stories of deaths to increase the sense of chaos within the prison system.

There are many factors which help to explain how journalists, and quite a lot of others, misread events. But the papers are not totally guiltless: there are several developments which might have suggested greater caution, despite the Home Office's apparent unwillingness or inability to confirm deaths inside the prison.

On the morning after the riot, Philip Randall, consultant in accident and emergency medicine at North Manchester General Hospital, gave a press conference in which he stated categorically that he had not admitted any prisoners with injuries from attempted hanging, castration or other mutilation. Only the broadsheet papers reported Mr Randall's comments. He later told the Press Council that he was surprised and distressed that stories reporting such injuries continued to appear. 'Such treatment of authentic information serves to give credence to a public view that some newspapers will reject, deliberately or subconsciously, any report that might spoil a good or sensational story,' the Press Council said.

As early as the second day of the siege, the prisoners on the prison roof held up a sheet with the words 'No Bodies' scrawled on it. Although it is easy to see why they were not considered the most reliable of sources, the press coverage of Strangeways would have been rather more accurate if the papers had paid a little more attention to primary sources who were at least in a position to know.

In the end, after every allowance has been made for the difficulties in covering the riot and siege, the account that the public was offered of events in Strangeways prison cannot be justified. As the Press Council recommended, when covering such situations newspapers should pay particular attention to the need to distinguish hard fact from speculation and conjecture; and headlines, however dramatic editors would like them to be, must be soundly based on facts and not overstate the text below.

5

'Unduly complacent and deficient in the practice of self-criticism' Inquiries into the press, 1947–77

On average once a decade over the past forty years or so, a British government has set up either a Royal Commission or a major inquiry into the financial structure, ownership or performance of the British press. There were Royal Commissions in 1947–9, 1961–2 and 1974–7; the Younger Committee on Privacy sat in 1970; and 1989 saw the Calcutt Committee into Privacy and Related Matters.

In 1947 the main motivation for a Royal Commission was a fear that a small number of proprietors were gaining too much power over too many newspapers, although press standards also became an issue. The second Royal Commission, in 1961–2, was primarily concerned with the financial health of the press following the closure of the *News Chronicle* and the *Star*, a London evening paper, in 1960; it also examined renewed fears about the concentration of ownership. The 1974–7 Commission held the broadest remit: to look at ever aspect of the structure and performance of the press. An underlying purpose was the search for the best balance between allowing the press as much freedom as possible and protecting the public's privacy from harmful intrusions.

These concerns fit under neat and familiar headings – political bias, intrusion into privacy, inaccuracy, triviality and sensationalism – and are supplemented by fears about monopoly and the extent to which some newspapers have become the playthings of rich and powerful men.

All the various Commissions and Committees took extensive written and oral evidence from leaders of the newspaper industry, organizations and members of the public. This was usually supplemented by some original research – public-opinion polls on the issue involved, such as privacy, or academic studies based on content-analysis of newspapers. For example, the 1947–9 Royal Commission commissioned a major investigation into 'the contents of newspapers and their methods of presenting news in the period 1927–1947', looking at both the space given to particular categories of article and the treatment of specific important stories of the day. The 1961–2 Royal Commission relied largely on detailed questionnaires sent to those involved in the newspaper industry, but also held sixty-three full-day meetings and visited a number of newspaper offices. The Younger Committee set up separate working parties on topics such as computers and privacy and the law and privacy, and also made use of very detailed questions on hypothetical stories or potential stories to investigate attitudes on what was and was not a legitimate topic for press coverage. The findings of the original research commissioned by the 1974–7 Royal Commission, including public-attitude surveys and studies of industrial relations, new technology, concentration of ownership, periodicals and the alternative press, and content-analysis of newspapers, were so massive that they were printed as a separate volume from the main report.

Despite all their endeavours, however, in terms of policies changed or visible effects on press behaviour the 'achievements' of the string of inquiries over more than forty years are modest indeed. Most of their conclusions and recommendations for intervention and action were quietly ignored. The main exception was the setting-up of the body for the self-regulation of the press. This was the General Council of the Press, which became the Press Council, which in turn was replaced by the Press Complaints Commission, as successive inquiries tinkered with its name, constitution and membership.

Though their recommendations may largely have been neglected, the more than 1,000 pages of official reports do usefully reveal the main preoccupations of politicians and public, and the strengths and weaknesses of the press. Above all else, the reports show how constant the main areas of concern about the press have been.

The reaction of much of the press to criticism hasn't altered much over the years either. Its policy might be summarized as: where possible, ignore calls for reform – citing the intensity of competitive pressures and the fact that the public must approve of what newspapers do because it continues to buy them; play for time when the calls for reform cannot be ignored; and take action only when threatened with legislation by politicians who sound unusually determined.

The evidence given to the first Royal Commission by a sub-editor in the Manchester office of Lord Kemsley's *Daily Sketch* in 1947 offers an insight into the enduring nature of the problem of press standards. He told the Commission, set up by the post-war Labour government, what had happened to him on the night in March 1939 when Hitler entered Prague. No authentic account of the events in the Czech capital was available for the early editions of the paper, so the unnamed sub-editor was instructed to 'jump' the news by writing an imaginative account for the first edition, attributing it to 'Our Prague Reporter'. His proprietor, Lord Kemsley, owner of the then largest newspaper chain, accounting for more than 17 per cent of daily and Sunday sales, told the Royal Commission he did not think the sub-editor had been given such an instruction. However, under questioning, he conceded, 'I think a thing like that might happen in any newspaper office.' The incident illustrates that the use of imagination in newspaper offices is not a recent phenomenon, and that generation after generation have consequently worried about the state of the press and the apparent 'decline' in standards.

Yet, while the press did not always live up to its grand reputation as a fourth estate of the realm, it remained an indispensable part of the political process and, especially in pre-broadcasting days, the main link between politicians and the electorate. There has also been a recognition by politicians that, although on the surface the newspaper industry is an industry like any other, it is also something more and should be judged by standards other than profit.

The first Royal Commission had its origins in a debate in the House of Commons in October 1946. Two MPs who were themselves journalists moved a motion calling for a commission to look into the financing, management and ownership of the press because of the increasing public concern at the growth of monopolistic tendencies. They pointed to a handful of men with the power to distort and suppress the news: notably Lord Rothermere of the *Daily Mail*, Lord Beaverbrook of the *Daily Express* and Lord Kemsley, owner of the *Daily Sketch*, the *Daily Graphic* and the *Sunday Times*.

One of the MPs, Hayden Davies, said that journalists had for years watched the freedom of the press being whittled away and had seen the honourable profession of journalism degraded by high finance and big business. The other MP, Michael Foot, a future leader of the Labour Party, spoke of the serious decline in press quality over the previous thirty years: in the face of strong proprietors, many editors had become little more than 'stooges, cyphers and sycophants'.

The opponents of the motion, mainly Conservatives, declared the British press to be a shining example of freedom and independence, but the motion was carried by 270 votes to 157.

The Commission terms of reference included looking at allegations that advertisers were directly influencing the editorial content of newspapers –

in particular, the allegation that in 1938 the advertising industry had complained that too great an emphasis on 'the international situation' was bad for trade and commerce. There were also allegations that owners were operating blacklists to ensure that the doings and sayings of politicians and personalities they did not like were either routinely played down or simply not reported. Winston Churchill, it was said, was hardly ever mentioned in Lord Kemsley's *Courier and Advertiser* in Dundee, where he had been MP, after he had displeased the proprietor. An eclectic blacklist at the *Daily Express* and the *Evening Standard* was said to have included the singer Paul Robeson, the author Noël Coward, Emperor Haile Selassie and the conductor Sir Thomas Beecham.

The 1947–9 Commission was chaired by the philosopher Sir William Ross, vice-chancellor of Oxford University, and included such notables as the president of the Liberal Party, Lady Violet Bonham Carter; the economist, social scientist and later Labour peer Barbara Wootton; and, until his resignation, the author J. B. Priestley. It investigated the fairness of press coverage of everything from bread rationing to strikes over increased 'stints', or work quotas, in the nationalized coal industry. Today, many of its preoccupations seem to belong to the age of post-war austerity, yet in its 361 pages reside all the issues now being tackled anew by the Press Complaints Commission which began operating in 1991.

The Royal Commission began by emphasizing its belief that a newspaper was one of the most remarkable products of modern society:

> To gather news from five continents; to print and distribute it so fast that what happens at dawn in India may be read before breakfast in England; to perform the feat afresh every twenty-four hours; and to sell the product for less than the price of a box of matches – this, were it not so familiar, would be recognized as an astonishing achievement.

This is an important point which still remains true, even though television is today the main national news-provider for most of the public.

As part of its investigations, the Commission heard from that 'handful of men' widely seen as holding the power to distort the news. This included one of the most colourful of them all – Lord Beaverbrook, proprietor of the *Daily Express*.

In 1930 Beaverbook and his fellow press baron Lord Rothermere of the *Daily Mail* had become the butt of perhaps the most famous condemnation ever made by a politician about newspapers and their owners. 'The papers conducted by Lord Rothermere and Lord Beaverbrook are not newspapers in the ordinary acceptance of the term,' said the former Conservative Prime Minister Stanley Baldwin. 'They are engines of propaganda for the constantly changing policies, desires . . . personal likes and dislikes of the two men. What the proprietorship of these papers is aiming at is power; but power without responsibility – the prerogative of the harlot throughout the ages.'

Seventeen years later this was a charge that Beaverbrook was happy to plead at least partially guilty to. When asked by the Royal Commission about his principal purpose in publishing the *Daily Express*, Beaverbrook replied, 'I run the paper purely for the purpose of making propaganda, and with no other motive.' He added, however, that the propaganda was on behalf of issues that he considered important, rather than in support of one political party.

On important issues such as the possibility of war, Beaverbrook claimed that he did not overrule his editors. Like many proprietors before and since, he did not need to – they were like-minded men or those able and willing to anticipate their bosses' every desire. It was fortunate, for example, that the *Daily Express* editor agreed with his boss that there was going to be no war in Europe. As a result the paper, and presumably many of its readers, was still confident of peace thirty days before Britain and France declared war on Germany.

Asked what happened when editors took divergent views on Lord Beaverbrook's great crusade in favour of Empire Free Trade, he replied, 'I talked them out of it.'

Had he instructed his papers to oppose British participation in the Marshall Plan, the US aid plain designed to help rebuild a Europe shattered by war? 'No, that is my teaching. That comes from my cooperation with my colleagues. We are all thinking together and thinking alike,' Lord Beaverbrook claimed.

A lot of people at the *Daily Express* were clearly thinking alike on the evening of 18 December 1947, when US Secretary of State George Marshall delivered an important speech on American foreign policy two days before leaving for a Council of Foreign Ministers meeting in London. The *Daily Express* carried a story under the headline 'Conflict Will Lessen' and reported Marshall as saying that if Europe were restored to solvency and vigour the disturbing conflict between Russian and the USA would decrease. However, Marshall's speech had in fact been a weighty and detailed attack on the 'inflammatory practices' of the Soviet Union, Soviet propaganda against the USA, and Soviet endeavours to prolong indefinitely the unsatisfactory state of affairs in Europe.

The Royal Commission decided that a few lines had been quoted out of context to bring the story into line with the paper's editorial policy. It said, 'We cannot escape in this instance the conclusion that a very important piece of news was gravely distorted in order to prevent it from telling against a line of policy pursued by the paper's principal proprietor. That any distortion could be pushed to such an extreme length reflects very seriously upon all concerned.'

Lord Kemsley might not have been such an overt propagandist as Lord Beaverbrook, but he held the title of editor-in-chief of the *Sunday Times* and said that he was in the closest possible touch with his papers, which included the pictured-based popular paper of conservative views the *Daily Graphic*. He declared himself 'entirely responsible' for a leading article advocating a national government published in the *Sunday Times* on 9 March 1947 – a leader picked up in turn the following day by the provincial newspapers of the Kemsley chain, the largest in the UK. He too said that his editors were all 'men with similar ideas to my own and it is quite unnecessary to tell them of my views on a subject'.

Yet, despite evidence of the influence of some individual proprietors, the Royal Commission found that on the whole there had been a move away from concentration of ownership in the previous twenty-five years. No two of the nine national mornings or three London evenings were in the same ownership. Three of the national Sunday papers were owned by Lord Kemsley – the *Sunday Times*, the *Sunday Chronicle* and the *Sunday Graphic* – but the other seven national Sundays were separately owned. This did not constitute a dangerous monopoly, the Commission decided, although the situation had to be closely monitored. Neither was the number of national newspapers so small as to prejudice either the free expression of opinion or the accurate presentation of news.

The Commission failed to find any evidence of concerted attempts by advertisers to influence the policies of newspapers or the operation of blacklists. Many of the names featuring on blacklists, it turned out, were people who were legally dangerous – who it was feared would sue if anything even mildly derogatory were written about them.

But the Commission was less than flattering about some aspects of press performance. The British press was pronounced to be second to none, notably free of corruption and financially independent from outside influences, but it did not always live up to its own high ideals of fairness and balance. Detailed examination of the coverage of a series of political stories showed evidence of political bias by almost all the papers.

The Commission looked at reporting of the Gravesend by-election in November 1947, which was seen as an important indicator of the level of support for the Labour government. The seat was finally retained for Labour by Sir Richard Acland, but with a greatly reduced majority.

With the exception of *The Times*, the national press showed a complete lack of objectivity in reporting the by-election, the Commission believed. Every other paper's coverage reflected its own political perspective, with news and views interwoven, spotlighting the paper's favoured candidate and either ignoring or deprecating his opponent.

The *Daily Herald* openly supported the Labour candidate in its news columns. On 25 November, the day before the election, there were three front-page headlines:

20,774 HOMES IN A MONTH

COAL UP 400,000 tons on 1946

POOR LAW DIES — AMID CHEERS

Over each headline was a subhead — 'Memo To The By-Election Voters'.

The *Daily Graphic* managed some equally biased headlines:

BRITAIN TIRED OF SOCIALISM

and

TORY CANDIDATE 'RESCUED' FROM GRAVESEND ADMIRERS

The Tory paper also gave a rather terse summary of Sir Richard's election address: 'Sir Richard Acland, the prospective Socialist candidate, says in his election address, that he is rather proud of "all these Government controls".'

At other times too, newspapers supporting the Conservative Party played up reports of food shortages and implied that such shortages as existed were due merely to bad distribution and the shortcomings of the new Labour government rather than a feature common to much of the post-war world. Papers that supported the Labour Party, such as the *Daily Mirror*, reported favourably on the activities of the government and the progress of major policies such as coal nationalization.

One bizarre example of bias, in December 1946, involved the *Daily Graphic*'s report of a New Year's Eve party being given by the Ministry of Fuel to celebrate the transfer of the coal industry to state ownership. One thousand guests, the paper forecast, would assemble in the Coal Board's panelled boardroom. Drinks would be plentiful, as the minister responsible, Manny Shinwell, had sent his experts out to search London for whisky, port and sherry. Waiters would serve sandwiches from silver salvers. And, at a time of fuel shortages and extreme austerity, it was emphasized that arrangements had been made to maintain the temperature of the entire building at a set level so that nobody would catch cold. The truth was rather different. The party was actually being held at the Ministry of Fuel, not the Coal Board. There were forty guests, one toast, no waiters and no special heating arrangements. Had the reporter exaggerated, or had he been sent up by a mischievous official? 'In either case the incident indicates a readiness to believe the improbable which we can attribute only to the effect of excessive political bias,' the Commission noted.

In another example, from April 1947, the *Sunday Express* published a front-page story that 11,000 people were employed at the Berkeley Square headquarters of the National Coal Board at a cost to the nation of £1 million a year in wages. This was clearly another instance of a bloated bureaucracy created by nationalization. The only problem with the story was that the real number of staff working at the NCB's Berkeley Square headquarters was 850.

Ironically, John Gordon, the editor of the *Sunday Express*, had less than a year earlier sent a memo on the subject of accuracy to all his staff, which was read out in evidence. 'I do not wish to be hyper-critical,' he had said, 'but the plain fact is – and we all know it to be true – that whenever we see a story in a newspaper concerning something we know about, it is more often wrong than right.' He had continued in words that should be framed on the wall of every newspaper office and copied out in every young journalist's first notebook:

I wish with all the emphasis possible to impress on everyone the supreme necessity for accuracy ... When you report an event do not distort the facts in order to make a better story ... Keep a balanced sense of judgment in writing the story. Do not force it all out of focus in order to 'find a better angle' ... the value of a story lies in its quality not its length. Don't overwrite. Don't strain to make a clever headline at the expense of the facts. The headline should go no further than the facts warrant. We sin grievously in that respect at times.

The 1947 Royal Commission was even able to supply an example of newspaper inaccuracy from its own experience – a story forecasting the contents of its own report. An *Observer* article predicted that the Commission would recommend that the government set up a Press Council and went on to suggest that the idea for a Press Council had been an uneasy compromise between warring factions on the Commission. The 'leftist' group on the Commission was said to have wanted to eliminate proprietors as the 'villains of the piece' and to have argued that only public bodies should be allowed to own newspapers. This split could lead to a minority report from the 'leftists', the article concluded.

The Commission, which did indeed proceed to recommend the creation of a General Council of the Press, observed rather tartly that it had never at any stage proposed that the Council should be appointed by the government and that the accounts of internal divisions in the Commission were 'not only untrue but devoid of any semblance to the truth'. To present speculation as a categorical statement of fact is a flagrant breach of standards which the press professes to set for itself, the Commission pointed out, and results in an inexcusable misleading of the public.

Apart from the issues of political bias and inaccuracy, the Commission expressed alarm at the dangers of trivialization. Was it right to present the matrimonial adventures of a film star as of the same intrinsic significance as events threatening the peace of a continent?

There was also disapproval of the invasion of privacy for no good reason, such as attempts to gather personal details on those unexpectedly in the news. The Commission pointed out that in 1937 the then Home Secretary had complained about press harassment of the bereaved, and that both the main newspaper industry organizations, the Newspaper Proprietors Association and the Newspaper Society, had passed motions condemning such behaviour. It was one thing to be questioned in a considerate manner by one reporter, a quite different matter for the bereaved to be harassed by telephone inquiries and besieged by reporters and photographers. 'Even if the journalists concerned were individually considerate and refrained from pressing for information not willingly given, the volume of inquiry could hardly fail to cause distress,' the Commission commented. That this is a perennial problem was shown in 1991, when the press started looking for information from the families of pilots shot down in the Gulf War. Indeed there may be no obvious solution except for greater discretion, sensitivity and courtesy on the part of individual reporters.

There was a danger, too, that notable events were given an exaggerated importance, so that long-term developments which give rise to no sudden changes tended to be ignored. Also, 'Some of our witnesses suggested that with our popular papers technique was becoming an end in itself and that the staff of these papers were concerned to impress their rivals in Fleet Street rather than to serve the public,' the Commission said. It was a tendency that had to be watched, because 'smart' journalism carried to extremes could produce a result as inaccurate as carelessness or inefficiency.

The Commission's conclusions were critical. They were that, with few exceptions, newspapers were failing to give the electorate adequate materials for sound political judgement. This was partly due to the 'modern conception of news value' and partly because of the failure of the press to keep pace with ever more exacting social requirements.

At the end of its deliberations the 1947–9 Royal Commission was convinced of one thing – the complexity of the problem. In an intensely competitive industry there was always the danger of the more scrupulous being undermined by the less. In any other industry such problems could be easily tackled by either legislation or the creation of a monopoly through nationalization. In the case of newspapers, both these approaches were dangerous. Instead, the industry had to try to live up to its own professed high standards. 'We cannot accept the view that the Press is doing everything it can reasonably be expected to do: some of the spokesmen of the press who gave evidence appeared to us unduly complacent and deficient in the practice of self-criticism,' the Commission reported. The British press had taken fewer steps to safeguard its standards of performance than any other institution of comparable importance.

The Commission rejected, as too heavy handed, interventionist appeals to set limits to newspaper circulations or profits, or to introduce legislation to prevent intrusion into privacy. Kingsley Martin, the editor of the *New Statesman and Nation*, had suggested that a column should be reserved daily in every newspaper for comments from an outside critic or expert – an early form of ombudsman – but this was seen as too impractical.

The Commission's main recommendation was for the newspaper industry to fund the setting up of a General Council of the Press, both to safeguard the freedom of the press and to encourage the growth of a sense of public responsibility and public service among all journalists. The new Council would have a lay chairman and at least twenty-five members representing proprietors, editors and other journalists, with 20 per cent lay members. It was to study the problem of formulating and implementing high standards of professional conduct and the problem of recruitment and training. 'If a journalist lacks the background that makes an event, a speech, or a discovery significant, he cannot make it significant or even intelligible to his readers;

and being unable to make the subject itself interesting, he will have to fall back on the trivialities incidental to it,' the Commission pointed out.

The new Council should also take any action it saw fit in order to keep under review developments likely to restrict the supply of publicly important information and to study developments in the press tending towards greater concentration in power or monopoly. It was also proposed that newspapers belonging to chains should be required by law to make that fact clear on their front pages.

In many ways the report produced by the 1947–9 Royal Commission was a remarkable document. It clearly identified both the strengths and weaknesses of the press, and pointed to areas of growing tension between press and public, such as the treatment of the bereaved; yet it totally rejected government intervention and gave the newspaper industry itself the responsibility for reform.

Parliament accepted the recommendations of the Commission without a vote, but it took more than four years to set up the General Council of the Press. In July 1952 Lady Bonham Carter wrote to complain about the inaction, and it took the threat of a private member's bill, introduced by the Labour MP C. J. Simmons, to get things moving.

The Council met for the first time at the headquarters of the Press Association and Reuters, in Fleet Street, on 21 July 1953. But over the following years it would have no lay chairman or indeed lay members, as recommended by the 1947–9 Commission, and it concentrated mainly on professional standards. It did little to increase public knowledge about the problems faced by the press. Its impact was slight.

Its first judgement involved the *Daily Mirror*'s coverage of Princess Margaret's romance with Group Captain Peter Townsend and seems ludicrous today, given the present state of royal reporting. The General Council ruled that a *Mirror* readership poll on whether Princes Margaret should marry Group Captain Townsend was 'contrary to the best traditions of British journalism'.

Largely in response to growing fears that the financial problems of the newspaper industry might lead to concentration of press power, another Royal Commission on the Press was established in 1961. Its chairman was Lord Shawcross, the chief UK prosecutor at the Nuremberg war-crimes tribunal and Attorney General in the post-war Labour government.

Since the 1947 Commission, seventeen daily and Sunday newspapers had closed, including the *News Chronicle* and the London evening paper the *Star*, which in 1960 merged with the *Evening News*. Only four had opened, and the ownership of those that remained had become more concentrated. In 1948, for example, the three leading newspaper groups – Beaverbrook Newspapers, Associated Newspapers and the *Daily Mirror* Group – controlled a total of 45 per cent of daily newspaper circulations. By 1961 their total had risen to 67 per cent, partly because of the closure of the *News Chronicle* and the absorption of the *Daily Herald* into the *Mirror* Group.

The new Commission was critical of the newspaper industry's response to the recommendations of its predecessor. The General Council set up after the 1947–9 Commission had been asked to study the long-term development of the press and, in particular, any tendency towards greater monopoly. 'Had these recommendations been carried out much of our own inquiry might have been unnecessary,' the Shawcross Commission pointed out. Nevertheless the 1961–2 Commission ruled that the press should be given another opportunity 'voluntarily to establish an authorative General Council with a lay element as recommended by the 1949 Commission'. But the government was urged to set a time limit after which there would be legislation to set up such a body.

Once again the threat of legislation had the desired effect, and in July 1963 the General Council of the Press was duly superseded by the Press Council, under an independent chairman, the distinguished lawyer Lord Devlin, with twenty members nominated by industry organizations and five lay members.

The 1961–2 Shawcross Commission had reviewed and rejected a wide range of proposals to regulate the competitive and economic forces of the newspaper industry so as to ensure diversity. These included suggestions of government subsidies for weaker newspapers, limits on the amount of advertising permitted and a levy on advertising to rise in line with a newspaper's circulation. The use of statutory devices to inhibit commercially successful newspapers was, it concluded, incompatible with the political realities of a free society. Rather, 'The only hope of the weaker newspapers is to secure – as some have done in the past – managers and editors of such enterprise and originality as will enable these publications to overcome the economic forces affecting them.'

The Commission also recommended the creation of a Press Amalgamations Court to look at take-overs of daily and Sunday newspapers which would lead to aggregate circulations of more than 3 million. Only those take-overs judged to be in the public interest would be permitted. Some elements of this proposal were later incorporated in monopolies and mergers legislation in 1965. Today newspaper take-overs involving a combined circulation of more than 500,000 have to be approved by the Department of Trade and Industry Secretary, who has the power to refer them automatically to the Monopoly and Mergers Commission unless there is a danger of either paper going out of business in the meantime.

Newspaper standards came to the fore again in 1970, with the setting-up of the Younger Committee on Privacy. This followed the second reading in the House of Commons of a Right of Privacy Bill introduced by Brian Walden, the political interviewer, who was then a Labour MP. The bill, largely based on a report on *Privacy and the Law* produced by a committee of Justice, the British section of the International Commission of Jurists, would have created a general right of privacy in Britain for the first time. James Callaghan, the then Home Secretary, rejected the bill on behalf of the government but, in the traditional British way, set up a committee of inquiry – the Younger Committee – to report on the subject.

The Younger Committee looked at everything from the prying of neighbours and landlords to the effects of computerization of bank records, protection of medical records and the activities of credit-rating agencies. It received more complaints about the activities of the press than about any other aspect of privacy, although it conceded that these complaints were mainly from organizations and companies rather than from individuals. In a survey of public attitudes to privacy, only 1 per cent of the 1,590 people questioned said that their privacy had been invaded by newspaper reports.

The inquiry raised the old conflict between the right to know and the right to be protected from intrusive journalism. It emphasized an important point about the role of the press in chronicling how public and private customs evolve, from marriage customs and the upbringing of children to entertainment and social life. 'Where customs vary between different regions, age groups, and social classes, the wide dissemination of knowledge about how others live is a necessary way of preventing the undue fragmentation of society,' the Committee declared. But there was, of course, another side, and complaints came to the inquiry from individuals and organizations arguing that the personal suffering caused by publicity might outweigh the possible public good.

There was the case of a woman who took part in 'white witchcraft' in her own home – behaviour that did not breach any law. Yet her name, photographs and address were published in a hostile newspaper article, and the photographs, she claimed, were obtained by unethical means. As a result, her property was damaged by local hooligans and she received a stream of offensive letters and phone calls. Was the press right in arguing that it had a duty to inform the public about issues like witchcraft which it considered important?

The difficulty of determining where the public interest lies is well illustrated by another example. West Sussex Council complained of press coverage after the Council decided that an 8-year-old who had been living with foster parents in Sussex should be returned to her natural mother. The decision was enforced, and the protesting child had to be sedated before she could be taken away. 'There was no question of the press doing public good by highlighting the irregularities of a local authority and no one could honestly argue that the publicity given could in any way be in the [child's] interests,' the clerk to the Council said. But many would now feel – thanks not least to campaigning journalism over the decades – that the policy of removing sedated, protesting children from foster homes does seem to merit some examination by newspapers, as long as this can be done without invading the privacy of the individual children.

The controversy surrounding the publication of the names of donors and recipients in heart-transplant cases in 1969 and 1970 was also not clear-cut. According to their critics, the newspapers who published the names of those involved displayed 'a singularly callous disregard for privacy' which had distressed relatives and was unnecessary for proper public debate of the medical and social issues surrounding organ transplants. The Press Council decided that the identities of those involved not only contributed to the realism of the news but were essential to establish its authenticity. When a heart transplant was a new, controversial and highly newsworthy event, it was probably inevitable that identities should be revealed. Now that organ transplants have become almost routine, the wishes of the families of those involved should surely be respected, though.

The Younger Committee also considered whether it was right that those who had committed minor offences, such as petty theft from a supermarket or drunkenness, should have to suffer what some saw as a worse 'penalty' than that imposed by the magistrates – loss of job, ridicule or ostracism suffered because of the publicity given to the case.

A former schoolmaster gave evidence of how he had been dismissed from his teaching job because of the publicity given to a minor sexual offence, even though the Department of Education and Science had ruled that he was not an unfit person to teach. But the Younger Committee concluded that the principle that ordinary legal proceedings should be conducted openly and that the press should be free to report them had to prevail over other interests in all but exceptional circumstances. There was no yardstick to decide whether the public importance of a story should override the privacy of the people and the personal information involved: the decision, at least initially, had to be left to the press. It did however, recommend that half of the Press Council should in future be drawn from outside the press, and that newspapers should, if possible, publish critical adjudications with as much prominence as the original article.

There was not total agreement among the 1970 Committee. In a minority report, Alex Lyon, later chairman of the Labour Party, advocated the creation of what Brian Walden had asked for – a general law of privacy. He argued that this would allow Britain to fulfil its obligations under the United Nations Declaration of Human Rights and the European Convention for the Protection of Human Rights.

Alex Lyon told the story of Mrs X, whose policeman husband had taken a mistress. The wife persuaded her husband to give up the mistress and the two were reconciled. The jealous lover told a national newspaper, and her account was printed under the headline 'The Love Life of a Detective'. As a result, Mr Lyon said, the couple's child was teased at school, the husband had to give up his job and the family had to move. 'What do I tell Mrs X?' Mr Lyon asked. 'Truth must prevail? We cannot protect privacy except where there has been a breach of confidence or the intruder used offensive new methods like bugging devices? A reformed Press Council will censure the newspaper?'

Little notice was taken of the minority report, and it is only now that the Press Complaints Commission is starting to address the issue of whether there is any legitimate public interest at all in publication of stories such as 'The Love Life of a Detective'.

In 1974 when the Labour government set up the third Royal Commission on the press its preoccupations were familiar. Apart from Labour's firmly held belief that the press was generally biased against the party, the Commission was faced with the old dilemma of how to ensure for the press 'as much freedom as possible on matters of public interest while leaving the individual better protected from harmful intrusions into his privacy'.

Sir Maurice Finer, a High Court judge specializing in family law, was appointed chairman of the Commission, but on his death, soon after, he was succeeded by the man who would later be chosen to head the Press Complaints Commission, Lord McGregor of Durris, the professor of social institutions at London University and chairman of the Advertising Standards

Authority. The Royal Commission took a realistic view of the nature of newspapers:

> In our opinion, it is humbug for newspapers to defend the publication of stories obtained by invasions of privacy, written so as to contain sexual innuendo and to excite the prurient curiosity of readers, with the justification that such stuff strengthens the nation's moral fibre. Equally we think it humbug to criticize items intended simply to divert and entertain for failing to provide material for instruction and serious political debate.

And journalists facing tight deadlines could not be judged as if they were workers in research centres, with as much time as required.

A detailed comparison of the contents of newspapers in 1975 and 1947 carried out for the Royal Commission found remarkably little change in how newspapers handled the news itself, but the growth of television had led to an expansion of features at the expense of hard news. It was usually broadcasters who now provided details of the big news stories first, and the popular newspapers were compensating with softer material, particularly about television, its stars and its programmes. Also, the gap between the 'popular' and 'quality' papers had become more marked, with the *Daily Mail* and the *Daily Express* giving a smaller proportion of their space to political, social and economic features while *The Times* and the *Daily Telegraph* gave more. This gap was even wider in the coverage of foreign news: the *Daily Mirror* gave 9 per cent of its news space to foreign news, compared with the *Guardian*'s 27 per cent.

Research on public attitudes to the press revealed a generally high level of satisfaction with newspapers, but over 60 per cent of *Daily Mirror* and *Sun* readers thought their papers exaggerated the more sensational parts of the news, and between 40 and 50 per cent thought that they invaded private grief and printed too many trivial stories. This was further confirmation of the old rule that people seem to enjoy their newspapers at the same time as they view them critically.

Still more critical in the survey were a group of 'influentials' – individuals such as councillors, managing directors and trade-union secretaries who had regular contact with the press. Most had fairly good relations with the press, but 46 per cent made 'very unfavourable' comments about stories of which they had direct knowledge. More than half had at some time felt like complaining about something in a regional or local paper, although only 29 per cent actually had done so. No satisfaction had been obtained in over half of those cases.

Many organizations were also critical. The Confederation of British Industry was at one with the Trades Union Congress in arguing that the press was more interested in disputes than in the positive achievements of British industry and that this emphasis damaged the country's image abroad. Local-authority associations attacked inaccuracy and sensationalism, and groups representing women, racial minorities and homosexuals all alleged unfair treatment.

Despite these criticisms, the Press Council's evidence to the Commission insisted that newspaper standards were rising. It claimed that newspaper groups were taking note of Council precedents in difficult cases and now often issued general directives to staff on behaviour. Serious cases of chequebook journalism had declined.

Some of the Commission's sharpest comments were reserved for the issue of privacy. The way in which a few national newspapers invaded private lives was one of the worst aspects of the performance of the press. Everyone had a right to privacy and it should be breached only when a demonstrable and important public interest was involved.

It soon became apparent that journalists like their own privacy respected. There was controversy when the Commission decided to find out about the earnings and voting habits of editors and journalists by carrying out a postal survey with questionnaires. Even though anonymity was guaranteed, the response rate was too low to be meaningful. The *UK Press Gazette*, the industry's trade magazine, campaigned against the survey, and Bernard Shrimsley, the then editor of the *News of the World*, made a speech attacking the Royal Commission for trying to carry it out. 'We found it ironical that some editors should have complained directly to the Commission about the impropriety of questions which invaded their privacy by asking about earnings or voting habits even when their anonymity was guaranteed,' the Commission noted.

In the end the McGregor Commission was of the view that, as a general principle, the press should not have special laws imposed upon it, but should, as far as possible, be treated like any other organization or citizen.

The Royal Commission's recommendations included measures to strengthen the Press Council and make it more effective. The newspaper industry should provide more money, so that the Press Council could advertise its services, in the manner of the Advertising Complaints Commission. The doctrine of 'right of reply' should be extended so that the replies of those criticized inaccurately were given equal prominence and space. There should be a code of behaviour. The Press Council should be able to review the record of a publication and journalist involved in a complaint. These were familiar recommendations that on the whole received a familiar response from the industry: inaction and prevarication.

The report also issued the inevitable warning. Some irresponsibility could be tolerated from newspapers as part of the price of living in a free society. But the policy of no special legal regime for the press was unlikely to continue 'unless those who control the press ensure that it behaves with proper restraint and provides its readers with the fair and accurate and comment essential for responsible judgements'.

Again there was some internal dissent. There was a minority report written by the journalist Geoffrey Goodman, the then industrial editor of the *Daily Mirror*, and supported by David Bassnett, general secretary of the Municipal and General Workers Union. They accepted much of the report but criticized its timidity. They said they would have preferred stronger reforms – in particular, measures that would have reflected the implications of the *Daily Mail* attacks on Lord Ryder and the British Leyland 'slush fund' story (mentioned in Chapter 2) by helping to increase the diversity of newspaper ownership and so reduce the effects of political bias. They believed that commercial pressures were diminishing the stature of much that was excellent in popular journalism and highlighting that which was questionable, objectionable and even obscene. And the gap between the broadsheets and the tabloids was widening: 'At one extreme the excellence of some of our quality newspapers and at the other edge the vacuity and irresponsibility of some of our popular newspapers is now more glaring then ever.'

Reflecting on their report today, Goodman believes it is all too evident that his pessimistic predictions came true. Some efforts should have been made to increase the diversity of the press by mitigating the ferocious effect of market forces – perhaps by means of a launch fund for new newspapers which would tide them over the worst and highest initial hurdle. 'It may be a dream, he says, 'but greater diversity might perhaps have done something to tame the worst aspects of the jungle.'

Commissions and Councils come and go, but there are still individuals of energy and optimism in the newspaper industry. Geoffrey Goodman, without the benefit of a launch fund, is hoping to raise the money to start a new quality middle-market paper, perhaps as early as autumn 1992. If he succeeds, it could have more influence towards higher standards in the newspaper industry than all the Royal Commissions put together.

6

'The press – the popular press – is drinking in the Last Chance Saloon'

The Calcutt Report into Privacy and Related Matters

IN 1990 the UK press very nearly came under statutory control, and all because of a storm, a comedy actor and a newspaper whose freaks, pin-ups and sexual advertising lead many to think it scarcely qualifies for the title of newspaper at all.

The actor was Gorden Kaye, who plays the café-owner René in the long-running BBC comedy hit *'Allo 'Allo*. On 25 January 1990 a hurricane hit much of Britain. As Kaye was driving into London, a piece of wood from an advertising hoarding was detached by the storm and was blown through his windscreen, lodging a splinter of wood in his brain. His injuries were so severe that he nearly became the thirty-eighth fatality of the storm. For three days he was on a life-support system in London's Charing Cross Hospital. *'Allo 'Allo Star in Fight For Life While Killer Winds Batter Britain* was how the *Sun*'s headline-writer described it.

As Gorden Kaye lay recovering in hospital, his right to privacy became the subject of a battle involving Drew Robertson, the then editor of the *Sunday Sport*, Britain's sleaziest newspaper; two of the paper's journalists; three Lord Justices of Appeal and, ultimately, the members of the Calcutt Committee into Privacy and Related Matters. Gorden Kaye eventually made a full recovery. For the press, thanks to the *Sunday Sport*, it had been a much more close-run thing.

The *Sunday Sport* is the creation of multi-millionaire David Sullivan who combines a degree from the London School of Economics with a lurid past as a publisher of pornography. For a time the *Sport* attracted a cult following, with stories about the difficult sex lives of women with 77-inch breasts, each weighing 7 lb, or women who slept with pigs or 'bonked' an entire ship's company of forty in a single night. Hitler and Elvis Presley were often found alive in the columns of the *Sport*.

On 13 February 1990, *Sunday Sport* journalists Gazza Thompson and Ray Levine arrived at Charing Cross Hospital. Previous Gazza Thompson stories had included 'John Wayne Ghost Saved My Life' and 'Pensioner Killed By Killer Sprout'. Ray Levine's investigative skills had unearthed 'Hubby Turns Wife Into Egyptian Mummy' and 'Peeping Tom Aliens Spy On Our Sex Romps'. Inside the hospital, the reporting duo ignored the notice listing the few people allowed to visit the still seriously ill actor, entered the room, photographed him and even attempted to conduct an interview. Sister Anne O'Kane, alerted to what was going on by the camera flashes, intervened and saw that the interlopers were shown off the premises. Gorden Kaye was so groggy that fifteen minutes after the incident he had forgotten it had ever happened.

Drew Robertson was proud of his paper's 'old-fashioned scoop' and issued a press release about it. He had obtained the interview all the popular papers wanted, and for nothing.

The ensuing row that broke out over the head of the *Sunday Sport*'s editor probably seemed like a fuss over very little. After all, in the old days, dressing up as a doctor to get a hospital interview was just one of the tricks of the trade. When television presenter Russell Harty was in hospital during his final illness in 1988, not only were there attempts to bribe a hospital window-cleaner to climb up his ladder to snatch a picture but 'gentlemen of the press' turned up in white coats and tried, unsuccessfully, to trick a nursing sister into parting with Harty's medical notes.

The *Sunday Sport* played its picture exclusive on its front page: 'This is the picture you nearly didn't see. Brave *'Allo 'Allo* Star Recovering From Surgery.' In a small front-page box the paper went on to boast, 'The snap was taken when *Sunday Sport* newsmen SNEAKED to the actor's bedside for the showbiz scoop of the year.'

Robertson later issued a rather disingenuous statement. He apologized if any distress or hurt had been caused to the actor's feelings but then declared 'we take the view that our readers would agree it [the exclusive] was compassionate, accurate and in no way detrimental.'

Even before this incident, Gorden Kaye had had considerable experience of the press and invasion of privacy. He once felt obliged to call in a 'friendly' journalist to write a story about his homosexuality and so defuse another article, due to appear in another national tabloid, that he feared would be more hostile. The comedy actor was afraid then that his career might be over, although it turned out that his public was more broadminded than some of the press and didn't mind his sexual preference.

Kaye is totally devoid of vindictiveness, and even now, when he has long since recovered from his accident, he is reluctant to advocate serious curbs on press freedom. He does think, however, that something should be done to protect people's privacy in future. 'It [regulation] hasn't protected me so far, not sufficiently. But one hopes that one day it will protect other people who might find themselves in hospital,' the actor said.

When the row broke out over the *Sunday Sport* story there was little sign that Drew Robertson realized how public attitudes towards the press were changing, or just how poor his timing had been – an invasion of privacy that was impossible to justify had been committed just as yet another committee of enquiry – the Calcutt Committee – was working on the final draft of its report on privacy and the press. Before the year was out he had been fired as editor of the *Sunday Sport* because of declining circulation and an ill-considered attack on the Press Council under the headline 'Bollocks to the Press Council'.

Readers of the *Sport* nearly didn't see the Gorden Kaye picture or interview because the actor's friend and agent Peter Froggatt applied for and obtained a High Court injunction preventing publication of the photographs or any comments made to the *Sport* by Gorden Kaye. On 23 February 1990 the *Sunday Sport*'s appeal against this injunction came up before Lord Justice Glidewell, Lord Justice Bingham and Lord Justice Leggatt. The judges were forced to recognize their near total impotence. 'It is well-known that in English law there is no right of privacy, and accordingly there is no right of action for breach of a person's privacy,' said Lord Justice Glidewell. He went on to argue that Parliament should consider whether the law should be changed to protect the privacy of individuals.

As the law stood there was little the Court of Appeal could do for Gorden Kaye. Arguments involving libel, trespass to the person and passing off were all considered and rejected. Only the argument of malicious falsehood – an argument with more than a touch of judicial goodwill and creativity – could be pressed into service. Although he did not go into detail, Lord Justice Glidewell decided it would be totally unreasonable for any jury to decide that the words about to be published about Gorden Kaye were anything other than false. But there was clear malice because the journalist must have known that Gorden Kaye was in no condition to give informed consent to the interview. The publication would also cause financial damage, because the actor would not be able to sell his exclusive story elsewhere.

94

Partially overturning the original injunction preventing publication, the Appeal Court ruled that the story and pictures could be published by the *Sport*, but only if it was made clear that they had been obtained without consent.

Lord Justice Bingham said the case highlighted yet again the failure of both the common law of England and statute law to protect effectively the privacy of individual citizens. 'If ever a person has a right to be let alone by strangers with no public interest to pursue, it must surely be when he lies in hospital recovering from brain surgery and in no more than partial command of his faculties,' he argued.

Lord Justice Leggatt added that there was no need for an equivalent of the USA's First Amendment to preserve the freedom of the press in the UK, but there was a need for a right of privacy to prevent the abuse of that freedom. 'It is hoped that the making good of this signal shortcoming in our law will not be long delayed,' he said.

Ironically, before the Gorden Kaye case the Calcutt Committee had been moving away from proposing a new law of privacy in favour of offering one final chance for self-regulation of the newspaper industry.

It was a mark of the degree of parliamentary concern about press standards that in 1989 the MPs who topped the ballot for private member's bills, which enable MPs to put forward legislation not in the government's programme, had used the opportunity to present bills designed to tackle press excesses. One was a Right of Reply Bill introduced by Tony Worthington, the Labour MP for Clydebank and Milngavie, to provide for a statutory right of reply for those who had been the subject of inaccurate reporting; the other was a Privacy Bill, introduced by John Browne, the Conservative MP for Winchester, which would have provided a general right of privacy and, as he described it, 'put water in the moat of everyone's castle'.

There was considerable support for both bills on the floor of the House of Commons, and the debates turned into attacks on the tabloid press. Gerald Howarth, the Conservative MP for Cannock and Burntwood, complained that the career of an actor he knew was being destroyed by exposure of his private life by a 'bunch of unscrupulous and disgraceful and disreputable hacks whose own private lives, I suspect, would fail to stand up to the scrutiny of a lighted candle'. Julian Critchley, the Conservative MP for Aldershot, argued that tabloid journalists were 'as British as football hooliganism and just as welcome', and he went on to attack the *Sun*, a paper for which he had once written a column. 'The truth is that as standards drop circulation figures rise. Such newspapers lie in search of profit,' he added.

The Browne bill fell unexpectedly on 27 January 1989, when only ninety-eight MPs supported a motion to force a vote to give the bill a second reading – two short of the number needed. (Peter Bottomley was the only MP who voted against.) It failed to make it partly because of political apathy – not enough MPs felt strongly enough about the issue to turn up – but also because it became tangled in procedural wrangling over another private member's bill, on abortion.

The government had made it clear that, although it was sympathetic to the feelings of outrage at invasion of privacy, it was one thing to feel a sense of outrage and another to devise sensible means of putting things right in legislative terms. The Privacy Bill went to the bottom of the queue for parliamentary time, so John Browne, whose own private life and undeclared business interests had featured in the headlines – he was censured by the House of Commons for lack of candour about his business interests and decided not to stand again for Parliament – withdrew his bill to make more time for a more mundane, albeit worthy, Weights and Measures Bill.

From the start there had been more government opposition to Tony Worthington's Right of Reply Bill, and it was clear that the government would not make parliamentary time available for it. (Private member's bills rarely make it to the statute-book without a measure of government acquiescence.)

The bill would have created a Press Commission with twenty-one members appointed by the Home Secretary. The Commission would have the power, ultimately backed by the High Court, to force a newspaper to publish a correction in the same place as the offending article. The bill would also have extended legal aid to cover actions for defamation.

As a result of the two bills, the then Home Office Minister, Tim Renton, 'bought' off the pressure for government action in the traditional British way – he set up an official committee of inquiry. This was the Calcutt Committee into Privacy and Related Matters.

The government did not want to introduce curbs on press freedom, but the setting up of the committee of inquiry was accompanied by much tough political talking; this was the 'last chance' for self-regulation; the press was 'on probation'. But was the Calcutt Committee more than a cynical political manoeuvre designed to divert back-bench pressure?

'The bills were bought off by the whips with the assurance that some action would be taken following a relevant committee, and that was why Calcutt was set up,' says Simon Jenkins, who joined the Committee as a *Sunday Times* columnist but became editor of *The Times* before it submitted its report. 'Those of us who were involved in the discussions early on in the gestation of that committee were fully aware that we were there to say either "yes" or "no" to statutory regulation of the press,' says Jenkins. As a Conservative, and one of those involved in the planning of the 1987 Conservative Party manifesto, *The Next Move Forward*, Jenkins had no doubt that most backbenchers felt there was a need for some sort of statutory legislation of the press.

Initially, according to Jenkins, the Calcutt Committee looked as if it was dominated by lawyers intent on action. Not only was the chairman, David Calcutt, a QC, but two other members of the seven-strong committee were also lawyers – David Eady, who had represented many newspapers in the past and had an affection for the industry, and John Spencer, a law lecturer at Cambridge University. From the start, both Eady and Spencer were predisposed to an immediate law on privacy. David Calcutt adopted a listening role, while both Jenkins and Sheila Black, a businesswoman and former journalist, were against legislation.

The only politician on the committee was John Cartwright, the SDP President and MP for Woolwich, who is also a magistrate. He had been one of the sponsors of John Browne's Privacy Bill, although he did not speak in its debate. Press behaviour, he argued at the time of the Privacy Bill, had raised a great deal of disquiet. 'It may be it's going to be impossible to find a legislative solution but it's worth looking at seriously,' he said.

The other member of the Committee was Professor John Last, director of the Charities Trust and a former lay member of the Press Council.

David Calcutt is a tall, spare figure with a domed brow who looks as if he might be the kindly small-town pharmacist his father actually was. The master of Magdalene College, Cambridge, he has the lawyer's habit of taking a brief, arguing his way through it, and – another problem solved – then moving on to the next case. This was very much the approach he took to the press and privacy, and he seems slightly surprised at the interest and controversy his efforts aroused.

Calcutt has gradually built up a formidable reputation as a judicious, reliable and efficient solver of tricky problems for governments. It was he who was called in to see whether Colin Wallace, the former Northern Ireland security man who made allegations of disinformation campaigns in the province in the 1960s, had been unfairly dismissed and, if so, what compensation he should receive. He found in Wallace's favour. He was also dispatched to the Falkland Islands to investigate a fatal fire in a hospital.

As he is chairman of the Panel on Takeovers and Mergers, a City regulatory body, self-regulation is clearly a concept he profoundly believes in.

Whatever its place in the history of British journalism, the Calcutt Committee will probably go down as one of the most frugal government inquiries in living memory. The Committee held its first meetings over sandwich lunches in an obscure Home Office building near Goodge Street station, but soon moved to the beautiful dining-room of the master's lodge at Magdelene College. Here the future of the press was discussed over lunch produced by the college staff for well within the £8 expenses limit set by the Home Office for members of the Committee. Once a month the members travelled to Cambridge second class, and even Simon Jenkins, who as a director of British Rail had a first-class pass, joined the others in the second-class compartment. They then all travelled from the station to Magdelene by bus. According to Sheila Black, 'David Calcutt always asked us what the committee meeting on the train had to say.'

During the meeting on the train and around the Magdalene dining-room table, the Committee gradually moved towards yet one more final chance for self-regulation and away from immediate legislation on privacy. As their deliberations continued, the Committee became more aware of the possibilities for redress that the law already offered those aggrieved by their treatment at the hands of the press. But many members were equally convinced that, for most victims of newspapers, the law was inaccessible because of lack of money, lack of knowledge or both. A new civil right to sue for damages for breach of privacy was unlikely to change that.

The Committee was initially faced with the sort of dilemmas encountered by all previous inquiries into the press. 'Many [press] witnesses argued strongly for press freedom to investigate wrongdoing,' the Calcutt Report pointed out. Yet most members of the public who wrote to the committee were seeking new restrictions on the press. 'These ranged from the outright prohibition of particular activities to various forms of recompense and to a variety of punishments for editors and journalists.'

The Committee, to its irritation, found it impossible to come up with evidence to prove in any objective way whether or not standards of journalism were really declining, as so many claimed. It admitted, 'We have found no reliable evidence to show whether unwarranted intrusion into individual privacy has or has not risen over the last 20 years.' Although during the past century there had been frequent accusations of increased intrusions by the press, 'we have no evidence of a golden age of media responsibility, and anecdotal evidence to the contrary is probably tinged with nostalgia.'

'Try as we did to sift through cuttings, files, past Royal Commissions and opinion polls it was extremely difficult to say that the press today in its behaviour was worse than it had ever been,' Simon Jenkins told a Bar Council conference. 'Many of the most appalling cases that were sent to us, often with the date cut off, came from way back in the 1930s and even earlier than that,' he said. It was extremely difficult to justify legislation without proof of some appreciable worsening of the state of affairs in society.

What had recently changed, the Committee was sure, was the intense degree of tabloid competition: the only comparison was with the pre-war circulation battles. As a result, some tabloid editors may have felt 'let off the leash'. It was also agreed that the content of the tabloids had become less political and more concerned with revelations about the lives of show-business personalities and royalty.

Despite the lack of clear-cut evidence, the Committee became convinced that both people and Parliament thought there was a problem that had to be tackled. That perception and the weight of evidence that built up before the Committee was enough to justify a serious look at the issue.

Among the evidence of public concern about the press that impressed the Committee was the boycott of the *Sun* in Liverpool because of its Hillsborough coverage, a boycott that had hit the paper's sales in the area, as Peter Chippendale and Chris Horrie showed in their portrait of the *Sun* – *Stick It Up Your Punter!* The Committee also attached weight to the fact that Tesco had withdrawn its advertising from the *Daily Star* when, under the editorship of the late Mike Gabbert, the paper had been obsessed with nipples and bonking. It was also noted that MPs were getting an increasing number of complaints about press behaviour from their constituents.

There were written submissions too. For example, Peter Scarboro wrote to the Committee about how his son David, once an actor in EastEnders, had been treated by the press. In a fit of depression David had thrown himself to his death off Beachy Head. Peter Scarboro had complained to the Press Council about an earlier *News of the World* front-page lead headlined 'Eastend Mark in Suicide Bid', saying that the paper had published an article containing inaccuracies when the actor was known to be in a vulnerable state, and that the behaviour of reporters had amounted to harassment. The Council had ruled that there was no evidence directly linking David Scarboro's eventual tragic death with the article, or that the *News of the*

World knew there was a major inaccuracy in the story when it was published, but the Council had also ruled that the article should not have been published, and the complaint had therefore been upheld. A similar complaint against the *Sun* had been rejected, although the Council said there were 'inaccuracies and controversial phrases' in a story about a planned television tribute to the young actor.

Paul Lamplugh, father of missing estate agent Suzy Lamplugh, also sent evidence to the Committee. A Press Council complaint against the *People* for a story headlined 'Missing Suzy's 50 Lovers', allegedly based on a book being written about the case, had been upheld in 1989.

One of the most dramatic personal appearances before the Calcutt Committee was by Sonia Sutcliffe, the wife of Peter Sutcliffe – 'the Yorkshire Ripper' – the man arrested on 2 January 1981 and later convicted of the murders of thirteen women. Mrs Sutcliffe had asked to come and give evidence – the Committee hadn't thought of inviting her – and was accompanied by her solicitor. She had kept a diary from the day of her husband's arrest, and she supplied the Committee with photostats from it. She said that every time her name appeared in the newspapers, eggs were pelted at her windows, she was screamed at and graffiti appeared on her front door. She had become a prisoner in her own home and was terrified.

Mrs Sutcliffe also told the Committee of the night the police came to tell her about her husband's arrest and how one of their main concerns was how to protect her from the press. She was moved to her parents' home, although they had not been warned and were found cowering in a corner as people banged on windows and doors and shouted and screamed.

The Committee also heard compelling evidence from Lord Alexander of Weedon QC, the famous libel lawyer. In the past, lawyers had defended newspapers with pride and conviction, but Lord Alexander said a great many people felt they wouldn't or couldn't do so now. As far as the legal profession was concerned, there was no question that newspapers were not behaving well.

'We were impressed by the weight of individual argument. It was obvious that the people and MPs knew it was bad and getting worse, and, whether or not they were right factually, qualitatively there was no way it could be ignored,' Sheila Black recalls.

Another influence on the Committee was *Hard News*, the Channel-4 programme on the press which began broadcasting in April 1989, the same month as the establishment of the Calcutt Committee was announced. I was presenter of the first forty-eight programmes. 'Everyone always switched on to *Hard News* at once, from the day the Committee was appointed, and everyone was most impressed by it. It entered a lot of the deliberations, but I'm afraid not on the side of the press,' said Ms Black.

In one programme during the first series of *Hard News*, in December 1989, members of the Committee were able to watch the then Home Office Minister David Mellor attack the popular press for its intrusion into the private lives of individuals and its morbid coverage of national tragedies such as the Hillsborough football-stadium disaster, when close-up pictures of the dead and dying were printed. 'I feel almost embarrassed to live in the same society as people who can produce that sort of stuff,' he said.

The press, said Mr Mellor, presented one of the more serious dilemmas the UK faced as a nation. 'On the one hand the government is very reluctant to interfere, certainly by way of statute, knowing it [the press] to be one of the foundation-stones of a free society. But equally government has to become aware of the widespread detestation in Parliament at some things that have been happening in recent years in the popular press.' And, in one of the most unambiguous attacks on press standards in recent years, he added an additional warning in the colourful language that has become his trademark: 'I do believe the press – the popular press – is drinking in the Last Chance Saloon,' he said. Some of the things published displayed a willingness if not to break the law then to sail closer to the wind 'than any of us could actually defend, perhaps than any of them would care to defend publicly.'

Ironically, although there were some signs of an improvement in press behaviour while the Committee was deliberating – caution was being shown in the face of large libel settlements, and a new code of practice has been signed by the editors of all the national newspapers – this counted against the press rather than in its favour. If the press could change so quickly as a result of a few high-profile cases, the argument went, couldn't it just as easily change back again once the pressure was off? Surely that made it even more sensible to put a firm disciplinary framework in place, to ensure there would be no subsequent backsliding.

But the Committee was also considerably influenced by witnesses such as Robert Maxwell, publisher of Mirror Group Newspapers, and Kelvin MacKenzie, editor of the *Sun*. They convinced the Committee that there was a genuine determination on the part of the press to change its ways. 'They sat there saying we don't want to be hated, we want to be loved – not quite in those words – basically saying, "We'd like to go to heaven too." We were persuaded by their attitude and their support of what by then had appeared, the editors' code of conduct, which also made a big difference to us,' recalled Sheila Black.

Kelvin MacKenzie, rarely seen outside his Wapping headquarters, was one of the few national newspaper editors to bother to take up the invitation to give the Committee evidence in person. He was the editor ultimately responsible for the stories that had led to a £1 million settlement with pop singer Elton John and the notorious headline 'The Truth' over controversial allegations of misbehaviour by Liverpool football fans at the time of the Hillsborough football-stadium disaster. MacKenzie told the Committee that pressure for change on his paper was now coming from the very top (proprietor Rupert Murdoch) and that he would be fired if he got it wrong again. He said he had been frightened into changing his ways and, anyway, he realized that readers didn't like some of the things the *Sun* was doing – 'My desk is getting pretty laden with angry readers' letters.'

He was asked if he thought he could produce as interesting and saleable a newspaper without intruding into privacy. 'I'm going to have to do it. If I don't do it Rupert will chop me. I don't want to be fired. I'm looking at this personally.'

The *Sun*'s editor also threw down a challenge to the Calcutt Committee. He brought along a number of issues of his paper and asked them to say what was wrong with them. 'Tabloid journalism', MacKenzie pointed out, 'cannot be condemned simply because it is brash or noisy or declamatory. It must only be called to order if it is false, irresponsible or reports untruths.' This argument impressed the Committee.

MacKenzie's boss, Rupert Murdoch, chief executive of The News Corporation and owner of five of Britain's national newspapers, commanding 34 per cent of total national circulation, was also in contrite mood when he appeared before the Committee. He too was looking for another chance for the press. When a Committee member remarked with arched eyebrows 'Another chance?' the Australian-American publisher conceded that it was a fair question to ask, but this time the press really did mean it. Sheila Black recalls that, 'Every time someone said to us, "Give us one last chance," the interesting thing was they were not denying that things had got bad.'

Just when discussion had shifted to the idea of creating a workable form of self-regulation – one that people would understand and be able to use – along came the case of Gorden Kaye. The *Sunday Sport*'s activities, Committee members recall, was decisive in pushing arguments back. The two lawyers argued once again for immediate legislation, and David Eady insisted that he could not put his name to anything that would allow mavericks such as the *Sunday Sport* to flourish. That case alone, some Committee members say, almost brought a recommendation for legislation – something that the government would have found difficult to resist.

Before then the Committee had been considering a non-legislative adjudicating body – perhaps even the Press Council, although there was scepticism about whether the Council could really become an effective force after it and its predecessor had tried unsuccessfully to stamp their authority on press behaviour for more than thirty years. The fact that the *Sunday Sport* was not a member of any of the newspaper bodies represented on the Press Council was an additional problem, because it made it less accountable.

At that point David Calcutt intervened. Until then he had been a listening chairman, not revealing his hand, unwilling to pre-empt discussion. He had always wanted an unanimous report, but he is also a believer in self-regulation where possible. To help achieve unanimity and to bridge the gap between the journalists who opposed legislation and the lawyers who favoured it, the chairman advanced a compromise. This fell well short of recommending an immediate general law on privacy, but it was a measure that would be seen to have teeth. And this measure enabled all members to sign the report without expressing formal reservations – a rarity in the history of press commissions and official inquiries.

When it was published, on 21 June 1990, the report of the Calcutt Committee came as a shock to the press. The fact that there was a last chance for self-regulation and there was to be no immediate general law on privacy had been well signposted, but the tone was rather fiercer than had been expected, and the press found itself facing a carefully drawn up regime of threats and inducements. There were immediate worries that the 'last chance' was in fact a 'slippery slope' leading inexorably to statutory regulation.

'The press doesn't realize how lucky they've been. They could have been hit quite hard. But we didn't think it would help the victims much. It was really the impracticality [of awarding damages or compensation for invasions of privacy] that convinced us,' says Sheila Black.

The blow the Calcutt Committee did deliver was seen as pretty severe by most of the press. It included the abolition of the Press Council and its replacement by a Press Complaints Commission, with the threat that if the 'last chance' for self-regulation did not work it would be replaced by a statutory tribunal presided over by a judge.

There was also a recommendation that three new criminal offences should be created that in practice could only be committed by journalists. These covered physical intrusion into people's homes, gardens, hotel rooms or hospital wards – the Kaye factor – without any public-interest justification.

According to the Committee, the activities of the new Press Complaints Commission should include

- running a 24-hour hotline for those who thought their privacy was about to be invaded – the Commission would inform the relevant editor that a protest had been made but would not be able to prevent publication;
- publishing, implementing and monitoring a comprehensive code of practice;
- recommending apologies to victims as well as corrections, and specifying the nature and form of the publishing of corrections.

The aggrieved would not have to waive their legal rights under libel law before having a complaint accepted for adjudication – something the Press Council insisted upon – and, unlike the Press Council, the Commission would be simply a complaints body and would not have the Council's additional role of defender of press freedom.

If any maverick publications – and clearly the Committee had the *Sunday Sport* very much in mind – refused to respond to the Commission's inquiries about complaints, or would not publish its findings, the Commission would be put on a statutory footing. Such publications would then be required to carry corrections and apologies and could be ordered to pay compensation.

Much more serious for the press, the Calcutt Committee went one stage further. It recommended two separate triggers which would lead to the Press Complaints Commission being swept away and replaced by a Press Complaints Tribunal, headed by a judge. This would implement a statutory code of practice and would also have the power to award compensation. The first trigger would be the failure of the press to set up a properly funded Complaints Commission within twelve months of the publication of the Calcutt Report. The second would be a serious breakdown of the system of self-regulation – if compliance with Commission adjudications was poor, or if papers deliberately flouted the code of practice.

Even more controversial were the recommended new criminal offences of physical intrusion – of entering private property without permission to obtain personal information with a view to publication, to take photographs or to place surveillance devices. The main defences would be that the intrusion was to prevent, detect or expose the commission of any crime or any seriously anti-social conduct.

The popular newspapers immediately fastened on to the extreme nature of the physical-intrusion proposals. *Today*, whose then editor, David Montgomery, was happy to see the replacement of the Press Council, warned of editors being sent to jail 'to protect Royals'. The paper said the Calcutt recommendations would throw a cloak of legal secrecy around the royal family, TV stars, politicians and powerful businessmen. 'Criminal prosecutions would be brought against reporters and photographers. But editors and proprietors could also be charged as accessories or even as part of a conspiracy.'

The *Sun* carried a cartoon showing a prison riot – the understandable reaction of the inmates to the news that the paper's editor was about to join them. (Needless to say, Calcutt had not at any time mentioned imprisonment.)

In a perceptive leader, the *Daily Express* acknowledged that the government had at least blocked the Right of Reply and Privacy Bills and conceded that the cowboy element in the press had shot itself in the foot once too often.

The *Daily Mail* argued that Calcutt had confronted the British press with its greatest challenge. And if the publishers and the politicians got the answer wrong, it would represent 'a paradise for those who fear the light, a picnic for the lawyers – and a Press that is not worth the paper it is printed on'.

The *Daily Telegraph* admitted there had been misconduct by some newspapers, but warned that the effect of the Calcutt proposals would be unquestionably to diminish press freedom. 'This seems a bitter price to pay for the behaviour of certain irresponsible newspaper proprietors,' the paper said.

Simon Jenkins condemned much of the press coverage of the Calcutt Report as itself misleading and not very accurate. 'Calcutt came to three central conclusions,' said Jenkins. 'One: that it was impossible to say that the performance and behaviour of the press in the matter of intrusion into privacy had been any worse than it had been throughout history. The second conclusion was that there should not be a privacy tort, and the third thing was that there should not be a statutory framework for regulating the industry.' The editor of *The Times* assumes here that the chances of further regulation through a statutory tribunal are so slight as to not represent a serious threat to press freedom. In fact the threat implied by Calcutt is very real, and the report provides a ready-made timetable and agenda, to justify a future government taking action against the press.

Jenkins makes no secret of the fact that he would have preferred the statutory 'sticks' to have appeared in appendices, rather than in the main body of the report. Sheila Black also had reservations about all the details of the report she signed. 'I would have preferred not to go quite so far, but we were a committee of seven. I would have made it a last chance, but I would have given it [self-regulation] three years as a system. I wouldn't have threatened legislation at this stage – perhaps a suggestion that next time around you won't escape legislation. I felt it was a bit aggressively threatening, but it could have been a lot worse,' she said.

One article in response to Calcutt that could not be ignored appeared in *The Times* the day after the report was published. Its author was David Waddington, the then Home Secretary, now leader of the House of Lords. With almost indecent haste, Mr Waddington, a right-wing former judge and a supporter of Margaret Thatcher, rushed to praise the report and accept its recommendations in principle, although in some places there was evidence that civil servants had chosen his words carefully.

The Home Secretary was happy to accept the abolition of the Press Council – its attempts at reform had not been enough – and to adopt the recommendation that a non-statutory Press Complaints Commission be funded and set up by the press. But he also issued warnings and made threatening noises. 'Some will say Calcutt should have recommended immediate statutory control. If this last chance is spurned their voices will be impossible to resist,' he said.

On extra restrictions on the reporting of court cases involving sexual offences, Waddington warmly welcomed only the Committee's 'general approach'. And on the new offences of physical intrusion the Home Secretary came very close to using the political language of polite rejection: 'We will consider the detail of the proposed criminal offences of physical intrusion and the scope of the defence (along with the recommendation on court reporting restrictions) very carefully in the next few months with a view to bringing forward our conclusions later in the year.'

The Home Office saw the physical-intrusion offences as politically sensitive, because they would really apply only to journalists. The main opportunity to legislate – the Criminal Justice Bill – was published in November 1990 without any mention of them.

As the full implications of the Calcutt Report sank in, so opposition began to grow.

One of the most direct attacks on it came from the chairman of the Australian Press Council, Professor David Flint. He is also chairman of a group trying to set up a World Association of Press Councils at a time when such bodies are increasingly looking like an endangered species. According to Professor Flint, the central flaw of Calcutt was that it failed to realize that freedom of speech and the press and the requirement that the press be responsible formed a single indivisible concept.

The Calcutt 'triggers' were weapons aimed at the freedom of the British press, which included a great many 'responsible and fearless newspapers whose titles are known and respected throughout the world'. It was a paradox, he said, that, at a time when so many countries were emerging from tyranny and beginning to enjoy freedoms that Britain had known for so long, the British government should be urged to impose such a draconian limitation on freedom of speech.

Professor Flint argued disapprovingly that 'this series of assaults, this intimidation of a free press and indirectly a free people, is justified [in government eyes] by the actions of a minority of mavericks.' But the problem was that the *Sunday Sport* was not the only 'maverick' – others, such as the *Sun* and the *News of the World*, had circulations that ran into the millions.

The Calcutt proposals were viewed with a mixture of anger and incomprehension by the editors of local and regional papers. Their attitude was understandable: they were being found guilty in their absence largely for the crimes of others – errors of taste and judgement made by high-profile national newspapers. The Press Council did, of course, receive complaints about the sins, omissions and intrusions of local newspapers, but their misdeeds and follies usually lacked the grandeur and inventiveness of the racier national newspapers. For local journalists, tied into their local communities and with contacts who cannot be permanently alienated for the sake of a single questionable story, virtue is usually a necessity. 'I am fast moving towards getting the hell out of this country before the tide of regulations disguised as deregulation engulfs us all,' was how one regional editor put it. A Scottish newspaper editor commented, 'My general thinking, even months after the event, is one of depression. I regard Calcutt as a sad day for the industry.'

David Calcutt himself has maintained a Trappist silence on the issue. He did not hold a press conference on publication day or make himself available for questions from journalists, and for a year he said virtually nothing on the subject. The only exception was an interview given to *Hard*

News on the day of publication of his report – an interview asked for formally in writing months before.

He was asked at what point the press would come under statutory control. He replied,

> 'If there is a flouting of the rulings of the Press Complaints Commission and if they demonstrate that they are not prepared to be bound by the code of practice then those are matters which can be looked at, and make a judgement as to whether or not self-regulation is capable of working. I don't think it's a question so much of waiting for another Gorden Kaye but seeing objectively whether the press is doing all it can to put its house in order. One maverick newspaper is one situation. But if there is a decline in standards then I'm afraid we have to face up to the fact that there has got to be statutory control. If the press can get its house in order then there need be no threat to freedom of the press.'

Calcutt believes he has provided a blueprint for the preservation of self-regulation. Suggest to him that he might also have produced a blueprint for the introduction of statutory controls and his attitude is, 'So be it.'

The Newspaper Publishers Association, the body representing the national newspaper publishers, was quick to recognize the logic of the Last Chance Saloon. Under the chairmanship of one of the UK's most experienced publishers, Sir Frank Rogers, deputy chairman of the *Daily Telegraph* group and a long time ago a sports reporter on the *Daily Mirror*, the NPA and the other newspaper industry bodies moved swiftly to implement Calcutt and set up a new Press Complaints Commission. There was a last spasm of defiance from the Press Council, which declared that it was the newspaper industry and not the government which had the right to close it down. Then the newspaper industry, which funded the Council, quietly got on with setting up the new body.

By 1 January 1991 the Press Complaints Commission was open for business in the Press Council's old headquarters in Salisbury Square, just off Fleet Street. Its chairman was Lord McGregor of Durris, the chairman of the last Royal Commission on the Press and former chairman of the Advertising Standards Authority, the body that regulates the advertising industry. In record time – a sure sign of how serious the threat was perceived to be – a board of finance had been created to ensure the new Commission had the resources to do its job, and a new code of practice was produced for journalists. As Louis Blom-Cooper, the last chairman of the Press Council, observed, the newspaper industry that had obstinately refused to increase the Council's budget for 1991 from £600,000 to £700,000 managed to promise £1.5 million for the new Commission for each of its first two years.

Despite better funding, the Commission still faced a daunting task: persuading the public and politicians that self-regulation can be made to work. 'It has by all accounts only two years to demonstrate that it can curb at least the worst excesses of some sections of the national press,' Blom-Cooper believes.

When the members of the Commission were announced, they included the editors of three national newspapers: two tabloid editors – Brian Hitchen of the *Daily Star* and Patsy Chapman of the *News of the World* – and the *Daily Telegraph*'s editor Max Hastings, a long-standing critic of tabloid newspapers and an editor who has been pessimistic about the long-term chances of self-regulation surviving.

Max Hastings is aware of the gulf dividing editors who come from different newspaper traditions. 'Will self-regulation work? No. In the editor's meetings you always get a straightforward divide. The pops all regard us, if they were expressing themselves frankly, as a bunch of middle-class wankers. We sit there thinking what are we doing round the table with all these animals. It is a mildly absurd situation,' said Hastings as he lit another cigar in his Docklands office in an interview held before his appointment to the PCC. Clearly he, like Calcutt and the government, is prepared to give self-regulation one last chance. But before the Commission was actually set up he had little doubt about the ultimate outcome: 'As long as people are making very large sums of money out of peddling rubbish, it seems reasonable to assume that they will go on peddling rubbish as long as they are allowed to.'

Lord McGregor managed to assemble a very high-powered team for his new Commission. Apart from the three serving national editors, those who came from the world of journalism included Sir Edward Pickering, executive vice-chairman of Times Newspapers and a former editor of the *Daily Express*; Sir Richard Francis, director-general of the British Council and a former BBC Radio managing director; David Chipp, a former editor-in-chief of the Press Association and a director of TV-am News; and Andrew Hughes, editor of the *Sunderland Echo* and a past president of the Guild of British Newspaper Editors. The 'lay' members included Dame Mary Donaldson, a former Lord Mayor of London; Lord Colnbrook, a former Northern Ireland Secretary; and Professor Robert Pinker, professor of social-work studies at the London School of Economics.

The first test for Lord McGregor came before he had even taken his coat off on 2 January 1991, the first working day of the new Commission. As he came through the door, the phone was ringing. It was Buckingham Palace on the line. Would he please come to Sandringham straight away to see how Prince Charles and Princess Diana were being hounded by the press? Lord McGregor, a courteous and kindly man, politely declined. He did not envisage chasing all over the country in pursuit of errant journalists.

Later that month the Commission encountered its first serious case – a complaint involving the privacy of a politician. This was the treatment of Clare Short, the Labour MP for Birmingham Ladywood, who has no doubt about what needs to be done to improve press standards. 'The only thing that will get the British press out of the gutter is legislation on privacy,' says Ms Short, who has become something of an expert on tabloid values after a number of years on the receiving end.

Clare Short is never going to be a tabloid heroine: she has backed too many unpopular causes for that, including support for the Birmingham Six and opposition to the Gulf War. But the issue that really divided Clare Short and the tabloids was her 1986 private member's bill to ban page-3 girls – the daily display in papers such as the *Sun* and the *Daily Star* of pictures of young ladies with large, naked breasts. She believes such pictures degrade women and set the tone for 'a shameful and objectionable part of the British newspaper tradition'. The bill failed, but there were fireworks from the *Sun*, which ran a campaign against 'Killjoy Clare' and invited readers to write in for 'Stop Crazy Clare' car-stickers. The pictures of her carried in the paper were usually unflattering.

That could all be easily dismissed as a very eccentric British confrontation between a radical MP and a tabloid defending its business interest in boobs. But in May 1991 Clare Short and her treatment at the hands of the press became the subject of the first major adjudication of the new Press Complaints Commission – a benchmark decision on which the new body's initial effectiveness was judged. The affair was given extra spice and significance by the fact that Clare Short's complaints were against the *News of the World* and its editor, Patsy Chapman, who was not only a member of the Commission but had chaired the committee that drew up the new regulatory body's code of practice. Ms Chapman was accused of breaking her own code in the first month of its operation. Labour politicians such as Roy Hattersley looked over the Commission's shoulder to see how it would cope.

Clare Short complained that her privacy had been invaded without any public-interest justification, and that inaccurate and misleading material had been published about her as part of a vendetta in revenge for her page-3 campaign.

The first story had been bizarre: a picture of Ms Short had appeared with two large old-fashioned naughty pictures under the headline 'Labour's Lovelies – Ad in Clare's Paper That Thrilled Grandad'. The story had been based on a small advertisement in the Labour weekly *Tribune* suggesting that people 'send for grandad's naughty pictures'. The only link between Clare Short and the advertisement was that the MP was a reader of the magazine.

The second story, under the headline 'Anti-Porn MP's Ex-Aide Quizzed Over Porn', claimed that a woman who had worked for Clare Short on the page-3 bill had been raided by the Obscene Publications Squad in connection with pornographic videos. In fact the woman had worked for Clare Short for only a brief period in 1983, three years before the bill, and Ms Short had not seen the woman since.

The Commission took the view that the two stories raised an inescapable suspicion that the *News of the World* was pursuing its private interest against Ms Short to embarrass her in retaliation for the campaign against page-3 pictures. The Sunday tabloid had gone beyond legitimate argument about the issues and had tried to link the MP with pornography.

But it was preparations for a third story about Clare Short that had the most significance, and which may set a precedent for press treatment of the private lives of public figures. When the *News of the World* started asking questions about her private life, Ms Short went for a pre-emptive strike in an adjournment debate (which allows MPs to raise a topic of their choice) in the House of Commons on 23 January 1991.

Clare Short accused *News of the World* reporter John Chapman of contacting her first husband – the marriage ended twenty years ago – and asking personal questions about her life. 'Questions had been asked with horrendous, deeply hurtful, unbelievable and completely false implications. Had he any "naughty" photographs of me? Photographs of me in a nightdress were discussed. Five thousand pounds was firmly offered and the possibility of as much as £20,000 was discussed. I know the photos, they are not improper, but I would find it terrible to see them published in the *News of the World*.'

The *News of the World*'s inquiries had involved John Daniels, a close friend of Ms Short in the early 1970s who was killed in Birmingham in 1979 – a murder that is still unsolved. The man had a number of convictions, although the *News of the World* did not suggest that Ms Short knew about them.

The Commission unanimously condemned the *News of the World*. The paper's dealings with Clare Short's former husband were indefensible, dealt with matters that were irrelevant to any proper inquiry and amounted to a serious breach of the provision on privacy in the code of practice which all national newspapers had accepted. It had been fair for the paper to ask questions about John Daniels, but it would only have been right to publish if facts were uncovered which were in the public interest. The code is quite specific: the public interest includes detecting or exposing crime, serious misdemeanour or seriously anti-social conduct; protecting public health; and preventing the public from being misled. The public interest does not include whatever the public is interested in, and it was of crucial importance to maintain the distinction – especially for those in public life. This is a distinction which will cause considerable problems for many tabloid editors in future.

In a break with the past in the UK, the *News of the World* carried out its obligation to carry a full report of the criticisms and gave over an entire page to publish the complete adjudication. There was even a nice photograph of Clare Short. However, as with many press 'victims' of the past, there was no sign of any regret and even less trace of an apology.

The Press Complaints Commission had a less satisfactory experience over the case of the *People*, Robert Maxwell and the pictures of a naked baby – Princess Eugenie.

The Duke of York complained to the Commission after the *People* on 14 July 1991 published two photographs of his daughter, Princess Eugenie, running naked in the high-walled garden of her home. The main picture was published again in August, together with an old picture from a French magazine of the Duke himself running naked into a stream. The headline read, 'Come on Andy . . . Where is your sense of fun?' and asked readers to phone to say whether they found either picture offensive.

The Press Complaints Commission ruled that the Princess Eugenie pictures were flagrant breaches of two clauses of the code of practice: that privacy should not be invaded unless it could be justified as being in the public interest and the rule that journalists should not normally photograph children without their parents' consent. Whether the pictures were offensive or not was irrelevant.

That should have been the end of the matter, but Robert Maxwell could not leave it alone. Together with Bill Haggerty, editor of the *People*, he published an article criticizing the adjudication and accused the Commission of trying to threaten newspapers with statutory enforcement unless they accepted the non-statutory variety. Lord McGregor pronounced himself 'dismayed' by Robert Maxwell's defiance, which was also criticized by Roy Hattersley for the Labour Party.

In October 1991 the Press Complaints Commission came down strongly on a paper edited by another of its members when it criticized Brian Hitchen's *Daily Star* for a front-page story headlined 'Poofters on Parade'. This, the Commission decided, had given a factually incorrect and distorted impression of a special report of the House of Commons Select Committee on the Armed Forces Bill, by claiming that its recommendations constituted a 'Gay Charter' which would make it lawful for homosexuals to serve in the armed forces. It had breached the code's clauses on accuracy and the need to distinguish comment, conjecture and fact.

The article had referred to homosexual pressure groups as 'strident, mincing preachers of filth', and a later article by the editor, headed 'Shove your queer ideas in the closet', had said that 'with a wink and a giggle' homosexuals had persuaded the Committee to legalize 'poofs in uniform'. In response to complaints that the paper had used insulting, offensive and derogatory language, inciting hatred and prejudice against homosexuals, the Commission said that it strongly upheld the right of editors to criticize and attack public policies, even in the most vigorous of language; nevertheless, 'they should not ride roughshod over the sensitivities of their fellow citizens, in this case, the minority who are homosexuals who, as far as the law is concerned, are behaving blamelessly. The paper failed to make a clear distinction between its legitimate expression of strong opinions and their publication in terms which could encourage the persecution of a minority. This was contrary to the spirit of clause 14(i) of the code.'

Earlier, in September 1991, Lord McGregor had expressed some overall satisfaction when he reviewed the Commission's first six months' work. The Commission had received 'helpful co-operation' from all editors facing complaints. But Lord McGregor also warned that he would in future be publishing detailed analyses of how far the press was observing its code of practice and observing formal adjudications of the Commission. 'On this, the continuance of self-regulation will in large measure depend,' he said.

David Calcutt – now Sir David – broke his silence in an article in the *Guardian* in June 1991. He was encouraged by the Commission's ruling on the public interest in the Clare Short case but disappointed that no hotline had been introduced to enable those who feared their privacy was about to be invaded to register a protest in advance. He still also wanted legal action against blatant physical intrusion. 'Criminal laws of France, Germany, Denmark and the Netherlands all cover physical intrusion. So why not England's? There are undoubtedly difficult questions of drafting. But we set out the bare bones and they formed an important part of the overall package. Something should be done sooner rather than later,' Sir David argued.

September 1991 also saw publication of the Press Council's epitaph in its final annual report. Its reason for existence, Louis Blom-Cooper wrote, had been negated by Calcutt's rejection of 'the logic and practice of consonant functions' – the dual role of handling complaints and fighting for press freedom. 'Given the unhappy demise of the Press Council and the absence of any successor to take on anything other than swift adjudication on complaints from persons directly affected by single instances of breaches of a code of conduct, who, now, will perform the role of safeguarding the freedom of the press?' Blom-Cooper asked a little plaintively.

7

'If we were dealing with evil men there really would be something to worry about'
Proprietors and press standards

EVERY year, just before Christmas, Lady Rothermere holds an 'At Home' in the ballroom at Claridge's. Hundreds come to drink champagne – when they can find room to lift their glasses. It is a grand occasion, and it would be a very poor year if there were not a couple of Cabinet ministers or at the very least the Chief Whip in the throng, rubbing shoulders with some of Fleet Street's most distinguished editors and columnists.

Lady Rothermere stands by the door, her own personal ice bucket of vintage champagne and tray of delicacies at her side, and receives guests. Beside her is the third Lord Rothermere, chairman of Associated Newspapers, publishers of the *Daily Mail*, the *Mail on Sunday*, the *Evening Standard* and a host of regional and local newspapers. The event is symbolic of continuity and old money: the last of the hereditary press barons dispensing Christmas hospitality to retainers, associates, contacts and friends.

The great-nephew of Lord Northcliffe, a founder of the *Daily Mail* and of the modern concept of popular journalism, the Viscount looks every inch the newspaper proprietor he was born to be. He is a tall, physically solid man, who in repose could pass – for a moment or two – as a severe Victorian of enormous respectability. But the impression vanishes as soon as he starts to talk, and in its place there is the mischievous smile of a rather naughty schoolboy.

Newspapers and politics were part of Vere Harmsworth's life from early childhood; he never wanted to do anything else but enter the family business. After school and a brief period working in a company-owned papermill in Quebec, he began his apprenticeship in 1951, at the *Daily Mail*, and worked in all the commercial departments of the company for twenty years, before becoming chairman of Associated Newspapers in 1971.

In the early days of his newspaper apprenticeship, some thought he appeared lost in the shadow of his father, the second Lord Rothermere, and he acquired the nickname 'Mere Vere'. This was probably never more than an obvious play on words and it is certainly not how he is described now. His achievements, marked by patience and the willingness to go on spending money in pursuit of a strategy he believes in, amount to nothing less than the saving from extinction of the newspaper group he inherited. When he took over, Associated Newspapers was completely eclipsed by the *Express* group and could have ended up being absorbed by it. It no longer is.

In 1971 Rothermere, with David English on the editorial side and Mick Shields on the management, master-minded the relaunch of the *Daily Mail* in tabloid form – or, as he prefers to call it, as a 'compact'. He then closed down the loss-making London *Evening News* in 1980 and, as part of the deal, obtained a half share in the *Evening Standard* with an option to buy the other half if the then owners of Express Newspapers, the property company Trafalgar House, ever wanted to sell. Rather like a move in a game of Monopoly, Lord Rothermere was finally able to get control of the London evening-newspaper market in 1985 when he bought the other half of the *Evening Standard* for £20 million.

He stood by the *Mail on Sunday* after a disastrous launch in 1982 and funded its losses for more than five years until the corner was turned and the paper became a powerful force in the middle market. A fainter heart might simply have given up.

In 1987 he personally planned the counter-attack on Robert Maxwell's new 24-hours-a-day paper the London *Daily News* with a classic Fleet Street spoiler – reviving the ghost of his London *Evening News* in a cheap and cheerful guise for a few months to cause maximum confusion for the opposition. The aim was to protect the *Evening Standard* by doing everything possible to prevent the *Daily News* getting a foothold. When the *Daily News* failed, after only five months, the *Evening News*, by then selling little more than 30,000 copies a night, was quietly reinterred, its job done.

More than a year later, Lord Rothermere would still wheeze with delight at the very mention of the name Maxwell and the memory of how he protected his *Evening Standard*. 'What gave me the greatest pleasure recently was the squashing of Bob Maxwell's *Daily News*,' Lord Rothermere said in an interview in 1988. 'His product was aimed at the wrong market. It was badly thought out, poorly constructed and mechanically he didn't have the means of getting it to the places he should have got it to. The whole thing was an ill-thought-out performance from beginning to end. It would have died anyway. The whole question was whether we could speed up his demise.' They could.

Lord Rothermere is one of five men who in recent years have virtually controlled the British national press. There are other proprietors besides these, such as Roland 'Tiny' Rowland, owner of the *Observer*, and the journalist founders who own stakes in the *Independent* and the *Independent on Sunday*, led by Andreas Whittam Smith, the *Independent*'s editor and chief executive, but – at least until the death of Robert Maxwell in November 1991 – the dominance of the Big Five was formidable. Together they owned or had effective power over, fifteen of the country's national newspapers, representing over 90 per cent of national sales – a dominance that has led to renewed fears about an unhealthy concentration of power in the national newspaper industry. They were and still are a strange bunch of assorted characters who rarely meet as a group and have few personal interests in common. Some are deadly rivals.

Apart from Lord Rothermere and the late Robert Maxwell, chairman of the Maxwell Communication Corporation and publisher of the *Daily Mirror*, the *Sunday Mirror* and the *People*, there is Rupert Murdoch, chief executive of The News Corporation, publishers of the *Sun*, *Today*, *The Times*, the *Sunday Times* and the *News of the World*; Conrad Black, chairman of the *Daily Telegraph* group, publishers of the *Daily Telegraph* and the *Sunday Telegraph*; and Lord Stevens, chairman of United Newspapers, publishers of the *Daily Express*, the *Sunday Express* and the *Daily Star*. To varying degrees they share strange egos and a taste for power and influence, and they take pleasure in having a permanently reserved box at the grand opera of politics. It goes without saying that most of them are also very rich.

Rupert Murdoch once succinctly described Robert Maxwell in a private conversation with Conrad Black as 'a thug, a buffoon and a KGB agent'. At the time this seemed an amusing piece of hyperbole by one rival newspaper tycoon about another, but a month after Maxwell's death the description appeared barely adequate to cover the enormity of the revelations about the man and his business dealings. In early December 1991 Maxwell's private companies were in the hands of administrators and with them a 51 per cent stake in Mirror Group Newspapers. The Serious Fraud Office were investigating allegations that nearly £100 million had been removed from the MGN and more than £400 million from the company pension funds in what looked like a final reckless and illegal gamble to prevent the Maxwell business empire being dragged down by debts that totalled more than £2,000 million. If Robert Maxwell had lived, he would almost certainly have ended up in prison.

Of the big UK newspaper proprietors he had certainly come the furthest. He was born Jan Ludvik Hoch in the Ruthenian town of Solotvino, in what was then Czechoslovakia, and his early life was one of poverty and often real hunger. At the height of his career it was claimed that he was worth £1,000 million – although that now looks like a colourful Maxwell exaggeration. By the end of his life the receivers were already knocking on the door, and all that was left was debt and a ruined reputation. The one-time Labour MP for Buckingham always said he did not believe in inherited wealth and would leave his children nothing, and this was one Maxwell prophecy that really did come true. On 3 December 1991 his sons Kevin and Ian Maxwell resigned from the chairmanships of Maxwell Communication Corporation and Mirror Group Newspapers respectively after being in charge for only a month.

Maxwell had remained a member of the Labour Party and claimed some of the credit for making Labour electable, because of Mirror Group Newspapers' attacks on the extreme left in the Labour Party and on the leadership of unions such as the National Union of Mineworkers. Yet Margaret Thatcher, when Prime Minister, once provoked Maxwell by describing him playfully as really 'one of us'.

All the other members of the Big Five are not just supporters of the Conservative Party: they were, and almost certainly still are, unambiguous admirers of Mrs Thatcher and what she stood for. It is inconceivable that any of their editors would be allowed to campaign vigorously for Labour – certainly not for long – even if they wanted to. As a result, there have been knighthoods for Larry Lamb, former editor of the *Sun*, David English of the *Daily Mail* and, the latest, Nicholas Lloyd of the *Daily Express*.

Rupert Murdoch's inheritance was nothing like as grand as Lord Rothermere's, but it still involved a newspaper tradition to live up to. His father, Sir Keith Murdoch, was a distinguished Australian journalist who controlled papers in Adelaide and Brisbane and was chief executive of the *Melbourne Herald*, without owning much stock. When his father died, in 1952, Rupert Murdoch inherited the *Adelaide News* and the *Sunday Mail*, after death duties and rationalizations. He was twenty-two. The rest of his international multi-media empire, The News Corporation, he built himself. As a result, Murdoch, a man of considerable charm and honesty whose anti-trade-union horns just do not show, is the only one of the proprietors who can do every job on a newspaper from editing a story to laying out a page.

Conrad Black came from a background of general business rather than newspapers. His father, George M. Black, was president of Canadian Breweries and a major shareholder in the Argus Corporation, a large Canadian holding company that his sons Conrad and Montagu would one day control. When he was eight, Conrad used his C$60 savings to buy a share in General Motors – a share he still has.

Of all the proprietors, Black probably has the greatest intellectual ambitions – he has history degrees from Carleton and McGill universities and a law degree from Laval, he has written a 700-page biography of the Quebec premier Maurice Duplessis and he hopes one day to write a work on historical philosophy. He has been caricatured as a brooding admirer of the Emperor Napoleon who likes nothing better than playing war games with his toy soldiers. In fact he does not own any toy soldiers, although there is a portrait of Napoleon in his *Daily Telegraph* office. Conrad Black's defining characteristic is a taste for political philosophy, expressed in sentences of inordinate length which somehow contrive to be none the less syntactically correct.

The *Daily Telegraph* chairman has also acquired a small stake in United Newspapers, although he has insisted to Lord Stevens, the United chairman, that his intentions are friendly.

Lord Stevens must be given at least honorary membership of the Big Five group of proprietors, even though he is technically not a newspaper proprietor at all. He is, as he happily acknowledges, 'an employee' who merely runs a public company. He does not own a substantial slice of its shares and is not as rich as the others, though he is almost certainly a millionaire. David Stevens is a diminutive financier, merchant banker and fund manager with a precise turn of mind and a puckish sense of humour. He became chairman of United Newspapers almost by accident after the death of his predecessor, Lord Barnetson. He had been on the board to represent the interests of a major City investor.

Despite his background in the financial world, he increasingly sees himself as a 'newspaperman'. Occasionally he shows he's getting the hang of being an opinionated newspaper proprietor by making appearances in the pages of the *Sunday Express* or the *Daily Star* to give his opinion on momentous events. In 1987 he advised the world that the stock-market fall was only a computer glitch that should be ignored, and in November 1990 he warned members of the Cabinet who might be plotting against Mrs Thatcher that they were confusing their own and the country's priorities and should support their leader. In February 1990, when the government cut interest rates by 0.5 per cent, under the byline 'Lord Stevens of Ludgate, Chairman of the *Daily Star*' he condemned the government for getting interest rates wrong and called for a reduction of 2 or even 3 per cent.

None of the Big Five is as mad as Lord Northcliffe, who launched the *Daily Mail* in May 1896 and died in August 1922 suffering, at least towards the end of his life, from paranoid megalomania. None is as manipulative or mischievous as Lord Beaverbrook of the *Daily Express*, or as politically unbalanced as the first Lord Rothermere, who admired Hitler, flirted with Mosley and in January 1934 wrote a *Daily Mail* leader article headed 'Hurrah for the Brownshirts'.

The one incontestable thing that they have in common is that they have the power to change national newspaper standards and journalistic practices in the UK. To date, this power seems to be exercised only when the public or major advertisers start to complain and circulations or revenues are threatened, or when politicians issue final warnings.

None of the proprietors is a total absentee landlord, although Rothermere spends more of his time in France and Murdoch most of his in the USA. All are responsible for hiring and firing editors and, however much leeway they give the editors they have chosen, all of them take a very detailed interest in what appears in their papers, even if they are thousands of miles away from London. The proprietors, as a group, have done little about the growing public concern over newspaper standards in recent years. This is particularly true of Robert Maxwell and Rupert Murdoch, who are largely responsible for standards at the mass tabloid end of the market. The problems the press faced, from threats of legislation to Calcutt, could have been avoided if this small group had put standards before sales.

Lord Rothermere makes no bones about his ultimate power over the content of his newspapers. If an editor were not producing the paper he wants, then, he says, he would 'have to take steps'. His papers are unashamedly Conservative. For a brief period in the late 1980s Stewart Steven, editor of the *Mail on Sunday*, asked for and was given permission for a flirtation with the SDP. It seems to have been a hard-headed business decision: the young middle classes were flocking to the SDP banner, and the paper couldn't afford to be totally out of tune with its target readership. But when SDP support started to melt away, the *Mail on Sunday* quickly tip-toed back to the Tories.

With the air of a man who has seen more newspapers headlines than most, Lord Rothermere takes a relaxed view of changing newspaper standards: 'The press reflects public taste at large and public fashions and standards. Certainly in the late eighteenth century public acceptability of the raucous press was considerable, and that could be because they didn't take it very seriously. In the nineteenth century the press fairly reflected the standards of the time. There were papers as sensational as papers today, but they didn't have much impact on the general middle-class public of Victorian England. The newspapers that were successful in Victorian England and Edwardian England were highly respectable, and Northcliffe's *Daily Mail* was exceedingly respectable.'

Apart from the occasional lapse of taste and judgement, Lord Rothermere's papers are not sensation sheets. They are professionally designed and packaged to be an 'interesting read' for an audience that Lord Rothermere estimates would probably have at least some GCSEs or 'O' levels and maybe also an 'A' level or two. They reflect, he believes, what are seen as the current family values of Middle England. In turn, his papers reinforce those very values.

The *Mirror*, Lord Rothermere adds, was considered scandalous in the 1930s – so much so that the first Lord Rothermere wouldn't allow it in the house and eventually sold his shares in the company. The *Sun*, widely seen as outrageous, merely started to reflect fairly accurately changes in mass public values. 'The *Sun*'s great offence was to start publishing scandalous and sometimes untrue stories about well-known people, whereas the *News of the World*, which was the scandal sheet in the old days, only reported the goings on of vicars and other relatively unimportant people,' he said. As a gold-plated member of the Establishment he is the first to concede the hypocrisy involved in such an attitude – the powerful can kick up a lot more fuss about the activities of the press than a few hapless vicars.

Lord Rothermere is a robust critic of special laws for journalists, and has condemned the Calcutt Committee for apparently threatening all the press with statutory controls if one of its number, however, marginal or eccentric, steps out of line. 'You might just as well argue that because one Rottweiler bites someone, every dog in Britain, no matter what its breed or pedigree or disposition, must by law be muzzled. That line of reasoning is as illogical as it is unjust,' he told a reception in June 1990 to mark the centenary of Queen Victoria's recognition of the Institute of Journalists as a professional body.

He believes that the greatest problem the press faces is the lack of accuracy in its reporting. Like many a more humble reader, Lord Rothermere has found that reports about him in newspapers are frequently wrong. 'Large numbers of people will have had direct or indirect connections with press reporting on a personal level and they have found it to be wildly inaccurate,' he claims. Some inaccuracy is clearly inevitable, he believes, because the pressure is always on journalists to produce a story, write it quickly and make it as lively as possible. Some yield to temptation and push the available facts too far. But others don't struggle too much to resist temptation in the first place.

Another problem the press faces, according to Lord Rothermere, is that major errors of taste or judgement by one title are highlighted by competing newspapers or television programmes. As a result, an anti-press atmosphere is kindled which plays into the hands of the sort of politician who is instinctively hostile to a free press. 'Governments have never liked press freedom. Without press freedom there would never have been a Profumo case. [In 1963 John Profumo, the War Minister, was found to be sharing a lover, Christine Keeler, with the Soviet naval attaché. After lying to Parliament during intense press interest in the affair, Profumo was forced to resign.] Under Calcutt, I doubt very much whether it would have been allowed,' he says.

Despite everything, Robert Maxwell did have some real achievements as a newspaper proprietor. He modernized the *Daily Mirror* and cut costs, and newspapers he published were neither the sleaziest nor the most dishonest. He was the first to introduce high-quality colour to a mass-circulation daily, a move that gave the *Mirror* an edge for more than a year in the circulation battle with Rupert Murdoch's *Sun*. Murdoch had made a rare strategic error when he convinced himself that colour didn't sell popular newspapers. When he changed his mind, there was a waiting-list for suitable presses – made by the German engineering company M. A. N. Roland – and colour was not available to all Murdoch titles in the UK until the end of 1990.

Robert Maxwell was also one of the first to make some effort to improve standards, by sacking Wendy Henry, the editor of the *People*, after the paper carried a picture of Prince William peeing in a park in November 1989, under the headline 'The Royal Wee'. Wendy Henry described it as a charming picture taken in a public place. The main reason for her dismissal, Maxwell insisted, was because of another picture in the same issue – a tasteless colour picture of the late Sammy Davis Jr showing the wounds from his throat-cancer operation. These followed previous assorted pictures of physical freaks and colour shots of dismembered bodies after the DC-10 aircrash in Sioux City, Iowa.

'I sacked Wendy Henry for lack of standards,' said Maxwell resolutely, although he continued to keep her on the payroll for a time. He believed her to be a talented journalist, if only she could be weaned away from the desire to publish shocking pictures of dismembered bodies.

Maxwell was, however, very slow to act on Wendy Henry, and presumably he should have known what he was getting into when he hired her in the first place. She had earlier resigned as editor of the *News of the World* before joining Maxwell. The reason was never publicly disclosed, but unconfirmed industry rumour suggested that Rupert Murdoch had asked her to tone down her act and she had declined. In 1990 she turned up in the USA as editor of the *Globe*, one of the supermarket checkout magazines which print fantastic stories about extraterrestrial creatures and suchlike, where her talents could be given a free rein. Defiant to the last, she declared, 'I can, and have been, accused of many things, but don't let anyone say I didn't know how to flog a few papers.'

Rather predictably, Robert Maxwell blamed competing newspapers – and in particular Rupert Murdoch's *Sun* – for the recent decline in standards. The two papers have frequently been at each other's throats – in print – over the past few years. When the Press Council upheld a complaint over a *Sun* 'world exclusive' interview with Mrs Marcia McKay, widow of the Falklands hero Sergeant Ian McKay – an interview that had never actually taken place – the *Mirror* went to town on its rival. The *Mirror* carried an editorial under the headline 'Lies, Damned Lies' and used as the sub-heading the words of the Press Council ruling that the *Sun* article had been 'A Deplorable, Insensitive Deception On The Public'.

'Standards have declined, led by the *Sun*, and the very shocking things they have done have brought about a reaction. At the *Mirror* we have removed tits and arses and we have overtaken the *Sun*,' Robert Maxwell said. (In fact the *Mirror* has overtaken the *Sun* only if the sales of the *Scottish Daily Record*, Maxwell's paper in Scotland, are included.) 'I don't suggest we don't make mistakes, but we are not in the gutter. The *Sun* took the popular press into the gutter and they were successful at it,' he added.

Maxwell insisted that editors and publishers have absolute responsibility for what appears in their newspapers. At the *Daily Mirror* there was little doubt that it was the publisher who had the last word – and many of the other words as well.

Robert Maxwell claimed he was in favour of tough action against newspapers miscreants but believed the action should be taken by the industry and not by the government. Statutory intervention would not in the end protect the individual and would certainly damage the press. He would have preferred to keep the Press Council, rather than have it replaced with a Press Complaints Commission, but it would have had to have been a Press Council with real teeth and a lay majority.

Maxwell, whose family had interests in football clubs such as Oxford United and Derby, suggested the yellow- and red-card system of soccer discipline could be applied to errant editors. 'The real teeth could include saying you can't hold an editorial chair if you transgress often enough. If you have done what MacKenzie [*Sun* editor Kelvin MacKenzie] has done – if you have been found ten times guilty – then you should be able to say this is a person who is not fit to be an editor.'

The American distinction between public and non-public figures should also be adopted, he believed. In the USA if you are a public figure and live by publicity and take advantage of it then almost anything is permissible unless the unwanted publicity is 'so exaggerated' that action for defamation is called for. Those who are not public figures have a right of privacy backed up, if necessary, by law. 'I have an absolute commitment [to the public figure principle] even though I have suffered so much from freedom of the press. There's no one more kicked around or maligned than I am,' claimed Maxwell. Maligned he may have been, but he also invariably issued writs if he believed he had been libelled, and he launched many law suits against journalists, including *Private Eye* and the authors of two unauthorized biographies.

If Robert Maxwell was right that it was the *Sun* that took the popular press into the gutter and that proprietors are ultimately responsible for what appears in their papers, then it must follow that Rupert Murdoch took the popular press into the gutter. Not surprisingly, this is not how Murdoch sees it. He is proud of the *Sun* and everything it stands for. He thoroughly approves of its raucous two fingers to the Establishment and believes the paper has been a positive force in British society: it has helped to destroy the obsequiousness of the workers towards their 'betters', and to break down outdated class barriers which stand in the way of people being free to realize their potential. 'In every sense it's been a mouthpiece for a new young generation in this country, and this country changes very slowly and you still have a class system to a certain extent. The elite here, the upper classes, see themselves threatened by papers like the *Sun*. We're saying to working-class people, "You are just as good as them." The *Sun* stands for opportunity for working people and for change in this society. It's a real catalyst for change. It's a very radical paper.'

In recent years the radicalism of the *Sun* has taken the form of support for Mrs Thatcher and the 'liberation' of the people from the nanny state as exemplified by 'looney-left' councils, social workers and do-gooders everywhere. The *Sun*, Murdoch believes, was a very important contributor to the social changes in Britain in the 1970s and 1980s, and has been 'brilliant' in handling the big stories of the day. Even notorious headlines like 'Gotcha' – written to commemorate the torpedoing of the Argentine cruiser *Belgrano* during the Falklands War but changed after the first edition, when it became clear that the ship had been sunk and there were many deaths – are fine by Rupert Murdoch. Such headlines celebrate patriotism, he says, and, in a war, patriotism is 'a good thing' and not something to apologize for. Battles won deserve celebration, and Britain as a nation hasn't got 'enough bloody pride' says Murdoch – the man who gave up his Australian nationality to become a US citizen mainly because the central focus of his media business had moved to America and foreign nationality would have been a hindrance there.

What has Murdoch's *Sun* contributed to the British press and society over more than twenty years? Has the overall effect of the Soaraway *Sun* really been benficial? 'Overall – absolutely. I'm proud of it,' says Murdoch, who has made millions of pounds in profit from the formerly broadsheet *Sun* since he bought it for £600,000 from Hugh Cudlipp's *Daily Mirror* group in 1969 and then transformed it into Britain's top-selling daily.

Although he always enjoys reading the paper, to see what editor Kelvin MacKenzie has got up to, the *Sun*'s number-one reader does concede that sometimes – just sometimes – the paper goes a bit too far. Then Kelvin MacKenzie gets a call from the man he calls 'Boss'. 'They've gone over the top on a few stories, but no more than any other paper and I think it's been right more often than not in its editorial policies and what it's stood up for. They've gone over the top when they've got a story wrong. I don't think it's gone over the top politically or on some of the things it's been criticized for, like the "Gotcha" headline,' says Murdoch.

The *Sun* definitely went over the top in August 1990, when the paper carried a picture, bought from a freelance photographer, of Prince Charles embracing Lady Romsey. The caption suggested that the Prince was embracing an old flame, with the implication that sparks of romance still lingered. What the *Sun* did not know was that the moment captured showed Prince Charles comforting his old friend, who had just heard that her child was suffering from cancer. The *Sun* admitted it had been wrong in its traditional way, by running a news story containing the true facts the next day – in effect a giant correction. Regrets came later. Kelvin got a call from the Boss. The paper was later heavily censured by the Press Council, but the censure that probably counted more with Kelvin was that call from Rupert Murdoch. 'That picture [of Prince Charles and Lady Romsey] by some Spanish photographer was unforgivable. That was really very wrong. They got the picture. Bang. Put it out without thinking. Sure I picked up the phone,' says Murdoch.

There have also been stories that verged on racism, The News Corporation's chief executive concedes – including an editorial on Australian Aborigines, in 1988, that went, he believes, '10 per cent too far'. This concerned Aborigine demonstrations over the celebrations of the bicentenary of European settlement of Australia, on 26 January 1988. Murdoch believes it was fair enough, in the face of demonstrations, for the *Sun* to give it assessment of what white men had done for Australia and what black men had done and what the remaining problems were. But the editorial, headlined 'Salute from The Poms', went further and described aborigines as treacherous and brutal people who had acquired none of the vital skills, arts or graces of civilization – of the sort so clearly displayed by *Sun* leader-writers. 'Left alone, the Abos would have wiped themselves out,' said the editorial. Rupert Murdoch, an Australian no longer, nevertheless picked up the phone to Kelvin.

But as for *Sun* headlines such as 'Stick It Up Yours Delors' as part of its campaign against the European Commission and its French president Jacques Delors, or calling Frenchmen 'Froggies' or Germans 'Krauts' – that's not racism, it's just a bit of good-natured fun.

Murdoch saw the Elton John case as a different matter. The *Sun* made a series of serious allegations against the pop singer. In February 1987 it published a story headlined 'Elton in Vice Boys Scandal', based on the 'confessions' of a rent boy, but Elton John could prove he was in the USA on the evening he was supposed to have been involved in scandalous events at his manager's house in the UK. The series of 'revelations' ended with a story accusing Elton John of having the barks removed from his Rottweiler dogs – 'Mystery of Elton's Silent Dogs' is how the paper put it. The pop singer had, in fact, Alsatians which could bark very well.

The lawyers moved in for the kill, and planned to take the ludicrous story about the dogs to court first. The *Sun* decided it could not substantiate its stories and instead made a record £1 million out-of-court settlement which included an enormous front-page apology under the headline 'Sorry Elton'. 'A very stupid lapse in judgement, but that's one paper in 6,000,' is how Murdoch describes the affair now.

It was around 1987, in the days when the *Star* was full of stories about 'bonking', that papers were at their worst. Since then, Murdoch believes, all the main popular papers – the *Mirror, Sun* and *Star* – have been a lot more careful. 'We said [to critics of the press], "This concern is right. It has gone too far but we have already tackled it and will continue to tackle it and we will go on having criticism from people about the press and the press will go on reacting to it." But the critics are not society . . .'

It is very difficult to imagine Murdoch allowing any of his British papers to back Labour – although this, he says, has happened in different circumstances in Australia. But David Montgomery, former editor of both the *News of the World* and *Today*, believes he did have a measure of political freedom. At the *News of the World*, Montgomery was politically independent most of the time but 'toed the Tory line' in general elections. At *Today*, where he was both editor and chief executive, he said Rupert Murdoch didn't interfere at all, and the search for a distinctive editorial voice even included a period of supporting the Green Party. 'He allows me to get on with it,' said Montgomery at the time. 'Clearly I'm not going to start campaigning for Labour. He would put his hand on my shoulder at that stage.'

Rupert Murdoch finds plenty to criticize in Britain's national newspapers. The country itself seems to him to be obsessed with sex. 'When you come here from puritanical America and see the British papers, you think "God!" ' His sense of shock has not, however, led him to do very much about the amount of sex in the papers he controls, or about the level of trivia – though 'Some of the show-business stories in the *Sun* and the *Mirror* are just too trivial and stupid,' he says.

Murdoch's main concern is over accuracy. 'My father had an old-fashioned belief that you got things right. That's all you had to do, and then you must never suppress what you know. If you had a good story you published it,' he says. The problem in the UK, he suggests, is that national newspapers are under such intense competitive pressure, whether it's the *Express, Mail, Mirror* or *Sun*, that editors don't take enough time to check things – they feel they can't afford to hold a story over for an extra day. And it's not just the tabloids – 'I see stories in *The Times* that horrify me.'

Murdoch says he will defend any story as long as it's right. If something is true then go ahead and publish? 'There'll probably be exceptions but yes, I'm saying that. If you start making exceptions you are on very difficult ground. Well, if you hurt someone's feelings . . . will it hurt national security? When someone has appealed to me [on national-security grounds] and I've given in to it, I've regretted it after,' he says.

Though Rupert Murdoch will never be more than a phone call away from erring editors, he has 'retired' from active crisis-management in the UK and now spends most of the time in the USA, where he has moved to Los Angeles to be close to his main film and television interests in Twentieth Century Fox studios. On a day-to-day basis, standards at the five national newspapers produced from the Wapping headquarters of his UK subsidiary News International are now in the hands of Andrew Knight, former editor of *The Economist* and former editor-in-chief of the *Daily Telegraph*. Knight is clearly a member of the British elite, yet he is one who greatly admires the *Sun* and even Kelvin Mackenzie, although he does wish that the *Sun*'s editor 'would grow up a bit'.

Rupert Murdoch first arrived in Fleet Street in 1968, when he beat Robert Maxwell to a large stake in, and eventual control of, the *News of the World*. Conrad Black is a much newer kid on the block. Black gained control of the ailing *Daily Telegraph* group in December 1985, when the chairman, Lord Hartwell, and the existing management urgently needed new investors, having overreached themselves on modernization plans at a time of declining circulation and revenues. In June that year Black had paid £10 million for a 14 per cent stake, but he had insisted on two conditions that turned out to be the making of his fortune. If any new shares were issued, he would have the right to buy a larger share than the Hartwell Family Trust, which controlled 60 per cent of the business, enabling him to increase his proportion of the company. He also won the right to match any takeover bid for the *Telegraph*.

In December 1985, when the *Daily Telegraph* desperately needed further new finance, it was Black who provided £30 million in return for increasing his stake to 50.1 per cent – a stake that has since been increased to around 80 per cent. He became chairman when Lord Hartwell retired, on 1 September 1987, although it was 1989 before Black, as executive chairman, formally took over his 'kingdom' in the Docklands and made London his main base.

Conrad Black believes that some British papers are among the worst to be found in the English language anywhere, yet he is indulgent about the men who own them. 'I know Murdoch and Maxwell are terribly controversial men, but they are not bad men,' he has said (prior to Maxwell's death). 'Lots of things can be said about them, but they are not miserable, misanthropic, anti-patriotic dishonest people. They're civilized, articulate and, in their own way, intelligent – and very generous in some ways. If we were dealing with evil men there really would be something to worry about.'

Black has inevitably been compared to fellow Canadian publishers Lord Beaverbrook and Lord Thomson of Fleet, who came to the UK in search of newspapers, money, power and peerages. Black probably fits somewhere between his two Canadian predecessors – interested in both politics and money, but not as irredeemably political as Lord Beaverbrook nor as single-mindedly interested in the bottom line as Lord Thomson.

There have, however, recently been echoes of the Beaverbrook past – particularly the Beaver's long but unsuccessful campaign against Britain's entry into the European Community. In October 1990 Black emerged as a public opponent of increased European integration and the loss of British sovereignty it would inevitably involve. His aim, he said in a lecture at Margaret Thatcher's last Conservative Party conference as leader, was 'to remind Conservatives who support European integration of their inherently Tory responsibility to safeguard the constitution of this sovereign nation'.

Black relishes living in London, which he believes is the greatest newspaper city in the world. But he sees an enormous divide between the broadsheet newspapers – of an outstandingly high quality, well written and offering every mainstream viewpoint from 'medium far left to furthest you can go on the intelligent right' – and the tabloids. 'The London tabloid journalist ranges from the saucy to the completely, dangerously scurrilous and, frankly, far worse than anything I've seen in any other English-speaking place,' he states emphatically. At the lower end of the market, he says, competition becomes so intense it ceases to beneficial and leads to a race to see who can be the most destructive and irresponsible.

Despite his views on the tabloids, Black believes the Calcutt Committee got it wrong by issuing threats to the press about last chances of avoiding statutory intervention. 'I find it terribly offensive. We cannot have Parliament setting up some Commission that monitors what appears in the press. Is this seriously acceptable to the British public? If anyone suggested this in either the US or Canada they would be taken to a mental home. I accept it as desirable to improve the standards of the lower echelons of the British press, but this isn't the way to do it.'

He believes that a way must be found urgently to reform the libel laws so that ordinary people can, if necessary, defend their reputations in the courts. At the moment there is no legal aid for libel, so usually only the rich or the dangerously foolhardy press a case. 'My sympathies are with the person who has been defamed, because I've been there myself. The power of individual members of the press to inflict terrible mental stress on unoffending members of the public is very great.'

Black has himself issued many writs for libel and has won all of them by getting apologies before the cases went to court. He would like to see a fund set up with public money to enable many more people to sue newspapers for libel. Such a fund should be run by a 'fair and independent-minded person' who would sift out the applications from vexatious litigants or those pursuing vendettas against the media to ensure that only well-founded cases went forward.

Black is not as opposed to a right of reply as other newspaper proprietors, who fear their columns will be cluttered as of right with the arguments of the unstable. A responsible right-of-reply system could, he suggests, be one of the functions of the Press Complaints Commission, and the *Telegraph*'s proprietor would not object to the Commission being able to require a paper to publish a right of reply rather than simply adjudicating on the rights or wrong of a particular case.

One of Black's main contributions to the maintenance of standards is to cast a cool eye on journalists – particularly on those he employs – to make sure they don't get carried away by their own arrogance. He employs several hundred, but he has an ambivalent attitude to the species – an attitude which seems to veer from admiration to contempt. 'Some of them are temperamental, tiresome and nauseatingly eccentric and simply just obnoxious,' is among the milder comments he makes on the subject. Not surprisingly, Black seems a remote figure to most of his journalists. (Among the other proprietors, it was Maxwell who most liked to think of himself as a journalist.)

Conrad Black values the professional skills even of journalists who are nauseatingly eccentric, yet he believes that a significant number are motivated by envy and are seriously frustrated at merely chronicling the doings and sayings of the great office-holders. 'It is up to the editors or publishers to provide some countervailing force to that. And this is one area where, despite the history of the capricious and eccentric press-owners in this country, it is preferable to have newspaper-company chairmen or proprietors who are active, who take an interest and who constitute a force for something in the formulation of the editorial product than to have the sort of eunuch publisher associated with newspaper chains where they are essentially paymasters.'

No one could accuse Black of being a eunuch publisher, although he intervenes in relatively restrained ways, usually on the grander issues of international – particularly Anglo-American – relationships. For example, he ended the *Daily Telegraph*'s habit of calling President Reagan's Iran-Contra problems 'Irangate' for short, because he believed there was no true comparison between the Watergate scandal and Ronald Reagan's mistakes. When the *Daily Telegraph* carried a leader attacking the US bombing of Libya in 1986, Conrad Black told Max Hastings, the *Telegraph*'s editor, that the leader and the article beside it by Ferdinand Mount were 'seriously fallacious analyses of what really happened'.

Often the *Telegraph*'s proprietor makes his views known in a more public way. He gets his right of reply by writing tough-minded letters to the *Telegraph* for publication, signed simply 'Conrad Black, London N6'. When the paper wrote in a leader that American opposition to compulsory repatriation of 30,000 boat people from Hong Kong was 'out of order', Black let loose both barrels in a letter to the editor – which was, of course, published. It was wrong, he said, to assert that the Americans had a particular duty to the Vietnamese when what they had done was to try, unsuccessfully, to resist the spread of totalitarianism in the region. It was 'completely spurious' to compare the Hong Kong situation with Mexicans illegally entering Texas. And, for good measure, Black added that, 'Britain must do better than compel the return of those wretched people to the source of their misery'.

Black does not interfere constantly in the editorial content of his papers, but, as he points out, 'What is the point in running a newspaper if you have absolutely no say?'

Lord Stevens would not disagree with that attitude: 'The idea that the chairman and chief executive has no control over the product is ludicrous. You are not in that position in a motor-car plant; why should you be in that position in a newspaper plant?' he says.

As chairman of United Newspapers, publishers of the *Daily Star*, Lord Stevens was ultimately responsible in the autumn of 1987 for what was probably the grossest lapse of standards in the recent history of British national newspapers. United did a deal with David Sullivan and the *Sunday Sport* – a deal designed to inject a little respectability into the *Sunday Sport* and an even greater amount of life into the *Daily Star*. The down-market tabloid, which started in Manchester and had its main readership roots in the north of England, had never quite made it into the first division of the popular press. With a circulation of less than 1 million it had not been in a position to challenge either the *Sun* or the *Daily Mirror*. Included in the *Sunday Sport* deal were understandings that the *Star* would not launch on Sundays and the *Sport* would be restrained during the week. Things did not go according to plan, and before long there was the ironic sight of the fastidious merchant banker David Stevens presiding, albeit for only a short period in 1987, over the bonking *Star* with proliferating 'pairs', as the nipple-count came to be calculated.

In a debate on press standards in the House of Lords, Lord Stevens faced an inevitable question from the tireless anti-pornography campaigner Lord Longford. Was it not the case that the noble lord's paper the *Star* tried to link up with the *Sunday Sport?* Lord Stevens came clean and admitted one major mistake – having hired Mike Gabbert, the wrong editor for the paper. 'The editor left after seven weeks. It was quite clear that the paper he produced was not what he was briefed to produce and he therefore departed. It was a very unsatisfactory episode,' Lord Stevens confessed to the House.

At the beginning of the 'unsatisfactory episode', the United chairman seemed to be amused by the notoriety the new *Star* was bringing him. In an interview with Andrew Cornelius in the *Guardian*, on 10 October 1987, Lord Stevens insisted that criticism of the newspaper had been greatly exaggerated and described it as a 'good read'. At the time, he also confessed to a sneaking admiration for Mike Gabbert: 'He's a lot of fun,' Lord Stevens said. 'You can feel there's a great amount of electricity there.' He did admit that there might be a bit too much 'bonking' in the *Star*, but he also chuckled and said, 'Bonking is a word, as I understand it, that is now in the *Oxford Dictionary.*'

One of the reasons why bonking rapidly fell out of fashion was the effect it was having on both readers and advertisers. The circulation started to drop, and Tesco, the supermarket chain, decided to withdraw its advertising from the *Star* because the company no longer perceived it as a family newspaper. An edict was sent to Gabbert – no more bonking. The next day the paper carried a story about a bonking horse. For Mike Gabbert this was one bonk too many. He was fired, and one of the most bizarre episodes in Fleet Street history came to an end.

Brian Hitchen, now a member of the Press Complaints Commission, was brought in as editor to clear up the mess and has on the whole been successful in producing a populist newspaper that also tackles serious stories – although the paper is almost as prone to jingoism as is the *Sun*. Lord Stevens is much encouraged. 'The *Star* is a good newspaper. It's better than the *Sun* now,' he says – although, at less than 900,000 copies, it has only a quarter of the *Sun*'s circulation.

In general Lord Stevens, who has been involved in publishing newspapers for ten years – 'longer than Maxwell' – does not believe there has been a general decline in standards. But he accepts that some papers have gone too far in paying people for stories and in invading privacy for no good reason.

He has also become convinced that the British newspaper tradition is a negative one – too critical, too reluctant to admit that people being savaged by journalists may simply be doing their best. 'Editors say people like attack, criticism and bad news – that's what sells newspapers. But I think there is a balance, and I'm not sure we've got the balance right in this country of having a bit more good news and praise for people,' Lord Stevens argues.

If he sees something that is unfair or wrong in Express Newspapers, he says, he has no hesitation in picking up the phone. Some years ago, for example, the *Sunday Express* had a story that the origin of the AIDS epidemic was a virus which had escaped from a germ-warfare laboratory in California. 'I rang the editor and said this was the most idiotic nonsense and I think you should stop it.'

The rules set by Lord Stevens for Express Newspapers are clear: preferably no sleaze or smut; preferably no invasion of privacy, because it's gone too far; and preferably no attacking people when they are dead, because he doesn't see the point in it.

Another fundamental rule is that the papers should on the whole support the Conservatives, although they do criticize the party sometimes – though perhaps not often enough, the Tory peer concedes. 'I think it would be very unlikely that I would have a newspaper that would support the socialist party. That isn't what some people would call press freedom, but why should I want a product I didn't approve of? I believe it is in the best interests of United Newspapers in term of its profits and shareholders to support the Conservatives,' Lord Stevens says.

Despite being a loyal Tory peer, he believes Mrs Thatcher's government became obsessed with secrecy and was 'a bit silly' in trying to prevent the publication of Peter Wright's book *Spycatcher*. As a result of such attitudes, there is now more danger of future press controls in the UK than in almost any other country, as the momentum for legislation already exists in Parliament.

The United chairman believes that the Press Complaints Commission would never have had to be set up if Lord McGregor had been chosen as chairman of the Press Council in the first place. The appointment of the barrister, penal reformer and *Financial Times* columnist Louis Blom-Cooper as Press Council chairman was, Lord Stevens believes, a 'mistake' because in the end Blom-Cooper did not make enough effort to, or was unable to, carry the newspaper industry with him in proposed reforms. The end result, though, with the help of 'a firm kick up the backside from the government' was a better system with a majority of press people as members – a prerequisite for effective self-regulation. 'We will see whether it works or not. It's a palliative to keep politicians off people's backs. But I don't think we will ever be in a position where politicians and other people don't complain about the press. It's going to be a question of degree,' he added.

Lord Stevens believes the press now has two or three years to correct its main excesses. The worse excess of all would be to ignore the rules and adjudications of the Commission. 'My view is that if the press doesn't abide by the rulings of the Press Complaints Commission they'll get statutory regulation and they'll deserve it.'

Despite their piety, the proprietors are all in their way guilty men – guilty of producing newspapers that are not as good as they should be. The one exception is perhaps Conrad Black – partly because he's new and partly because he doesn't own a tabloid newspaper. However, even the *Daily Telegraph* decided in 1991 to focus more on personality stories as part of the struggle to replace the 50,000 of its more elderly than average readers who die every year. In 1991 its circulation was only 70,000 copies a day above the symbolic 1 million mark.

The other proprietors have all been responsible for journalism that they would find it difficult to defend in public – stories that were untrue, ridiculous or destroyed privacy for no good reason. For purely pragmatic reasons they should do more about it. If proprietors are perfectly willing to breach concepts of editorial independence when it comes to dictating the political line of their papers, there seems little justification for holding back when it comes to promoting higher standards of journalism. The public is unlikely to complain about that sort of proprietorial manipulation and interference.

Lord Stevens, at least, seems to agree. He told the House of Lords in 1989, 'One of the main reasons we have reached this current pass is that some chairmen have been reluctant to dictate how their newspapers should operate. To do so would immediately give rise to charges of editorial interference, often – such is the contrariness of life – from the very people who now criticize us for not being strict enough on editors. However, it is, in my opinion, our job to set standards.'

8

'We can damage people's lives and health with our publications'
Editors and press standards

ROY Maddison is not the sort of editor who rides about in a chauffeur-driven limousine for drinks with celebrities at the American bar at the Savoy or lunches with Cabinet ministers. Nor does he have any prospect of a political knighthood for services rendered. But he is a power in his own land – the Whitehaven area of Cumbria. Roy Maddison edits the *Whitehaven News* – a weekly paper so close to and trusted by its readers that in some parts of its circulation area it manages to sell more copies than there are houses.

The Whitehaven newspaper combines the latest colour-printing technology with a marvellous Victorian masthead, featuring a Britannia-like figure atop the motto *Perseverantia Vincit Omnis* – perseverance conquers all.

With a circulation of around 20,000, it may be small, but the *Whitehaven News* is no sleepy parish-pump paper. In its area there is one ongoing national and potentially international story – Sellafield, the nuclear installation which combines a power station and a reprocessing plant and employs more than 13,000 people.

Despite the huge local economic influence of Sellafield, Roy Maddison gives equal prominence to the views of campaigners and supporters for and against nuclear power – a stand that is not always popular. He has looked into the sensitive question of leukaemia clusters in west Cumbria – areas of above-average incidence of the disease – to see whether they are linked with the nuclear industry.

The paper also campaigns vigorously for better roads in the area, because of the post-Chernobyl fear of nuclear accidents. In 1989 there was a bomb scare at the plant. The word spread like wildfire that there had been a leak of radioactive material, and the roads were blocked by people trying to flee. In fact there was no leak, but the *Whitehaven News* ran the story about the rumour because Roy Maddison thought it was in the public interest to do so. He wanted to draw attention to the inadequate state of the roads in the area. 'God forbid, but if there were ever a leak at Sellafield we'd not get out, the roads are so bad,' he says.

The way some of the nationals cover Sellafield and the complex issues it raises makes Maddison cringe, and he has decided simply not to talk to journalists from the national tabloids any more. 'The *Star* has a vendetta against Sellafield. In fact they have declared their intention to have it closed. They won't close it, so, as the years roll by, they are increasingly going to lose credibility as they try to get stories to support their case,' he says. At one stage British Nuclear Fuels had made seventy complaints against the *Star*, although the Press Council was abolished before the complaints could be adjudicated on and the Press Complaints Commission decided not to take on the Press Council's backlog as it wanted to make a fresh start.

Roy Maddison has no interest in vendettas. He describes himself as a journalist to his bootstraps, one who still gets enormous pleasure every week when the printer presses the button and the presses start to pick up speed to print *his* paper. Every Thursday he holds a copy clinic to see how the paper could have been better and to discuss the reason for any mistakes. There are also forums with readers, who are asked what they think of the paper and the stories it carries. And were their names spelled correctly when they appeared?

Quite apart from Sellafield coverage, Maddison, who worked for a time in Fleet Street himself, is horrified at how some national newspapers behave. He deeply resents the fact that, in the minds of many readers, he is tarred with the same brush as journalists from the more intrusive tabloids. The Calcutt Committee's findings are in his eyes the equivalent of being hung for a crime he hasn't committed.

The issue is symbolized for him by a front-page splash in the *Daily Mirror* on 10 April 1990. The enormous headline read:

PRINCE EDWARD
I'M NOT GAY

The story was labelled as a 'world exclusive' in which the Queen's son 'poured out his heart' to the *Mirror*. What had actually poured out was the prince's anger at being asked by *Daily Mirror* reporters about rumours that he was gay, at a party following the New York première of Andrew Lloyd Webber's *Aspects of Love*. At the time, with perhaps more candour than wisdom, Prince Edward reacted to the questions by saying it was outrageous and preposterous to suggest such a thing. Roy Maddison finds such behaviour by journalists appalling. 'You ask Prince Edward, "Are you a homosexual?" then run the denial story. I stuck that up on the wall for my trainees. If we ever get down to that level, boy have we got problems!'

Reporters on the *Whitehaven News*, he says, do not go in for double-dealing or doorstepping. Even if he believed in such behaviour, he could not get away with it. Unlike the readers of most national newspapers, Roy Maddison's readers walk through the door to deliver their complaints about the paper in person. When that happens, everything is put aside to discuss the paper, and if the paper has made a mistake it is corrected in the next issue. The attitude has more to it than the desire not to offend and to keep circulation up. 'It's identification with people you cater for and, dare I say, care about,' says Maddison, whose sincerity is enough to restore the greatest cynic's faith in newspapers.

Keith Parker would almost certainly agree with Roy Maddison's attitude, although his paper is much bigger and the pace he has to work at is more frenetic. Parker is the editor of the award-winning *Wolverhampton Express and Star* – a paper that has beaten the general trend of declining evening-paper circulations by offering news as up-to-the minute as the latest electronic technology allows. Every day he tailor-makes a series of very different newspapers, including different advertisements, for all the towns of the paper's circulation area. As a result, more than 160 journalists work for twelve editions of the paper, making changes to as many as 120 pages a day, with a deadline of some sort rarely more than twenty minutes away.

The paper, which has a circulation of 240,000, aims to be a complete newspaper, providing national and international as well as local and regional news. It is closing on the *Manchester Evening News* as the largest-selling evening newspaper outside London, and in its area it outsells the *Sun* and the *Daily Mirror* combined.

Like that of many middle-aged journalists, Keith Parker's working life has encompassed a total transformation of newspapers. When he began, as a 17-year-old indentured trainee on the *Wellington Journal and Shrewsbury News*, there were auctioneers' advertisements on the front page and journalists had to provide their own bicycle and typewriter – and, above all, make sure they got all the names of mourners at funerals absolutely correct. Now, at just over fifty, he is in charge of a highly competitive, fully computerized newspaper that has been publishing colour on its news pages since the mid-1980s.

Keith Parker knows exactly what makes a good evening-newspaper story for his paper. In a recent example, he got good colour pictures of a robbery that went wrong at a local building society. A freelance photographer happened to be passing just as the police held the robber on the ground with a revolver to his head. The robber was 'bang to rights', so the *Star* published the pictures, even though technically this was probably a contempt of court, because the robber was obviously about to be charged – the point at which restriction on what can be published come into play. It was, Parker believes, the very model of a good local news story.

'We cover everything that moves in the West Midlands,' says Parker, 'and more often than not beat everybody. We have an inquest if we are stuffed by national or local competition. I don't like the word "yesterday" in the paper.' The real opposition is the *News at Ten*, and he tries to make sure he has most of its stories in his paper.

Despite running a hard-nosed outfit, Keith Parker is emphatic that his reporters should avoid unnecessary intrusion into people's private lives. 'We'd come down very heavily on reporters if that was found, because you're closer to the public than a national newspaper that comes into a town and then buggers off. We are not in that business.' Parker is not all that impressed by what he sees when the pack of national reporters does hit town. This is partly due to the intimidating effect of numbers: as many as twenty journalists can turn up outside someone's door and stay there for several days. 'That's terrible. It can't be right really – although I don't know what the alternative is,' he admits.

The problems posed by the press pack aside, he also believes that truth is far from the first priority of some of the national reporters he encounters. 'The stories aren't totally wrong, but they are whammed up. That's old-fashioned 1950s journalism – *Boy's Own* stuff. Good stories tell themselves,' he adds.

The *Wolverhampton Express and Star* is a fiercely competitive newspaper, so it is not surprising that it has made the occasional appearance before both the Press Council and its successor, the Press Complaints Commission.

The paper was censured by the Press Council for using a colour picture of a body protruding from a blanket after the Hungerford massacre of seventeen people in 1987. Keith Parker is still vexed by the verdict. He feels he was condemned for his advanced technology: papers that used exactly the same picture in black and white were not criticized.

Another complaint, involving the former Liberal Party leader Jeremy Thorpe, was thrown out. The *Wolverhampton Express and Star* found out that Thorpe was having treatment for Parkinson's disease at a local hospital and published the story. The chairman of the local health authority complained, alleging intrusion into privacy. The Press Council ruled, however, that, as a former leader of a political party, Jeremy Thorpe was not a private individual and therefore did not have the same rights to privacy as an ordinary citizen. The new Press Complaints Commission would be far more likely to say that, despite being a former politician, he is still entitled to some privacy – extending to the state of his health and any medical treatment he is receiving. It is surely right to try to make such a distinction. There must come a time when, after someone retires from public life and gives up all ambitions for office, he or she should gradually be entitled to a private life if no public interest other than curiosity is involved.

The *Wolverhampton Express and Star* also won the doubtful privilege of being, with the *Daily Mail*, the subject of the first ruling of the Press Complaints Commission, in April 1991. It was accused of breaching the spirit of the newspaper industry's code of practice. The Commission decided the paper had been wrong to say in a report of an IRA shooting in the Midlands that a chief constable lived nearby. Even though the paper argued that this information was well known locally and had already been published elsewhere, there was a danger, the Commission said, of creating another target.

But Keith Parker is clearly not an editor for whom absolutely anything goes. In deciding whether to print a telling news story or picture, he does weigh up the balance between the distress it is likely to cause those involved and where the public interest lies. This is how he describes a concrete example of the way in which he exercises his judgement and where he draws the line. 'A minibus crashed and six teenagers died,' Parker recounts. 'In the background was a policeman and a man. It was obvious from the picture that the policeman was telling the man his son was dead. That would have been intrusion. We didn't use the picture. Local people would expect us to have a higher standard than that.'

In contrast to Roy Maddison and Keith Parker, Max Hastings edits a national institution, the *Daily Telegraph*. Indeed, Max Hastings is well on the way to being a national institution himself – during the Falklands War, he walked into Port Stanley ahead of the British troops, in order to be the first reporter on the scene.

In talking about newspaper standards, the editor of the *Daily Telegraph* is worried about sounding sanctimonious and looking down his Northamptonshire-county-set nose at tabloid editors from south London with a handful of O levels. He is the first to admit that the *Telegraph* gets things wrong, that it makes errors of judgement like everyone else.

It has long been an open secret that the place to get all the sexual details of particularly gruesome court cases is not on page 3 of the *Sun* but on page 3 of the *Telegraph*. A survey of all rape coverage in the national newspapers over a six-month period, conducted by Lorraine Heggessey and Jacqui Webster of *Hard News*, found that the *Daily Telegraph* carried more rape stories than any other broadsheet newspaper, and more even than any tabloid apart from the *Sun*. At the time, Hastings refused to discuss the survey, the question of how his paper covers rape or whether the *Telegraph* gives its readers a false coverage on the relatively atypical cases where women are raped by strangers rather than by someone they know.

Max Hastings does, however, take a robust view about milder forms of pornography and doesn't particularly object either to page-3 girls or to excesses of tabloid silliness. He can even cope with the activities of the *Sun's* editor, Kelvin MacKenzie. 'Kelvin MacKenzie you can see coming at twenty paces. There's a sort of brutish honesty about Kelvin,' Hastings says.

The real problem faced by the press, the *Daily Telegraph's* editor believes, goes much deeper. 'There are two kinds of journalism. There is the journalism that is trying to tell the truth and there's the journalism that treats the news as show business.' It is impossible, Hastings believes, to mount any coherent defence of the press to the public on behalf of those who are not making at least some attempt to tell the truth. 'There has been a spread and an increase in the number of titles and the number of editors who really don't mind whether a story is true or not. A significant number of titles are now carrying stories that you don't really believe in a million years that their editors can seriously suppose are true.'

Too much attention has been focused on the *Sun* in the debate about newspaper standards, when papers like *Today*, he argues, have had a far more persistent record of mendacity. 'The *Sun*'s stories which are untrue concern essentially trivial issues. What is striking about *Today* is that it is more likely to produce untrue stories about more serious issues.' (He was speaking before the former deputy editor of the *Sun*, Martin Dunn, took over as editor of *Today* at the end of March 1991.)

It is when Max Hastings starts to apply his mind to possible solutions to the intractable problem of newspaper standards that eccentricity – or, some would say, the English class system – starts to show through. He is prepared to resort to the ultimate weapons to bring erring newspaper proprietors to heel – withholding the lunch invitation and administering the social snub. 'I'm not suggesting that Rupert [Murdoch] would be on the phone to his editors at once if he didn't get invited to lunch, but there is at the moment no sense of real social disapprobation on those who are responsible for this' [the decline in standards],' the *Daily Telegraph*'s editor says.

If lack of lunch fails to persuade proprietors to behave themselves, Max Hastings is not at all sure what will work. Politicians, he believes, are on weak ground when they threaten legislation against the press, because over the years they have been perfectly willing to traffic with proprietors, such as Rupert Murdoch, for their own political advantage.

But, despite being a member of the Press Complaints Commission, Hastings has long been pessimistic about the chances for the ultimate survival of self-regulation. In conversation, he returns again and again to the difference in purpose and approach between the broadsheets and the tabloids. 'We will all do our best to make it [self-regulation] work, but sometimes one does feel fairly foolish that here we are all attempting to be good boy scouts, running corrections religiously on getting the date of Kitchener's expedition up the Nile wrong, while every day teams of people are driving a coach and horses through the whole situation.'

Roy Maddison, Keith Parker and Max Hastings are three very different editors, with different backgrounds and responsibilities – a local weekly, a regional evening and one of the great national dailies. Yet each of them acknowledges, albeit to a different degree, that there is a serious problem over the values and practices of some national newspapers, whether it's actually making up stories, failing to check them before publication or 'whamming' them up to such an extent that contact with reality is lost.

Talk to editors and former editors – and there are even more former editors than former football managers – and many concede that standards, particularly of accuracy, in broadsheet as well as in tabloid newspapers, have fallen within the living memory of the older generation of journalists, even though such subjective judgements can never be proved statistically, as the Calcutt Committee found.

By no stretch of the imagination can Arthur Brittenden be dismissed as a sanctimonious out-of-touch complainer looking down his broadsheet nose at the activities of the tabloids. He is a former editor of the *Daily Mail* and was for a time deputy editor of the *Sun*, under Kelvin MacKenzie. He started his career in journalism in 1940 in what was then a very traditional way – as a 16-year-old junior 'at 10 bob a week and 5 shillings expenses' and worked his way up first to Fleet Street and then to one of the most coveted editor's chairs. He has no doubt whatsoever that, during his working life, standards have fallen, although there was villainy among reporters then as now.

'What has changed along the line is now the reader suffers because now there is sheer invention. That did not happen in my day,' Brittenden says. 'If you made up quotes you would have been in serious trouble, and one of the reasons people got fired into the street from time to time without the pay-offs that people expect now was that if you got it wrong a time or two it was just accepted that, like a footballer who kicks the legs from under another, you got a red card and you went off.'

Competition and the pressure to find stories sensational enough to make papers walk off the newsagents' counters encourage invention, exaggeration and the invasion of privacy. In recent years a new dimension has been added to the competition that newspapers have faced from each other. An unequal battle has been joined with an opponent impossible to defeat and difficult even to contain – television.

Television brings the news as it is happening, and through more and more channels. ITV now has news bulletins throughout the night, and cable and satellite television bring up to thirty channels to a growing number of homes. Sky News broadcasts twenty-four hours a day, with half an hour of news on the hour. By mid-1991 it was available in only around 2 million homes, but that number is growing all the time. Forecasts by advertising agency Saatchi & Saatchi suggest that by the end of the century 68 per cent of UK homes will have multi-channel television via cable-TV networks or satellite dishes.

The total amount of television being watched has been increasing – in 1985 total viewing hours averaged just over 23 hours a week per person; by November 1991 it was over 28 hours. But the sheer volume of TV news, in particular, could slowly undermine newspaper circulations. The popular end of the market is particularly vulnerable.

Another ex-editor, Roy Greenslade, a talented editor of the *Daily Mirror* who left the paper 'by mutual agreement' at the beginning of March 1991, had earlier expressed pessimism about the future of tabloid newspapers. Perhaps, he suggested, the fears of the 1950s, that television would devastate the newspaper industry, were now belatedly coming to pass; young people were orientated more towards moving pictures than towards the printed word and would gradually desert newspapers. This is an argument that is easy to overstate, but the overall long-term circulation trends are downwards.

Professor Harry Henry, one of the pioneers of modern market research in the UK, revealed the good and the bad news for newspapers in a study of newspaper circulations and cover prices for the years 1961 to 1984. Over this period newspapers owners had been able to get away with considerable price rises, and what the public spent on papers had actually increased by 70 per cent in real terms. Circulation trends were much less healthy. The total number of newspapers sold fell from 10,200 million in 1961 to 8,610 million in 1984.

And for most of the popular papers the trend had continued down. For the six months to the end of February 1991, the mass-market tabloids showed an 8 per cent fall, to 8.533 million daily sales, compared with the same period five years ago. The equivalent figure for the mass-market Sunday tabloids was a 7 per cent decline, to 10.407 million. The picture continued to appear grim well into 1991, with the downward trend affecting most titles, with the exception of the *Guardian*, the *Financial Times* and the *Daily Mail*.

Recession clearly played a part. Some people saved money by cutting out their paper, or by buying only one paper instead of two. There is also a suspicion, that cannot be verified, that tabloid sales may also have been affected by a new cautiousness as editors try to respond to the new regulatory environment and the threat of legislation. Scandals do not appear to be quite so thick on pages of the papers as in the late 1980s.

Indeed, in 1991 one large question was exercising the minds of popular newspaper editors – could they pull off the trick of being a little more 'respectable,' as influential sections of society appeared to want, without inevitably losing circulation?

Apart from the growing pervasiveness of television, the tabloids could be slowly undermined as if the growing numbers of people going into higher or further education result in more sophisticated readers being lured up market. Those who have had tertiary education are likely to be broadsheet readers. At the other end of the scale of educational achievement, the growing numbers who find reading difficult are unlikely to become newspaper readers at all.

The death of Fleet Street as the geographical home of most national newspapers and the diaspora to Wapping, the Isle of Dogs or even, in the case of the *Daily Mail*, Kensington High Street has been part of the economic transformation of the industry. The sale of the old properties around Fleet Street, together with gains in productivity, has paid for the installation of sophisticated new presses. From 1985 to 1990, all the national newspapers either installed new computer-controlled colour presses, which seem as big as battleships, or decided to print under contract at modern printing plants around the country. For readers, this has meant sharper, crisper print and pictures and a growing use of run-of-press colour – colour that is printed at the same time as the newspaper is produced, rather than being printed on different presses and then inserted into the newspaper. But the dispersal may also have contributed to some of the excesses and the printing of stories that simply were not true.

In the past there may have been intense competition to get a story, but there was also considerable pressure to get it right. 'If you got something wrong, everyone would know you got it wrong, because other people were on the story and you would walk into El Vinos and you would be barracked. It didn't mean they wouldn't buy you a drink, but at least equal to the pressure from the reader was the pressure from your chums, knowing they were going to say: "Christ! Got it wrong again, Brittenden," ' says Arthur Brittenden.

Another factor that has put pressure on standards has been a greater tendency by journalists to stay in their offices chasing stories on the telephone rather than getting out and meeting the people they are writing about. The lack of human contact may make it easier for journalists, working in a near vacuum, to visualize the ideal pattern of a story without letting awkward facts or contradictory details get in the way. 'I think with some journalists they live in a fantasy land where they don't think that people will actually read it tomorrow and people who know it is a lie will say it is a lie.'

As Kelvin MacKenzie's deputy, Arthur Brittenden found that the editor of the *Sun* could be an enormously attractive character but one who could also be utterly irresponsible. When he was a young man new to Fleet Street and working as a reporter on the *News Chronicle*, one of Brittenden's jobs was to follow up missed stories from the first editions of the other papers. He would call bishops at midnight to see whether it really was true – as the *Daily Express* or some other paper was claiming – that a local curate had been caught assaulting small boys. If no one could be found to confirm the story it simply wasn't used. That wasn't how it was on the *Sun* when he was deputy editor. He would go to the night editor and draw his attention to a strong story on the front page of the *Daily Mail*. The *Sun* executive would say they already had got that story. Even though the paper had known about the story for only five or ten minutes, they already 'had' it. 'As I walked away I would see a reporter – probably a shift reporter, not even a staff reporter – who was sitting with a typewriter just lifting the *Mail* story. And he hadn't picked up the telephone. He hadn't checked,' Brittenden says.

Present concerns over accuracy and quality are not expressed just by those looking back over their shoulders at the apparently more innocuous naughtiness of the 1950s and 1960s. There are those with the courage and honesty to admit that sometimes the newspapers did indeed go too far. One of them is David Montgomery, who has edited both the *News of the World* and *Today* and is perhaps the archetypal tabloid journalist – although not as notorious as Kelvin MacKenzie. Unlike many of his tabloid colleagues, he did not hide in his office issuing 'no comment' statements to the press through his secretary; he was prepared to come out and defend what he did for a living.

'I think it became more permissive during the late seventies and eighties. We pushed things to the ultimate limit and it got badly out of hand, and one or two great exponents of tabloid journalism were not too fussy about the veracity of what they were saying sometimes. It happened because of the emphasis on competition and circulation battles, and the fact that kiss-and-tell stories were not building circulation fast enough,' reflects Montgomery.

Nobody inside the papers was warning against the dangers of stories that were becoming ever more strident and ever more stretched. And tabloid journalists were hardly likely to listen to the 'sneering and cynical' critics in the 'quality' press, who joined with politicians and broadcasters to create what David Montgomery believes became an anti-tabloid industry. Sneer at the tabloids and you are really sneering at their readers: you are rapidly back in the English class system and its upstairs-downstairs hierarchy of reading habits. Max Hastings, in particular, he believes, is a snob. 'On the occasions when Kelvin and I have met him, he has refused to shake our hands. That's not the sign of a gentleman for a start,' says David Montgomery.

The former editor of *Today* is concerned that few seem prepared to acknowledge that 99 per cent of tabloid journalism is decent and honest. What has also not been generally acknowledged is the greatest achievement of the tabloids – the fact that there is still a huge newspaper-reading public in the UK despite the competition from television. 'The tabloids have done their job brilliantly well to captivate such a vast audience – 20 million readers – despite breakfast television and new channels.' For many *Sun* and *Mirror* readers their morning newspaper may be the main printed matter they come across in a day. 'The tabloids bring a little colour into people's lives. They give them information about their favourite personalities and on wars, disasters, politics.'

David Montgomery receives full support for such views from an unexpected quarter – Andrew Knight, former editor of *The Economist*, one of Britain's most intellectual and successful weekly magazines.

Knight was also editor-in-chief of the *Daily Telegraph* until he became, in 1990, Rupert Murdoch's right hand in London as executive chairman of News International and the man with the final editorial say on the company's five national newspapers. He is a long-term reader of the *Sun*, a qualified admirer of Kelvin MacKenzie and not at all fastidious about how the *Sun* expresses itself. When the Press Council criticized the paper for describing homosexuals as 'poofters', Knight defended the usage as simply part of the everyday language of the British people.

They make an odd couple, the politically sophisticated former *Economist* editor and the *Sun* editor whom Rupert Murdoch himself is said to have once described as 'a political pygmy'.

Both admirers and detractors of MacKenzie agree that he sometimes gets a bit carried away – and rarely more than during Michael Heseltine's campaign to replace Margaret Thatcher as Prime Minister, when MacKenzie ran a front page with a headline 'The Adulterer, the Bungler and the Joker'. The story began, 'If you believe a man is best judged by the company he keeps, the *Sun* poses this crucial question today: Is Michael Heseltine the right person to succeed Maggie?' To fit the derogatory categories of the headline, the front page carried three photographs of named MPs who were supporting Heseltine. It was, Andrew Knight believes a classic example of someone trying to please his masters and going too far in the process.

The executive chairman of News International normally has a chat with Kelvin MacKenzie once or twice a day and tries to have a look at the early page layouts to see if there is any need to say 'Wait a minute.' The day of the Heseltine supporters 'story', Andrew Knight was in Los Angeles and Murdoch was in New York, and Kelvin had been left to his own devices. 'That's where Kelvin's lack of political nous comes in. He was seeking to help Margaret Thatcher. What did he do? He hurt her grievously. She actually had to disown it in Parliament. I rang Rupert straight away when I was told about it on the telephone. Both of us had words with Kelvin and he admitted he'd made a mistake. It all bubbles up quite naturally – he needs someone there,' says Andrew Knight.

Knight, who picked up around £12 million worth of *Telegraph* shares for his role in spotting the investment opportunity for Conrad Black and in helping to bring the paper back from the verge of bankruptcy, believes Kelvin MacKenzie is potentially the greatest asset News International has got. He has a delicate path to tread between harnessing Kelvin MacKenzie's tremendous energy and creativity and preventing him going over the top entirely. 'If I was to go in and totally confuse him and say from now on you're not going to do this, that or the other, he would lose his way. He's already got enough pressure on him from the change in the political complexion of the country, particularly his readers, the change in societal attitudes from the Press Complaints Commission and what lies behind that.'

The News International chairman is now a lot happier with the way the *Sun* is going – at least when he or Rupert Murdoch is in town. 'The *Sun* should be naughty, not nasty, and it's too often been nasty.'

On Saturdays Andrew Knight is usually phoned by *News of the World* editor Patsy Chapman with news on the main stories for Sunday's paper, and again he might offer advice if a story seems potentially dangerous. Andrew Neil, the editor of the *Sunday Times*, usually calls Knight as well, to check the paper's editorials with him or at least to have a chat about them, Knight says. But one Saturday the call didn't come. It was the day the *Sunday Times* ran an editorial attacking some members of the royal family for their activities, or lack of them, during the Gulf War.

By coincidence, that Saturday Rupert Murdoch, who is no royalist and who doesn't mind the royals being turned over a bit from time to time, arrived unexpectedly in London and picked up his copy of the *Sunday Times*. 'He regarded it [the editorial] as pompous and extremely inappropriate in the middle of a war. The one thing you don't do in the middle of a war is attack the symbol of unity, the royal family. Rupert rang me up and said "What on earth is Andrew up to?" Then the *Guardian* carries a headline saying the Murdoch press attacks the royal family, ignoring the fact that *The Times* and the *Sun* had leaders saying what rubbish this all was,' Andrew Knight says with exasperation.

Knight is clearly in a position to influence the content of five national newspapers, including several with a tradition of journalism and a view of the world that is liable to take them up to and sometimes beyond the ever-changing notional boundary of what society regards as acceptable. Though he denies riding shotgun to protect journalistic standards at Wapping, that is in effect is what he does when not diverted by other more pressing issues, as at the end of 1989 and the beginning of 1990, when he was one of the team working on the News Corporation's vital $7.4 billion refinancing.

As Rupert Murdoch has followed his empire westwards to Los Angeles, Andrew Knight has become a powerful viceroy. 'My view of the *Sun* is that it has suffered not by Rupert Murdoch's presence but by his absence. When he was there the paper was salacious, rough, tough and it made enemies but it never overstepped the mark. It overstepped the mark when he wasn't there.'

Andreas Whittam Smith, editor and chief executive of the *Independent*, is usually there running the paper. Although not strictly speaking a newspaper proprietor, he was the principal founder of the *Independent* and is a substantial shareholder in Newspaper Publishing, the paper's holding company – a company which started life with a 15 per cent limit on individual stakes, to prevent any single investor becoming too powerful. He is one of a new and still rarified breed of journalists who successfully combine editorial flair with business acumen and a strong streak of self-interest. Andreas Whittam Smith is, at least on paper, probably even richer than Andrew Knight.

To *Private Eye*, the editor of the *Independent* is 'Whittam Strobes', and often the adjectives 'saintly' or 'blessed' are added for good measure, perhaps reflecting the fact he is the son of a Church of England cleric. But anyone trying to take away what he regards as his would quickly discover there are limits to his saintliness. For example, Andreas Whittam Smith launched his *Independent on Sunday* directly at the *Sunday Correspondent* in January 1990, at its moment of maximum weakness, at least partly because he did not want to let the *Correspondent* get away with making use of 'his' idea.

The *Correspondent* folded but, as a result of the worst advertising recession for quality newspapers this century, Andreas Whittam Smith also overreached himself. In the summer of 1991, the *Independent on Sunday*, losing at one stage at the rate of £6 million a year, had to be integrated with the *Independent* to cut costs. The merger seems to have worked, although at considerable personal cost. Fifty-six jobs went under a redundancy programme, most of them on the Sunday title, and Stephen Glover, one of the founders of the *Independent* and editor of the *Independent on Sunday*, resigned. Costs have been cut, however, and by September 1991 circulation of the Sunday title had drifted up towards 400,000.

But the advertising recession, which deepened during 1991, has affected the finances of the *Independent* severely. Newspaper Publishing made a pretax loss of £6.45 million in the six months to March 1991, and in September 1991 it went for its second refinancing in less than a year, raising more than £16 million in new equity and loans – a refinancing underwritten by its two principal shareholders, the Continental European newspapers *La Repubblica* of Italy and *El Pais* of Spain, although at a cost of abandoning its initial 15 per cent limit on individual shareholdings.

Although not infallible, Andreas Whittam Smith has earned himself a place in the history of national newspapers. In March 1985 when he was City editor of the *Daily Telegraph*, he was rung by *Business Week* magazine and asked if Eddy Shah's plans for a revolutionary new paper, *Today*, would work. 'No,' was his instant reply. But almost as soon as he put the phone down he began wondering if he was wrong, and he asked to meet Eddy Shah the next day. Use of the latest computer technology and printing under contract rather than buying expensive presses could lower the entry costs enough to allow even journalists to launch a new national daily.

Andreas Whittam Smith not only saw the opportunity but also managed to raise the £21 million needed from the City to make the idea a reality and create a paper that is not just a broadsheet but one that earns the title 'quality' as well. By challenging *The Times*, the *Guardian* and the *Daily Telegraph*, the paper has expanded the market for serious newspapers in the UK. About half its near 400,000 circulation was taken from existing papers; the rest came by attracting readers who had not bought a regular daily paper.

It was in 1989 that the *Independent*'s editor really began to worry seriously about the various threats to the British press from the new Official Secrets legislation and from Right of Reply and Right of Privacy Bills. Yet, despite such threats, no collective or coherent opposition was being organized against measures that would reduce press freedom. 'We were like a group of people in the middle of a field without cover and everyone was shooting at us and we were just going to get shot. The first thing to do was to find high ground,' Andreas Whittam Smith remembers.

He had no doubt that the intense competition faced by the tabloids had increased the sleaze factor in the British press, but he was no disapproving maiden aunt tut-tutting at the tabloids. Social standards had changed and he was prepared to be earthy in his coverage when the occasion demanded it – within reason. When an *Independent* journalist presented him with a report of an impromptu performance by actor Oliver Reed with five 'fucks' in it, that was a few too many for Whittam Smith. He passed one or two, though, to convey the flavour of the occasion. A tabloid editor would have reached for his asterisks.

Controversial use of language was one thing, but newspapers were absolutely mad, he believes, not to consider the whole question of editorial standards and the trouble they were getting the press into. So it was that the unlikely figure of Andreas Whittam Smith set about persuading the lion to lie down with the lamb. The aim was to persuade the editors of all the national newspapers to agree to a common code of conduct and introduce ombudsmen or reader's representatives. It meant Sir Geoffrey Owen, the then editor of the *Financial Times*, making common cause with Kelvin MacKenzie and with Brian Hitchen, editor of the *Daily Star*.

A subcommittee of the Newspaper Publishers Association was set up to prepare a code. It was chaired by Whittam Smith and usually met at the offices of the *Independent*. It included Brian MacArthur, the founding editor of *Today*; Sir Frank Rogers, deputy chairman of the Newspaper Publishers Association; and Bernard Shrimsley, former editor of the *News of the World*.

'Andreas Whittam Smith seized the baton. His decisiveness was impressive, as was his recognition that this was a very potent issue on which newspapers were getting on the wrong side,' Brian MacArthur believes. Whittam Smith was very aware, though, that broadsheets couldn't lecture tabloids in a patronizing way. Apart from being counter-productive, it was obvious that if the code were to work it would be the tabloids which would have to give up the most.

If the initiative were to stand any chance of success, it would have to have the support of the newspaper proprietors. MacArthur advised tackling the biggest challenge first – Rupert Murdoch. It helped that Murdoch has a high personal regard for Whittam Smith and what he has achieved with the launch of the *Independent*. The timing was also good. The £1 million out-of-court settlement with Elton John had been a watershed. A backlog of out-of-court libel settlements was being cleared up, and there was growing pressure within News International to avoid such costly errors of judgement in future. Rupert Murdoch was supportive of the Whittam Smith proposals.

The next target was Robert Maxwell, who was also receptive to the idea of a code. When Whittam Smith arrived to see Mr Maxwell, the editors of the *Daily Mirror, Sunday Mirror* and *People* were already waiting in a sideroom. The publisher of Mirror Group Newspapers said there were two ways of proceeding. One was to tell the editors what they had to do; the other was to try to persuade them of the merits of a code. 'I said I'd seek to persuade them. Maxwell said he thought that was absolutely the wrong way to do this,' Whittam Smith says, but the *Independent*'s editor had his way.

There was a measure of opposition from Peter Preston, the editor of the *Guardian*, who predicted – correctly – that the initiative would undermine the Press Council. Whittam Smith didn't care. It was time, he believed, for national newspapers to look after their own immediate interests; the Press Council would fall into line.

A national code was approved at a remarkable five-hour meeting at the World Trade Centre, by the Tower of London, in December 1989. This was the first time in living memory that the editors of all Britain's national newspapers had sat down to consider matters of mutual concern.

The code – which called for prompt corrections for mistakes, an end to invasion of privacy where there was no public interest, and the appointing of readers' representatives – was remarkable less for its content than for the fact it was accepted by all but the *Financial Times*, which decided it wanted the editor to continue handling complaints rather than an ombudsman. 'People said this was a very weak code and that all those ombudsmen are patsies. I knew that and frankly didn't mind. So far as I was concerned, to get that far was a triumph and the next stage was to tighten up,' Andreas Whittam Smith commented.

Even the 'weak' code went too far for some. Peregrine Worsthorne warned readers of the *Sunday Telegraph* of the dangers of media priggishness. 'Journalism does less harm when it disgusts by its genuine vulgarity than when it deludes by its spurious sanctity,' he declared.

But there were larger issues at stake than priggishness or vulgarity. The question was much more whether the press could devise an effective form of self-regulation. The *Independent*'s editor is totally convinced of the need for regulation and for the setting of limits. 'I can scarcely think of any market that doesn't need some regulation. The stuff we are peddling is quite as dangerous as drugs or pharmaceutical products. We can damage people's lives and health with our publications.'

He sees a second wave of Fleet Street history taking shape. Over most of the past thirty years, all the efforts of managers had to be concentrated on the daily battle against the powerful and intransigent print unions. With that battle essentially over following the exodus from Fleet Street, newspaper executives now have more time and freedom to devote to improving their products, and that must include editorial standards.

But time is short, and the Press Complaints Commission is the last chance for self-regulation. 'If this doesn't work I won't make any further arguments. The industry has allowed me my shot. I have helped to set up and get running the system I think we should have, and if it now doesn't work then I'll have to shut up. I think it will be very hard to hold the line against legislation if this doesn't work,' Andreas Whittam Smith says. For newspapers, the test and the standards of excellence to be aimed for are quite simple. 'Can we have the same relationship with our readers as Marks & Spencer has with its customers? If it doesn't work, God help us,' he adds.

With the exception of Andreas Whittam Smith, there is very little sign that national newspaper owners and editors have ever begun to think about quality control for their products in a way that a Marks & Spencer would take for granted.

9

'Statements made by Sylvester the Cat were erroneously attributed to Daffy Duck' The press in the USA

IN marked contrast to the British, Americans take their journalism seriously. Debates are held about the power of newspapers, the role of the journalist in society and the difference between best practice and sharp practice. In the USA, there are even journalists who are prepared to utter the word 'ethics' in public without blushing.

Publications such as the *Journal of the Gannett Center For Media Studies* in New York, the *Columbia Journalism Review* or the *Washington Journalism Review* regularly examine questions of ethics and excellence. The first real attempt to create anything comparable in the UK came as recently as the autumn of 1989, when, with the support of journalists, newspapers and the Rowntree Trust, the *British Journalism Review* was launched to 'raise the flag of insurrection against the advance of those poisonous weeds that are now choking the life-blood out of British journalism'. In an editorial explaining 'Why We Are Here', the new review explained that British journalism was now subject to a contagious outbreak 'of squalid, banal, lazy and cowardly journalism whose only qualification is that it helps to make newspaper publishers (and some journalists) rich'.

In many respects the American newspaper industry differs widely from that in the UK. It has different traditions and different economics, and it operates in a different legal framework. Above all else, with the exception of the *Wall Street Journal*, American newspapers are largely city-based or regional, rather than national. Yet, despite such fundamental differences, British papers can learn from the American experience – particularly about maintaining the relationship between a paper and its readers, and what to do when things go wrong.

One reason for the variant approaches in the two countries may be that most American journalists have gone to university journalism schools and that, as a result, journalism has a more academic tradition. In Britain, although the number of graduates is increasing, many journalists still drift into the occupation and combine learning on the job with part-time training. Yet training alone does not account for the fact that there is a greater willingness for journalists in the USA, at least in the mainstream press, to ask serious questions about what they do – questions with a moral dimension. From the *Daily Camera* in Boulder, Colorado, or the *New Salisbury Post* in North Carolina, to the mighty *Washington Post*, there appears to be a much greater concern in the USA about everything from journalistic conflicts of interest to accuracy and fairness.

On papers such as the *Los Angeles Times*, for example, there is a written code of ethics for journalists. It includes instructions to shun gifts from news sources (except things of insignificant value), and the selling of review copies of books or records is forbidden. 'Within bounds of common sense and civil behaviour, staffers should not accept free transport or reduced rate travel, or free accommodation or meals,' the code says.

At the *Washington Post* they make a point of paying for their own tickets to review plays and concerts. And free trips abroad – the notorious 'freebies' so beloved by many British journalists – are generally frowned on in the USA. It is also made clear to *Post* journalists that they cannot take part in political activity – and that includes marching in demonstrations. When several *Washington Post* reporters were spotted in an abortion-rights march, they were immediately told that in future they would not be allowed to cover anything touching on the abortion issue. Corrections are also felt to be a serious matter. And the paper has a routine slot for correcting errors – down to the incorrect spelling of names.

Inevitably, in the land of specialist newsletters, there is a newsletter, called *FineLine*, published in Louisville, Kentucky, which is devoted entirely to the ethics of journalism. Journalists are encouraged to write articles for *FineLine* describing real newspaper dilemmas and how they coped with them. Its columns allow an outsider to eavesdrop on the preoccupations of American journalists as they wrestle in public over where moral lines should be drawn. Although many write in self-justification and conclude they behaved perfectly properly in the circumstances, they are nevertheless engaging in a debate that has hardly begun in the UK.

Many of *FineLine*'s articles address universal questions of where legitimate news ends and unwarranted intrusion into private grief begins. Take the all-too-common dilemma faced by Kevin Goddard, managing editor of the *Times Argus* in the small community of Barre, Vermont. He wrote in the newsletter of his dilemma over an emotionally powerful picture of a young couple embracing in grief as the body of their 5-year-old son Henry, covered by a sheet, lay on the road nearby. He had been the victim of a hit-and-run driver as he ran to his school bus-stop. The photographer had kept his distance and, by choosing his angle carefully, had made sure the faces of the parents could not be seen. Should the photograph be printed?

'We ran the picture three columns by eight inches above the fold on page one. Then we spent the next six months explaining our decision,' Goddard wrote in *FineLine*. The letters of complaint came by the dozen and accused the paper of being 'insensitive', 'exploitative' and 'sensational'. The *Times Argus* responded with an editorial explaining the positive side of what it had done. The coverage had showed that a family's loss was also a community's loss; it had made thousands of parents hug their children with a special understanding and discuss road safety a little more vigorously; and it had helped to encourage local transportation officials to try to reduce such risks in future.

According to Goddard, the most positive aspect of all was the response the controversy provoked in the newsroom. 'We call it missionary work: it's when editors and reporters are called upon in their "real lives" to explain what we do and why we do it.' The little paper, he promised, would continue to hold up the mirror to society and help the community to 'see itself as it is, day in and day out, on happy days and sad ones'.

Karen Schmidt, assistant regional editor of the *Waterbury Republican-American* in Connecticut, faced an even more difficult dilemma. Two weeks after a gunman had opened fire and murdered five children in a Californian school, she discovered that a letter threatening similar violence had been sent to police in a local town. It was probably media coverage of the California shootings that had given the unbalanced writer of the letter the idea of threatening to shoot 'Catholic pigs' in the schoolyard 'real soon, ladies first'. Security at the school in Connecticut had already been intensified, and parents had been warned of the threat by letter. Would the newspaper become an accomplice if it overplayed the story? How would a splashy story affect more than 3,000 children?

The *Waterbury Republican-American* decided to carry just a four-paragraph story, putting the incident on the public record but doing nothing that would excite a sick person craving attention. The paper held to this firm line even though the local television station opted to promote the story for all it was worth and used studio-background graphics of a target riddled with bullet holes. 'Looking back, I still think we did the right thing,' says

Ms Schmidt. 'We can't determine story-play only on how many people will read it: we have a responsibility to consider the consequences.'

The small-town daily newspapers of America are, inevitably, close to their readers and responsive to their moods and complaints. But it is papers like the *Washington Post*, a paper that has seen both the best and the worst of American journalism, that sets the agenda for how journalists should behave.

It is difficult to walk across the vast, cluttered *Post* newsroom without seeing ghosts of Watergate or imagining overhearing snatches of unattributable phone calls to a Bob Woodward or Carl Bernstein. Their stories of conspiracy to bug and burgle the headquarters of the Democrats' 1972 election campaign, written with the help of 'Deep Throat', the inside source who has still not definitively been identified, played a key role in forcing the resignation of President Richard Nixon on 9 August 1974.

The *Washington Post* was also the paper that published a feature that began with the following dramatic sentence: 'Jimmy is 8 years old with sandy hair, velvety brown eyes and needle marks freckling the baby-smooth skin of his brown arms.' The story, by *Post* reporter Janet Cooke, won a 1981 Pulitzer Prize. It was, however, untrue. An investigation by the *Post*'s then ombudsman Bill Green, the man who dealt with readers' complaints, found that Jimmy didn't exist. The Pulitzer was handed back and Cooke was fired.

Richard Harwood, the present ombudsman, is everyone's idea of what a tough-talking senior American journalist should be. He combines faded Ivy League elegance with the slightly weary demeanour of a man who has seen it all. In 1970 he became the *Post*'s first ombudsman, and one of the first to hold that position in America, although they didn't call it by that strange Swedish name then. Now retired as a journalist, he's come back for a second stint as ombudsman.

Many of the complaints he receives are minor, he says, involving a misspelt name or missing balancing detail – what the *Post*'s legendary executive editor Ben Bradlee, who retired in 1991, called 'picking the flyshit out of the pepper'. Many letters of complaint come from pedantic grammarians worried about split infinitives, and even more come from plain nuts. 'I told Don Graham [The *Post*'s publisher] a couple of months ago, I don't know who told you the customer is always right but he was full of shit,' says Harwood.

Among the fly-droppings, however, Richard Harwood finds some all-too-real complaints to deal with about articles that have appeared in the paper, and he has had to tackle controversial issues about how *Post* reporters behave in their 'private' lives.

He was critical of Stephanie Mansfield, a reporter who wrote a scathing profile of a government official she had never met. 'She passed all of those judgements from cuttings and I have never been able to ascertain from where else,' says Harwood. Another case, involving a summer trainee, was clear-cut. At a Congressional hearing, scientist after scientist had testified that there was no evidence suggesting that Agent Orange, the defoliant used in Vietnam, seriously affected people's health. Only one witness disagreed, but the young reporter had devoted his entire story to this, giving the impression this was the weight of the evidence given to Congress. Richard Harwood wrote a column about this incident.

Harwood confirms the universal truth that journalists everywhere are very sensitive of public criticism of them. They love reading his regular ombudsman column in the *Post*, however – as long as its not about them. He has also made himself less than popular with senior colleagues by ruling that in future journalists will not be able to accept honoraria for making speeches to special lobby groups. Some *Post* specialists made up to $100,000 a year in fees from this source, he says. One opponent of the new policy even complained that he used his *Post* salary only to pay his income tax. 'Over the years I have been highly critical of prominent members of staff attacking members of Congress for taking money from special-interest groups, when those same journalists were taking money from the same interest groups in the form of honoraria for speeches. We have now come to the point, and its going to hurt some people, where we are not going to allow that any more,' says Harwood.

It was the Vietnam war that led to the *Washington Post* establishing an ombudsman. In the minds of some readers, the *Post* was identified with the anti-war movement and the counter-culture of the 1960s, and hundreds and hundreds of readers were cancelling their subscriptions on ideological grounds. Richard Harwood took the 1969–70 group of summer interns, gave each of them a bundle of cancellation letters and sent them out to the suburbs to get a clearer picture of what was bugging people and why. A number of senior staff were then asked to write essays on how the paper should respond to the reader dissatisfaction they found, and the late Phil Foisie, the paper's foreign editor and a man addicted to writing memos to himself on his shirtcuffs, is credited with coming up with the idea of a reader's representative.

The importance of an ombudsman on a paper like the *Post*, which on a

Sunday often prints more than 1,000 pages and weighs in at 6lb, is obvious. The first time the editor sees most of the articles is when his own copy of the paper is delivered. The scale of the business matches the size of the paper: there are nearly 700 people involved in the editorial process.

Although there are 1,700 daily newspapers in the USA (many of them tiny by British standards), there are currently only around 30 ombudsmen. However, their presence is likely to grow as more papers address the issues of standards and ethics and introduce tough codes of conduct as part of standard business practice. No one wants to alienate the customer at a time when newspaper circulations are static and the total number of readers is in gradual decline.

In 1970, daily newspaper circulation in the USA fell below the total number of households for the first time in recent history, and by 1985 household penetration had fallen to 0.70 – a decline that is continuing. Newspaper circulations are failing to keep up with population growth and the generation of new households, although in absolute terms the number of papers sold is static. According to the International Federation of Newspaper Publishers, between 1986 and 1990 the total number of newspapers sold by daily newspapers in the USA rose slightly, from 62.5 billion a year in 1986 to 62.65 billion in 1990. The main reason for the slight increase is believed to be that some communities have increased in size and as a result have been able to support a daily rather than a weekly newspaper. Fierce competition from electronic media is seen as the main reason for the decline relative to population.

The greater sensitivity to ethics in the USA is, however, scarcely a sign of timidity. Compared with Britain, the legal position of American newspapers is enormously strong – mainly because of the First Amendment to the US constitution, which says emphatically that 'The Congress shall make no law . . . abridging the freedom of speech or of the press.' An army of lawyers specializing in First Amendment law makes sure there is no backsliding by politicians who, much like politicians everywhere, are more interested in the theory of press freedom than the practice. 'The First Amendment – that's the prize. That's where we are so far ahead of you guys,' says Dr Sally Taylor, a First Amendment specialist who now lives in the UK and has recently written *Shock! Horror!*, a surprisingly affectionate account of what she calls Britain's 'three-ring circus' – the country's national tabloid newspapers.

The staying power of the First Amendment was greatly reinforced in a famous 1964 Supreme Court case – *New York Times* v. *Sullivan*. In the

Sullivan case, the court ruled that in the case of public officials it is not enough to demonstrate that something written about them is untrue: they also have to show there was 'actual malice' and that a newspaper knew a statement was false but published 'with reckless disregard of whether it was false or not'. And in recent years the Supreme Court has continued in the view that law suits which inhibit freedom of speech cannot stand. American courts have become notorious for multi-million awards of damages against newspapers, but in most cases these rulings have been overturned on appeal because of the difficulty of proving malice. In fact, since the Sullivan case, the idea of a public official has been broadened to cover almost anyone who carries out business in public. A television evangelist, for instance, has been considered quite public enough. Some American editors clearly feel that by putting someone in the paper they have defined him or her as a public figure.

Conrad Black, the *Daily Telegraph* chairman, who owns small daily newspapers in both Canada and the USA, would like to see the *New York Times* v. *Sullivan* ruling overturned. 'It effectively abolished the tort of civil defamation. To prove malice is practically impossible unless the defendant wants to be convicted. It's the removal of a check and balance and they [the journalists] are not normally counterbalanced within American newspapers by assertive owners or editors,' he says.

The weakness of the libel law has encouraged lawyers to use privacy legislation to try to get redress for those defamed by newspapers, although anyone running for public office tends to be regarded as having forfeited the right to a private life. In December 1987 journalists from the *Miami Herald* effectively ended the presidential run of Democratic candidate Gary Hart with allegations of womanizing in his 'private' life, a purity test the late President John F. Kennedy, for one, could not have passed.

Ever since the publication of an article on 'The Right to Privacy' by Warren and Brandeis in the *Harvard Law Review* in 1890, more and more US states have introduced privacy legislation. This covers areas such as intrusion into an individual's physical solitude, portraying someone in a false light, publication of private matters that violate the ordinary decencies, or appropriating an individual's name or likeness for commercial gain. But the nature of the tort – the injury or wrong for which you can sue for damages – varies from state to state. Few cases have made it to the Supreme Court for adjudication, and it is far from clear how such state privacy laws square with the First Amendment.

Public figures have tended to use privacy laws designed to prevent the portraying of people in a false light. According to Sally Taylor, however, the privacy laws have generally been most successful against electronic surveillance of citizens. 'Home in the US is more of a castle than in the UK,' says Dr Taylor, who cites a case in which the courts found it was unreasonable for surreptitious pictures to be taken of a faith-healer in his home.

What needs to be remembered in any discussion of the American press is that the USA is a country almost sinking under the volume of available information, where everything from the state of the President's colon to the tax records of the spouse of those seeking public office forms part of the public record. Virtually anything that is not a national or commercial secret is available under the Freedom of Information Act.

The combination of ready access to information and the availability of inexpensive computers has even allowed American journalists to create a new form of reporting – computer-assisted investigative journalism – in which computer-literate reporters, sometimes using mainframe computers, plough through the electronic records of public bodies. *USA Today* reporters analysed the equivalent of more than 80 million words in the records of the Environmental Protection Agency to determine communities' state of readiness to cope with a toxic chemical accident. The *Providence Journal* matched a computerized list of all those registered to drive school buses with lists of those with traffic offences and drug-dealing convictions. The *Atlanta Journal* won a Pulitzer Prize in 1989 for a series analysing racial discrimination in bank-lending patterns in the Atlanta area – the practice of 'red-lining' particular areas for different treatment on loans. In the UK, if the Official Secrets Act didn't stop such stories then the Data Protection Act, which forbids unauthorized disclosure of personal information held in electronic form, probably would.

Growing public sensitivity about how American newspaper reporters behave is partly a reflection of the fact, that in most places, fierce circulation wars are a thing of the past. It is now the three or four television stations and the eight or nine radio stations crowding the airwaves in even medium-sized cities that have to fight for audiences. The local paper, often a monopoly and forced by circumstances to serve the entire community, has evolved into a publication expected to display a certain respectability. There is also a primness and puritanism about the American mainstream press which, for example, makes Britain's topless page-3 girls unthinkable in the USA.

There are stricter rules in the USA than in Britain on cross-media ownership – owning television stations as well as newspapers. Rupert Murdoch had to give up his ownership of the *New York Post* when he bought a television station in New York, because rules on concentration of media ownership prevented the possession of a television station and a daily newspaper in the same market. In the UK, by contrast, Murdoch can, and does, own five national newspapers and controls 50 per cent of British Sky Broadcasting, the six-channel satellite-television venture.

Murdoch believes the American press has gradually retreated as radio and television have won a larger slice of advertising revenue. Then, too, there is the problem of distribution. People don't go to work by public transport in the USA, so newspaper publishers have to deliver direct to the home. 'The paper that delivers eight copies in one street as opposed to two has an unapproachable economic advantage,' he points out. 'Simple market forces have led to the monopolization of the press in America.' He has himself looked seriously at the possibility of launching new competing newspapers in one-newspaper cities, but decided the sums simply didn't add up.

The future of the American newspaper, then, seems to be one of continuing local monopoly, and the inevitable tendency towards blandness that goes with it. This wasn't always the case. In the late eighteenth and the nineteenth centuries, America had a very partisan and, by modern standards, a very corrupt press, with close financial ties to political parties and factions. At one point President Jackson had no less than fifty-seven journalists on the official payroll. Yet, as Anthony Smith makes clear in his book *The Newspaper – an International History*, even before the middle of the last century there were publishers who were more interested in running an independent business than in seeking to influence, or be part of, an inner circle of policy-makers – publishers such as Benjamin H. Day, who launched the *Sun*, New York's first penny paper, in 1833. Day went straight to the readers on the streets for his profits, employing squads of young newspaper-sellers who shouted of the latest trials, suicides, fires or burglaries.

Some newspaper publishers in those days also had very high ambitions for their papers. As James Gordon Bennett, who in 1835 founded the *New York Herald* to compete with the *Sun*, put it, 'A newspaper can be made to take the lead . . . in the great movements of human thought, and human civilization. A newspaper can send more souls to Heaven, and save more from Hell, than all the churches or chapels in New York.'

There were, of course many less idealistic than Bennett: there is little in the UK experience, even at its most sensational, to match the New York circulation wars between William Randolph Hearst's *New York Journal* and Joseph Pulitzer's *New York World* in the final years of the last century. The jingoistic attitudes of the two press barons helped to stir up the war fever that would push the USA into the Spanish-American war in 1898 in Cuba and the Philippines – a war in which thousands died. The press coverage makes the UK *Sun*'s Kelvin MacKenzie's Falklands campaign against 'the Argies' seem positively even-handed. The flavour of the story is best caught in the infamous exchange of telegrams between Hearst and the *New York Journal*'s artist Frederic Remington, who was in Cuba. Remington wired Hearst: THERE IS NO TROUBLE HERE. THERE WILL BE NO WAR. WISH TO RETURN. REMINGTON. Hearst replied PLEASE REMAIN. YOU FURNISH THE PICTURES, AND I'LL FURNISH THE WAR. Which is more or less, given a little journalistic hyperbole, what he proceeded to do by whipping up pro-war sentiment.

Widespread concern about press standards in the USA after the Second World War led to the establishment of the Hutchins Commission, under the chairmanship of Robert Hutchins of the University of Chicago. The Commission looked at the articles of the sensationalist journalists and muckrakers to judge the extent of unfair reporting.

In its 1947 report, the Commission criticized journalism for 'meaningless-ness, flatness, distortion and the perpetuation of misunderstanding'. But, in what J. Herbert Altschull in *From Milton to McLuhan* describes as the most enduring of the Commission's demands, Hutchins also called on the press not only to present the facts in a meaningful context but to disclose 'the truth behind the facts' too. Objective facts were not enough – reporters also had to find out what lay behind them and to present the truth of what they had uncovered, 'thus sealing into the professional ideology the essence of investigative reporting'.

But if newspapers in the USA are much less sensational now than in the 1940s, this has less to do with the Hutchins Commission than with the lack of competition. There is still newspaper competition, of a less flamboyant sort, in New York, but it is not between the *Sun*, the *Herald*, the *Journal* or the *World* – all long deceased or merged into the declining number of survivors. Apart from the up-market *New York Times*, America's leading city has to make do with the *New York Post* and the *New York Daily News* – two papers with an uncertain hold on life.

In April 1991 the *Daily News* in particular seemed doomed. The paper was in the middle of a damaging strike, and its owners, the Tribune Group of Chicago, said that unless a buyer was found it would be closed. Robert

Maxwell turned out to be that buyer. He arrived in New York's East River on his ocean-going yacht the *Lady Ghislaine* and, his baseball hat at just the right jaunty angle, proceeded to take the city by storm.

New York is one of only twenty cities in the USA where there are competing newspapers. Some of these papers are hybrids which the government has given special dispensation from cartel rules to allow joint operating agreements. Under these arrangements, two rivals merge their businesses but run papers, usually one in the morning and one in the afternoon, that compete editorially – at least notionally.

In 1989, for example, America's two largest newspaper chains, Gannett and Knight-Ridder, did a sweetheart deal over Gannett's *Detroit News* and Knight-Ridder's *Detroit Free Press*. They decided that the two papers, which were together losing as much as $25 million a year, could move into profit if they merged and split Detroit, America's fifth largest newspaper market, with 1.5 million readers, between them. The *Free Press* would have the weekday mornings, the *News* the afternoons, and at the weekends there would be combined editions. Neither readers nor advertisers in Detroit were ecstatic about the deal, and so far it has not worked well. There were losses of $12 million in 1990, and by 1991 the combined newspaper company was into its third publisher and the circulation of both titles had dropped.

The trend to monopoly seems to be irreversible. The only reasons the *Washington Post* isn't a local monopoly is because of the massive subsidies poured into its rival, the *Washington Times*, by South Korean businessmen associated with the Revd Sun Myung Moon's Unification Church. All those local monopolies have, Richard Harwood believes, turned many newspapers into public utilities.

Apart from their robust treatment of public figures, many American newspapers can seem dull to British eyes. They may be accurate and fair, but there seems to be an almost religious determination to attribute even the most banal and uncontroversial information to named sources. The relative lack of partisanship, combined with the self-indulgent length of many articles in American papers, makes the British press seem very lively by comparison.

'There are vast numbers of newspapers in America which just feed in the agency copy until the paper is full – enormous papers full of stodge. They scarcely ever take up a local cause because they are afraid of the advertisers,' says Arthur Brittenden, former editor of the *Daily Mail* and a one-time New York correspondent for the *Daily Express*.

'I think it is a myth to say American papers have a great lesson for us. Yes indeed, two or three of them are excellent newspapers by world standards, but most of them are just dull,' he added.

Rupert Murdoch is similarly unimpressed by American newspapers, and that includes their apparent preoccupation with ethics. The *Washington Post*, he said, speaking before the retirement of Ben Bradlee in 1991, doesn't let ethics get in the way of a good story. 'Ben Bradlee can't resist a good story. He certainly won't admit to anyone's right of privacy,' says Murdoch. 'The real problem with most American newspapers is they're boring. They've all become monopolies. And opinion gets into all the writing: there is a prevailing liberal school of writing in the *New York Times* and *Washington Post* which gets repeated in every paper in the country,' says the one-time socialist who in recent years has been a passionate supporter of Margaret Thatcher.

Whether or not Murdoch is right about a liberal bias – a mind-set rather than a conspiracy, he believes – such papers and their ombudsmen can get themselves tangled in the most amusing ethical knots when confronted with conflicting orthodoxies.

The leading American dailies employ large numbers of young, highly educated women, who are understandably keen to promote equality and attack sexism. The papers have responded to these internal pressures by being quick to pounce on events or reporting which might demean women. Naturally the liberal dailies have in recent years ridiculed beauty contests as exploitative cattle-shows, when they didn't ignore them entirely. This enlightened policy was even followed when, for the first time, a black woman was chosen as Miss America. 'The telephone would not stop ringing. "You racist sons of bitches. You always put a photograph of Miss America on the front page with her gown and her crown, and when a black Miss America comes along it's two paragraphs," ' Richard Harwood remembers sardonically. Ombudsmen wrote endless columns and editors patiently explained at length that there had really only been a few paragraphs on the contest in the previous year, too, when Miss America had been white. 'It was rather difficult. We have done somersaults and backflips and there have been many fine articles and pictures on this young woman,' says Harwood.

Ombudsmen are only one source of ideas about standards and trends in the American press. There are also the professors of journalism – often retired newspapermen – who write and teach at the many schools of journalism or who serve as fellows at institutions such as the Gannett Center at New York's Columbia University.

Everette Dennis, executive director of the Gannett Center, has been warning the American newspaper industry for years of the need for news organizations to explain their activities to the public in more detail. Freedom of the press is not a self-evident virtue to many people, Dennis warned in *Reshaping The Media*, and some even saw the press as a barrier to their freedom. Journalism, he believes, must make a case for itself, 'to explain why thoughtful and orderly information presented with interpretative tools and in literate language is more beneficial than raw data ordered up through an information storage retrieval system'.

The argument about press standards in the USA is not a new one: it goes back to the frontier days, when editors who annoyed sources were sometimes lynched and their offices put to the torch. But as long ago as 1920, the distinguished columnist Walter Lippmann warned in a collection of essays called *Liberty and the News* that there was an increasingly angry disillusionment with the press. If publishers and authors did not face this fact and try to deal with it, Lippmann argued, 'Someday Congress in a fit of temper, egged on by an outraged public opinion, will operate on the press with an axe ... For somehow the community must find a way of making men who publish news accept responsibility for an honest effort not to misrepresent the facts.'

The search for the means to do this is still going on in the USA. Apart from the scattering of ombudsmen, the methods used have included codes of ethics, 'news councils' (as the American equivalent of Britain's Press Council have been called) and even an annual ethical audit.

The American Society of Newspaper Editors approved a code of ethics at its first meeting in 1923. Like such codes everywhere else, American codes tend to talk about fairness, honesty, objectivity, responsibility and other fine-sounding words as easy to list as they are difficult to define. As elsewhere, this language has more to do with public relations than with influencing journalistic behaviour in the pursuit of stories.

In his book *Ethical Journalism*, Philip Meyer, a journalism professor at the University of North Carolina, writes of a series of unwritten rules that really govern how journalists behave. They include the maxim that a story originated by another publication is never as newsworthy as one originated by one's own paper. This has been described by columnist Russell Baker as 'the tendency to piss all over the other guy's story, to hope that the story will go away because it makes you look bad for missing it'. Another unacknowledged rule is that newspapers are written for other newspaper people rather than the general reader. This, Meyer claims, makes journalists strive for the spectacular at the expense of less glamorous public-service stories. But one rule applied above all others: whenever possible, try to avoid directly admitting a mistake.

Despite Meyer's unwritten rules of journalism, however, there is considerable evidence that American newspapers *do* take corrections seriously. A recent study of the corrections policy at twelve US newspapers – six large and famous and six small – found that serious thought was being given to the issue and that corrections were being made, and made quickly – two-thirds of them within two days of the publication of the error. According to Charles Whitney, a professor of communication at the University of Illinois who wrote the study, all the editors talked to were willing and ready to correct any factual error. Most also honoured the maxim of Robert Phelps of the *Boston Globe*, that newspapers 'should be generous' on corrections.

The *Globe* is generous to a fault and knows it. It once apparently apologized because 'statements made by Sylvester the Cat were erroneously attributed to Daffy Duck'. More significantly, the *Boston Globe* and most of the newspapers surveyed not only correct errors but usually offer some explanation for how they occurred.

'A newspaper enhances its reputation for accuracy when it has a clear and complete policy, preferably a written one, for correcting its errors. If, in addition, a paper keeps a careful account of its errors and corrections, it enhances its usefulness to future generations as a historical record and to its reader as a reliable source of information,' concluded Whitney.

Another American media academic, Susan Shapiro, has even argued that the fact-checking system to maintain high standards of accuracy on magazines such as *Time, Newsweek* and *Rolling Stone* could be extended to daily newspapers – with the exception of stories that are developing too rapidly. She proposed letting some magazine fact-checkers loose on a sample of print and broadcast news stories and predicted that the researchers would uncover all sorts of errors that slip through the traditional editing process, although the suggestion does not seem to have been taken any further.

As a method of improving the standards of American newspapers, news councils have had less impact than codes of ethics. A National News Council, founded on the model of Britain's Press Council in 1973, collapsed in 1986 when the financing from charitable foundations dried up. 'The apparent moral of its eleven-year existence: news councils won't work in this country,' argues Philip Meyer, although he points out that the Minnesota News Council is still going strong.

One serious flaw in the establishment of the National News Council was that, although it was supported by papers such as the *Wall Street Journal* and the *Washington Post*, it was never accepted by the *New York Times*. The paper's then publisher, Arthur Ochs Sulzberger, saw news councils as a first step towards loss of independence. Sulzberger, quoted in Patrick Brogan's *Spiked: The Short Life and Death of the National News Council*, said, 'We do not think that the real threat of a free press in the United States arises from a failing of the press to be fair and accurate.' The real threat, Sulzberger argued, came from 'people who are attempting to intimidate or use the press for their own ends'.

In the USA it would be absolutely inconceivable – not to mention illegal – for the federal government to behave as the British government did and virtually instruct its newspaper industry to set up a Press Complaints Commission or face something far worse. In the absence of national or even much local regulation, Philip Meyer suggests that newspapers should do the job themselves by carrying out an annual ethical audit. This would involve the use of market research to determine how fair a paper's readers believed it to be, an analysis of the paper's contents for objectivity, and an assessment of whether it was providing the range of articles that a 'well-informed reader would need in order to understand the changing world'.

The ethical audit would also look into the affiliations and financial interests of a newspaper's journalists. But at the heart of the process would be an accuracy audit – a procedure pioneered in the USA by Michael Charnley in 1936, when he carried out regular checks on the *Minnesota Daily* by randomly clipping twenty-five stories a day and sending them off to those named in them to check their accuracy. The study found an average error rate of 0.77 per cent, or less than one mistake a story, although the rate went as high as 1.72 per cent on some occasions. Meyer concedes that what constitutes an error can be very subjective, and that the most bitter disputes often arise over matters of interpretation, but it would be very interesting to see how well some British newspapers – broadsheet as well as tabloid – would come out of an audit.

All of these tests could, Meyer argues, be combined into an annual audit which is either printed as a supplement to the paper or made available at a newspaper's offices to anyone who is interested.

However, as Meyer admits, the ethical problems of journalism go beyond anything that can be measured by simple evaluation. 'But improvement must begin somewhere, and if it cannot begin at that fundamental and simple level, perhaps news people should face the possibility that it cannot be achieved at all,' he says.

The debate about ethics in US journalism is in fact intensifying, and it is not at all clear that what is happening can be called improvement. Commentators have started worrying about an outbreak of what Howard Kurtz of the *Washington Post* has called 'sleaze, scandal, malicious gossip and gotcha-journalism'.

The soul-searching has been caused by the press coverage of the alleged rape of a young woman at the Kennedy family property in Florida during Easter-weekend celebrations in 1991. NBC, the US network television company, revealed the young woman's identity, and the *New York Times* followed suit on the ground that the issue of the woman's privacy had been taken out of their hands by the action of the NBC. But the *New York Times*, one of the main bastions of serious journalism in the US, went much further than naming the victim without her permission: the paper revealed that the woman had had a child with a man she did not marry and 'liked to drink and have fun with the ne'er-do-wells in café society'. This led Dan Schwartz, editor of the *National Enquirer*, the down-market supermarket tabloid, to say of the *New York Times*, 'I think we took a more ethical stand than they did.'

No direct comparisons are possible between the newspaper industries of the UK and the United States: the legislative framework, the traditions and the largely city-based structure in the USA are so different. But British national newspapers could benefit from a close look at some aspects of the American press – the greater willingness to at least consider ethical issues and to worry about possible conflicts of interest, the application of modern research tools such as computers to investigative journalism and the rigorous opposition to any attempt to undermine press freedom by the state. In an ideal world, the life and vigour of Britain's tabloid press would be allied with the best American practice in matters of accuracy and fairness.

10

'A modern democracy cannot function properly without a well-informed electorate'
Constraints on the press

ONE unfortunate consequence of the excesses of some newspapers is that talk of regulation and legislation has tended to dominate the official agenda on the press. But if journalists are to carry out their role of properly informing the public on everything from transport safety and the environment to health and the quality of products we buy, what is needed in the UK is greater freedom for the press. Compared with most western democracies, Britain is an unusually secretive society and it shows few signs of improvement in this respect. Press freedom, although real enough by most international standards, remains largely a matter of convention in a country without a written constitution and with no statute guaranteeing freedom of the press in the UK.

Harold Evans, the former editor of the *Sunday Times*, has referred in the past to Britain's 'half-free press'. He was commenting mainly on the 'prior restraints' on publication that afflict the British media, such as the gagging writs issued for libel, which prevent publication of further information or the repetition of the original story by other publications, and the rules on contempt of court that can be invoked to claim that further publication creates a substantial risk that the course of justice in the dispute concerned will be seriously impaired or prejudiced. Although the effect of these has been much reduced by the ruling that strict liability for contempt now runs only from when a case is put down for trial, not from when a writ is served, such restraints would certainly not be tolerated in the USA.

The case for more freedom for the press to report on the affairs of government has been put well by barrister Anthony Lester QC, who has specialized in human-rights issues. 'I do not believe that the choice is government without newspapers or newspapers without government. A modern democracy cannot function properly without a well-informed electorate. We could enjoy substantially more freedom of information in this country without endangering effective government. Greater freedom of information means more accountability and the ability to make wiser choices.'

The single most effective way to extend press freedom in Britain would be to pass a Freedom of Information Act. Such an act would declare all official information to be in the public domain with narrowly specified exceptions which would include any information that imperils defence or national security, helps the commission of crimes, breaches commercial confidentiality or identifies individuals who have given particular policy advice.

Such rights to freedom of information were first introduced in Scandinavia, in the Swedish constitution of 1776, spread to the USA in 1966 and are now part of the legislative framework in Commonwealth countries such as Australia, New Zealand and Canada. But in Britain Margaret Thatcher always set her face against innovations in this area. Indeed, her more than eleven years in office were marked by a tightening of control over official information and by often counter-productive prosecutions of those who tried to reveal more than the government wished.

One of the most notorious cases was that of the Ministry of Defence civil servant Clive Ponting, who leaked to Labour MP Tam Dalyell details of the sinking of the Argentine cruiser *Belgrano* during the Falklands War. Although the information – that the ship had been steaming away from the British task-force when it was torpedoed with heavy loss of life – was more a political embarrassment than a serious breach of security, Ponting was prosecuted. Even though he was clearly guilty of leaking the information, in February 1985 the jury acquitted him. The jurors explicitly accepted the civil servant's claim that he had acted in the public interest to prevent Parliament being misled.

There was nothing very surprising in the prosecution of Clive Ponting. When she first became Prime Minister, in 1979, Mrs Thatcher made her attitude on freedom of information very clear. She was asked by the Labour MP Renee Short whether she intended to bring forward legislation to establish a public right of access to official information. 'No,' was Mrs Thatcher's laconic reply. Was she, then, satisfied with the current public right of access to official information? 'Yes,' said the Prime Minister.

Throughout her years in Downing Street, Mrs Thatcher's view did not change: ministers were accountable to Parliament for the work of their departments, and that included official information. Ministers and no one else must decide what information should be made formally available to the public. The irony is, of course, that it is often ministers who are the source of leaks to the press – to fly a policy kite to see how it is received or to disparage the work of their political rivals.

If there were a statutory right of access to information, Mrs Thatcher argued, then control over what information is ultimately released to the public could pass from Parliament to the courts, and it would be they, rather than effectively the government of the day, who would decide what information should be made available to the public and what should not.

Maurice Frankel, director of the Campaign for Freedom of Information, which has being trying to persuade all political parties of the wisdom of a Freedom of Information Act, concedes that such an Act would not necessarily make the lives of politicians easier. But open policy-making, where all the options are explored before a final commitment is made, would be not only feasible but helpful. 'A policy seen to emerge in this way may have greater public acceptance. And the policy itself may be sounder because unworkable proposals can be identified and jettisoned before they are adopted, and without loss of face [by politicians],' Mr Frankel argued in his book *Glasnost in Britain?*

The desire to control information is not just a Conservative trait. Earlier in 1979, Renee Short could have put the same questions she asked Mrs Thatcher to her own party's Prime Minister, James Callaghan. She would probably have received similar answers.

The 1974 Labour election manifesto had promised to reform the Official Secrets Act with a measure which put the burden on the public authorities to justify withholding information – the essence of a Freedom of Information Act. But that promise was never kept. In 1990 Tony Benn, the former Labour Energy Secretary, revealed in a volume of political memoirs – *Conflicts of Interest: Diaries 1977–80* – just how blatantly that promise was ignored. At a Cabinet meeting in June 1978, according to Benn, the Labour premier declared himself against legislation on freedom of information. Those who had the responsibility for taking decisions were entitled to have their privacy respected, Callaghan argued.

Later, in March 1979, when the Liberal MP Clement Freud's private member's Official Information Bill was before the Commons, Callaghan told his Cabinet ministers that he found the subject utterly boring. Only articulate minorities wanted such a thing – the rest didn't care. Even the following month, when Freud's bill had been killed off by the fall of the government and the impending general election and there was a chance to include a promise on freedom of information in the Labour manifesto, Callaghan said he didn't want any of this 'statutory access' stuff put in.

Times have changed. Labour, influenced by more than a decade of opposition to Thatcherism and by the desire to offer something new and appealing to the electorate, decided in 1991 to put forward a Charter of Rights for all citizens. This would include a Freedom of Information Act and, for the first time in the UK, a law guaranteeing freedom of the press. The policy has been publicly endorsed by the Labour leader, Neil Kinnock.

Opposition parties are always more enthusiastic about freedom of information than governments. However, Roy Hattersley, deputy leader of the Labour Party and the man expected to be Home Secretary if a Labour government is elected, will have some explaining to do if his promises on freedom of information are not kept. On 21 January 1991, when he was presenting the annual awards of the Campaign for Freedom of Information, Hattersley said that a Freedom of Information Act was not only suitable for early enactment but was ready for early enactment. 'If a Labour government was elected on Thursday I would be able to send the headings of a bill to parliamentary draughtsmen on the following day. When you sit down to decide your awards for 1992 or 1993 you will be able to at least consider inviting me, not to present them but – on behalf of the Labour government – to receive one.'

John Major, although initially attracted to the idea of a public right of access to official information as part of his Citizen's Charter, in the end decided against. In July 1991 Francis Maude, the Financial Secretary to the Treasury, who co-ordinated policy initiatives for the Citizens' Charter argued, like an echo of Mrs Thatcher, that freedom of information 'would undermine the traditional concepts of ministerial responsibility under the Crown and accountability to Parliament'.

Francis Maude was in effect defending the tradition of unreasonable secrecy. The case for a Freedom of Information Act in Britain is now overwhelming: a full flow of information is essential in a democracy if citizens are to make informed judgements, and will also make government more efficient through all policy options having been discussed fully before a choice is made. Such an act should be simply a matter of good government, not a party-political issue. Only access to as much information as possible – as of right – can possibly begin to curb the abuse of secrecy perpetrated by governments of every political persuasion.

One notorious example was Harold Macmillan's decision to suppress for more than a generation the full details of an accident at the Windscale atomic-energy plant (now Sellafield) in 1957. The amount of radiation released reached levels 600 times greater than that in the far more notorious accident at the Three Mile Island plant in the USA. Although the press covered the Windscale accident at the time, the full official information on its extent came to light only in January 1988, under the 30-year-rule protecting the release of government papers.

There are many more recent examples of information that is clearly in the public interest and yet is not readily available to British newspapers. Britons have sometimes had to go to the USA to use the American Freedom of Information Act in order to obtain information that the British government has refused to disclose. In a July 1991 report, the Campaign For Freedom of Information showed just how ill-informed the British electorate is compared with the American. For instance, the safety of an ICI pesticide called Captan is under review in the UK but the details are confidential. They are available at the Environmental Protection Agency's reading-room in Washington. The Campaign says data on 90 per cent of pesticides remains secret in the UK, but information on most of them is available under the USA Freedom of Information Act.

Reports on kitchen-hygiene inspections carried out on British liners docking at US ports are made freely available in the USA. In Britain they would usually remain confidential. For example, Cunard's *Queen Elizabeth 2* failed two out of four hygiene inspections in seventeen months. In December 1989, cockroaches were found in the bread-slicing room, on grill surfaces and in the Grand Lounge pantry. The problem was tackled, but the cockroaches were again found in the kitchen areas in April 1991.

Reports by American inspectors on British drugs exported to the USA are available under the Freedom of Information Act. In the UK, a Department of Health official could get sent to jail for revealing the same information.

Transport safety is another area where the government and other official bodies have notoriously attempted to restrict access to sensitive information of public concern. The Department of Transport's refusal to identify seven passenger ferries which failed to meet enhanced safety recommendations following the Zeebrugge ferry disaster is an example of this attitude. The Department claimed the information involved commercial confidentiality, but it was forced to release it officially when the vessels concerned were correctly identified by the press, in March 1989.

If the fire brigade criticizes safety standards at a London Underground station, users can find out because the Underground now makes fire-brigade inspection reports public. However, the public is much less likely to know about safety standards at a British Rail station, because BR keeps such things confidential. In January 1990, *Secrets*, the journal of the Campaign for Freedom of Information, accused British Rail of giving too little information about safety, particularly near misses, to its passenger consultative bodies – and complained that these bodies in turn kept this information confidential. No one knows how many people may have died because of the lack of full disclosure of every aspect of public safety, and in particular of the early warnings that near misses can give.

In Britain, the disclosure of important information has to proceed haphazardly, through leaks. In the early 1980s the British government was still dismissing as 'exaggerated' and 'emotive' claims that lead in petrol was permanently damaging the IQs of many children living near motorways. This response had to be revised somewhat after the leaking of a confidential letter by Sir Henry Yellowlees, the then chief medical officer of the Department of Health and Social Security, acknowledging that in reality hundreds of thousands of children were at risk. The letter had been written more than a year earlier. Yet again, the public found out about important information only throughout the hit-and-miss mechanism of leaks to newspapers.

In 1988 the government was forced to drop its opposition to a ban on furniture filled with flammable foam, partly as a result of the leaking of a critical memorandum by the Crown Suppliers, the government purchasing agency. It pointed out that there was a safer foam available, of the kind already used in furniture in ministers' offices.

By contrast with the haphazard dependence on individual leaks in the UK, journalists in the USA can work methodically to expose threats to health and safety and potential waste of money in public projects. Thanks to the US Freedom of Information Act, passed in 1966 but made more effective by amendments in 1971, hundreds of scandals have been uncovered by the press. These have included unreported accidents at nuclear sites, and X-ray machines at cancer-detection centres which were emitting twenty-five to thirty times the correct level of radiation. Within months of disclosure, all such centres in the US had reduced the amount of radiation emitted.

There have been stories about security guards at sensitive weapons plants who either had records of instability or had committed criminal offences, and reports of anaesthetic drugs routinely given during childbirth even though they could cause brain damage to babies. A Louisville newspaper obtained federal inspection reports on nursing homes which showed that residents were being abused. As a result of the publicity, new state legislation was introduced, many homes were closed down and the owners of several were charged with fraud. On larger issues, the 1968 My Lai massacre in Vietnam (when a platoon of American soldiers under the command of Lieutenant William Calley killed around 300 innocent civilians, including many women and children) was finally made public eighteen months later when a Congressman involved in compiling a confidential report applied as a private citizen for a copy of the US Army report on the massacre under the Freedom of Information Act.

The British author William Shawcross was able to use the Freedom of Information Act to get inside information on the American invasion of Cambodia for his book *Sideshow: Kissinger, Nixon and the Destruction of Cambodia*. In the book, he quoted extensively from American documents, many marked 'Top Secret', obtained under the act. In many cases the government agency involved initially refused to supply the information, but when Shawcross appealed under the act he got most of the documents he was seeking. 'The Freedom of Information Act is a tribute to the self-confidence of American society; it recognizes rights of citizens that are hardly to be conceived anywhere else in the world,' Shawcross wrote at the time.

In Australia, too, Freedom of Information legislation has produced positive results. The Australian army, for instance, was insisting on a new £266 million tank training-area in New South Wales. The project was cancelled following the disclosure of an internal analysis, obtained through the Freedom of Information Act, which argued that both the terrain and the climate were unsuitable for the purpose.

Anthony Lewis, the lawyer and *New York Times* commentator, believes the state of the law in the UK and the limited access of British journalists to information has played its part in 'the visible degradation of British journalism'. This, he believes, is not just a case of popular newspapers going from the gutter to the sewer – that is a different issue. 'Even the more serious papers, most of them, act as if their duty to freedom were fulfilled by critical comment. There are encouraging exceptions. But too many cover political life largely as transmission belts for unexamined assertions by politicians.'

Some limited progress has been made in opening some official doors in the UK. Private member's bills have succeeded in allowing individuals access to medical records and in making public a register of all the enforcement notices served by the safety and environmental agencies on matters affecting public health and safety and environmental pollution. But such morsels for press and public are no substitute for a general Freedom of Information Act. At the moment, all information is secret unless officially authorized – apart, of course, from leaks.

A real danger for the press is that, in Britain, a Freedom of Information Act, if one is ever passed, will probably come with strings attached. A formula will be devised in which such an act will be balanced by oppressive legislation against the press, through a new privacy law and/or a statutory press tribunal.

Roy Hattersley is already limbering up with his own version of this trade-off argument. Labour, he argues, gives detailed and comprehensive support to the Calcutt Report – including the hair-triggers that would lead inevitably to statutory regulation of the press. While Labour welcomes the setting up of the new Press Complaints Commission and will wait to see if self-regulation can work, the party clearly has deep reservations about it.

The attacks on Labour MP Clare Short by the *News of the World* did not help matters, even though the Commission severely censured the paper in May 1991. There is doubt in the party over whether the Commission will be able to stop other similiar attacks by newspapers on the privacy of individuals.

'As Calcutt recommends, the next Labour government will make a careful assessment of the success of the Commission and if we consider it to have failed – when measured against the strict criteria set out by Calcutt itself – we will move to the second phase and introduce a statutory complaints tribunal,' Roy Hattersley promises.

Hattersley is well aware that many serious journalists believe this would be a restriction on their freedom of expression and a further weakening of press freedom in the UK. 'They must know that to be wrong. Calcutt's proposals are designed specifically to protect the private individual from the type of sensational exposure which can never be justified on the grounds of public interest but is simply salacious and is used to sell tabloid newspapers. Such material is both irrelevant and I presume distasteful to the work of serious journalists – journalists who will be greatly assisted in writing about matters of public interest once we have a Freedom of Information Act.'

Yet the future of the press should not be determined as a result of a crude trade-off. Press regulation and better access to official information are two entirely separate ideas and should be treated as such. A Freedom of Information Act should be implemented because it will improve the workings of government and democracy and will for the first time treat British citizens as full partners in the running of their society.

The scheme for self-regulation envisaged by Calcutt should now be given a proper chance to work and not be closed down under an arbitrary timetable. The transgressions of a single rogue publisher, unless perhaps if it is one of the biggest national newspaper publishers, should not be used as an excuse to bring the entire edifice of self-regulation crashing down. Statutory tribunals headed by judges – not all of whom seem to have a very firm grasp of the principles of press freedom and who too often in the past have equated the interests of the state with the interests of a particular government – should be a court of last resort for press and public.

The record shows that the media and freedom of expression came under increasing pressure during the Thatcher years. Broadcasters came under even more scrutiny than newspapers in a number of celebrated cases of government interference.

One of the most bizarre incidents was the *Real Lives* affair, in August 1985, when Leon Brittan, the then Home Secretary, publicly appealed to the BBC governors to intervene to prevent the transmission of a programme that portrayed the lives of two extremists on opposite sides of Northern Ireland's sectarian divide. When, after several months' delay, the governors finally approved the programme for transmission, only one small cosmetic change had been made. The result was that an interesting but unexceptional programme pulled a larger audience than expected because of all the publicity.

'More serious for broadcasters, and ultimately for the reputation of the government, was the *Secret Society* affair. In February 1987 police raided the Glasgow offices of the BBC and took away all the tapes for a television series being made by investigative reporter Duncan Campbell. The series included a programme on Zircon, a planned spy satellite – a project which, it was alleged, had been improperly concealed from parliamentary scrutiny. Eventually all six *Secret Society* programmes were broadcast – although the sixth, on the Cabinet, was not shown until a 1991 Channel-4 series on banned programmes – but the incident revealed the lengths to which the British government was prepared to go to prevent anyone making programmes about just how secret a society Britain really is.

There was pressure on broadcasters again in 1988, when the Thames Television programme *This Week* made a special programme on the fatal shooting of three IRA terrorists planning a bomb attack in Gibraltar. Sir Geoffrey Howe, the then Foreign Secretary, directly contacted the Independent Broadcasting Authority and asked for the programme to be postponed until after the inquest on the terrorists. This request was rejected and the programme was transmitted, to the great anger of the government. The programme asked legitimate questions about how the three met their deaths and about new evidence brought forward for consideration at the inquest. The eventual inquest did, however, bring in a verdict of justifiable homicide by a nine-to-two majority.

Aside from the pressure applied about individual programmes, controversy was aroused by the continuing ban on direct broadcasting of words spoken by representatives of Sinn Fein and other organizations proscribed under the Prevention of Terrorism Act. The ban, which does not apply to newspapers, has led to the strange but perfectly permissible practice of banned politicians appearing on screen with their words either subtitled or spoken by an actor.

Newspapers have also experienced a series of trials and tribulations which have tended to restrict their freedom of manoeuvre. These are best exemplified by the ludicrous affair of the retired MI5 officer Peter Wright, his book *Spycatcher* and the British government's unseemly chase around half the world trying, in vain, to limit the extent of its publication.

The book raised allegations of wrong-doing by members of MI5 and, in particular, claimed that some right-wing security officers had attempted to destabilize the Labour government led by Harold Wilson during the 1970s. Most of the allegations were not new but had been discussed in previous books to which the government had not apparently taken exception. In this case it was clearly the government's aim to enforce a life-long vow of confidentiality on its security officers.

It was in Australia, where the British government attempted to obtain a permanent injunction preventing local publication, that the drama reached its high point with the immortal admission by the government's main witness in the *Spycatcher* case, Sir Robert Armstrong, then the Cabinet Secretary, that he had been 'economical with the truth' in his earlier evidence.

In the New South Wales Appeal Court in September 1987, Mr Justice Kirby was scathing about the book and, by implication, those who were trying so hard to prevent its publication. He described *Spycatcher* as 'one rather cantankerous old man's perspective of things notorious, or description of technology long out-dated, people long since dead and controversies tirelessly worked over by numberless writers'.

Though the British government failed to prevent publication of *Spycatcher* in Australia, it never faltered in its attempts to limit publication in the UK through injunctions against British newspapers. In June 1986 there had been injunctions against the *Observer* and the *Guardian*, which had published some of the allegations in the book in advance of its publication. The government later obtained an injunction which prevented the rest of the British media from reporting the book's allegations until the outcome of the original case against the *Observer* and the *Guardian*. Then, in May 1989, the *Independent*, the *Sunday Times* and the *News on Sunday* were each fined £50,000 on the grounds that, by publishing information from the book, they had intended to prejudice legal proceedings in the original case, although these fines were later set aside on appeal.

Throughout the vastly expensive four-year legal process, there were at least some judges who were far from complimentary about the wisdom of the government's actions.

Mr Justice Scott set aside the injunction against the *Guardian* and the *Observer* and rejected the government's claim that national security must always take priority over freedom of the press. He argued that the absolute protection of the security services sought by Sir Robert Armstrong 'could not be achieved this side of the Iron Curtain'. A duty of confidentiality simply could not be imposed to protect information that was useless or already in the public domain. He also acknowledged an important role for the press: 'The press has a legitimate role in disclosing scandals in government. An open democratic society requires that to be so.'

Similarly, in the Court of Appeal, Lord Justice Bingham noted that 'the court will not seek to emulate the fifteenth-century pope who issued a papal bull against Halley's comet'. And in October 1988 the Law Lords put the final seal on the government's embarrassment when they ruled that, as a result of worldwide publication, all confidentiality in the contents of *Spycatcher* had been destroyed and no further harm could be done by further publication in the UK.

Although the affair has many farcical elements, it usefully illustrates the lengths to which the British government was prepared to go in order to prevent publication in an easily available form – a newspaper – of information by then already available between hard covers all over the country.

Rodney Austin, a senior law lecturer at University College, London, argues that the sensational nature of the *Spycatcher* case and its media coverage have tended to obscure an important point – the increasing recourse by the government to private law rights, such as the law of contract and confidentiality, in order to restrict the flow of public information. For the government, this approach offers a number of advantages. Such cases can be pursued in any country recognizing similiar rights and obligations and, unlike criminal prosecutions, the test is 'balance of probabilities' rather than 'beyond reasonable doubt'. Civil cases are heard by a judge alone. They can affect those not directly involved, and injunctions can be obtained for prior restraint on publication.

The government, Rodney Austin believes, already has more than sufficent public-law powers and administrative mechanisms to prevent and punish the disclosure of official information. 'The freedom of the press in a democratic society to expose, in the public interest, the wrongdoings, inefficiency or incompetence of government and its agencies ought not to be further strengthened by permitting government to resort to the inappropriate private law of confidence,' he argues. 'If government is to be permitted, in exceptional circumstances, to exercise prior restraint over publication of sensitive official information, it should be by way of public-law mechanisms with appropriate limitations and safeguards.'

In 1989 the government strengthened its public-law mechanisms with a new Official Secrets Act. The new act, which came into effect in March 1990, was a big disappointment for those trying to extend press freedom in the UK.

The original Official Secrets Act of 1911, with its notorious Section II which made it an offence for any civil servant to make public any information obtained in the course of his official duties, had become virtually unworkable. As the government discovered in the Ponting case, juries could not be relied upon to convict civil servants who passed on unauthorized information when they did so in the public interest.

The then Home Secretary, Douglas Hurd, promised much when he brought forward the new legislation that would sweep away Section II. It amounted, he claimed, to an earthquake in Whitehall and 'a substantial and unprecedented thrust in the direction of greater openness'. But Des Wilson, co-chairman of the Campaign for Freedom of Information, saw matters quite differently: the legislation was about the more efficient protection of information, not its disclosure. This was not a measure designed to give people enough information to meet their needs as citizens and to ensure their servants are running the country properly.

Under the new act, vast amounts of official information will no longer be protected by the criminal law, although civil servants will still be subject to internal discipline for leaking. There are now five main areas of information covered by the Act – security and intelligence, defence, international relations, information supplied in confidence by other governments and law enforcement – and journalists commit an offence if they print leaks on any of these. While in some cases an offence is committed only if the information published is likely to be harmful, in others the offence is absolute and there is no test of harm.

The biggest flaw in the legislation is that there is no public-interest defence. The benefits of disclosure can never be taken into account, no matter how great the wrong-doing disclosed or how imminent the danger to the public. Without a public-interest defence, journalists could be in grave danger of conviction under the act, although by the autumn of 1991 no case had actually been brought against journalists.

Revealing information supplied to another government in confidence is deemed to be an offence because of the breach of confidence alone, whether or not the information disclosed is damaging.

Any disclosure relating to the authorized tapping of telephones, opening of mail or action by the security services under a warrant is an absolute offence, and no evidence is needed that any harm has been caused by publishing the information. And it doesn't matter that the information is trivial or has been published many times before.

To prevent any new generation of Peter Wrights penning their memoirs, a lifelong duty of confidentiality is imposed on all Crown servants, including security and intelligence officers, and any disclosure is an absolute offence – motives are considered irrelevant.

The act as it applies to journalists and to those who disclose wrong-doing in the public interest looks likely to prove every bit as controversial, and possibly as unworkable, as the old Section II it was designed to replace.

There has been growing pressure on another essential journalistic practice which receives only limited recognition in law – the need to maintain confidentiality of sources. It is impossible to exaggerate the importance for a journalist of being able to obtain information in confidence from a private source and then being allowed to protect the confidentiality of that source. For example, the identity of 'Deep Throat', who guided the reporting of the *Washington Post's* Watergate reporters Bob Woodward and Carl Bernstein, is unknown to this day. But in recent years reporters in the UK have been taken to court to persuade or force them to disclose private sources.

In January 1988 Jeremy Warner, the financial correspondent of the *Independent*, was fined £20,000 for refusing to disclose the confidential sources who had provided information for his stories on insider information and take-over bids. More recently, in 1990, it was William Goodwin, a trainee journalist on the *Engineer* magazine, who found himself in the firing-line.

He was fined £5,000 because he refused to comply with a court order requiring him to reveal a confidential source who had given him information about a company's financial affairs. The House of Lords ruled that disclosure of the source was necessary for the administration of justice, even though the company already had an injunction to stop publication of the information.

Under the Contempt of Court Act 1981, journalists have the right to protect their sources except where disclosure is necessary in the interests of justice or national security, or for the prevention of disorder or crime. 'The decision against Goodwin is regarded by many journalists as rendering this limited statutory protection effectively valueless,' says the 1991 *World Report on Information Freedom and Censorship* published by Article 19, the pressure group that campaigns against censorship.

Goodwin is at present following the by now well-beaten path to the European Court of Human Rights, where an increasing number of British cases involving individual rights are heard.

A related controversy affecting the media involves the extent to which pictures and other news material should be handed over to the police. There has been increasing use of the Police and Criminal Evidence Act 1984 to compel journalists and media organizations to hand over unpublished material for use in police investigations. It seems a simple issue – journalists are citizens too, with the same interest as everyone else in ensuring that crimes do not go unpunished. But the matter is in fact much more complex. If journalists covering riots and demonstrations are seen as an extension of the law-enforcement agencies, they not only will be in physical danger but will be unable to do their job. Society will suffer, because it will be impossible to produce an independent view of events.

This is an issue where there is a great divide between the broadsheet newspapers, which are very worried about the issue, and the tabloids, which tend to bang the law-and-order drum. The difference of approach emerged at one of the meetings of national editors when the new code of practice was being finalized at the end of 1989. 'All the quality editors adopted the same position – that we did not want to find ourselves in the position of just handing photographs over,' Max Hastings recalls. In complete contrast, the popular editors said they saw it as their duty to help the police in every way and were happy to provide all the photographs they wanted. 'It was quite comic the difference between us on what we considered an issue of principle, as did they. Kelvin MacKenzie gave us a minute or two on social responsibility on that occasion,' the *Telegraph*'s editor added ironically.

John Wilson, policy controller of the BBC, produced a special report on *The Police and Journalistic Material* for the International Press Institute. His conclusion was that law enforcement and public enlightenment were different functions. 'One is now threatened by the other. Journalists in Britain are being required too often and too readily to serve the purposes of law enforcement in a stressed and divided society,' he decided. Judges have discretion as to whether or not such material should be handed over to the police. In many cases judges have been readily and almost routinely approving police applications for unpublished photographs to be handed over. The test was supposed to be that the material would likely to be of 'substantial value' to an inquiry; instead, this was becoming 'of possible help'.

John Wilson accepts that there are occasions when police should be able to get access to journalistic material, but before this happens judges should apply a stringent series of tests. Is it essential information that cannot be obtained from other sources? Is a serious offence being investigated which is likely to lead to prosecution? And is the material to be handed over the minimum required for the purpose?

Anthony Lester QC sees this as another example of the English courts failing to apply the test of 'necessity' to any interference with free speech. Such a test would place the burden of proof on the state to justify any such interference and show that the means used were in proportion to the stated aim.

A further serious constraint upon press freedom, at least until recently, has been the enormous awards handed down by juries in libel cases. Clearly a number of newspapers went too far and published stories they were completely unable to justify in court, and there have consequently been a series of big winners in libel actions. They have included Koo Stark, the former girlfriend of Prince Andrew, who according to some estimates may have been paid nearly £1 million from a number of actions, including £300,000 against the *People*, and Jeffrey Archer, the former deputy chairman of the Conservative Party, who was awarded £500,000 against the *Star*. The perception that juries were setting out to punish newspapers for their transgressions rather than to compensate the victim for any loss of reputation involved had a chilling effect on investigative reporting. The danger was that newspapers would either back off a story in the first place or settle out of court cases they ought to have defended.

The leading libel lawyer Charles Gray QC is worried about the present state of libel law and its effects on the press. 'If a point is reached where the level of awards and settlements is so high that it is having a cumulatively inhibiting effect on the performance of its [the press's] legitimate role investigating and exposing abuses, then there is reason for concern. I believe that there is a question to be answered: are we dealing with claims for libel in a just, fair and consistent manner?'

The worst may, in fact, be over. In May 1989 *Private Eye* was successful in its appeal against the £600,000 damages awarded to Mrs Sonia Sutcliffe, wife of the convicted mass murderer Peter Sutcliffe, for its allegation that she had sold her story to the newspapers (although she accepted a £60,000 settlement before a retrial of the case could be heard). When the *Private Eye* settlement was accepted in the High Court, Lord Donaldson, the Master of the Rolls, said that in future juries should be directed to take into account the financial implications of their awards. Later Mrs Sutcliffe lost a case against the *News of the World*, which had alleged that she had had a holiday affair with a man who looked like her husband, something she vigorously denied. She faced an estimated bill for costs of around £300,000. It meant she lost virtually all the £334,000 she had won over several years in a series of actions against local and national newspapers for libel and breach of copyright.

Charles Gray believes that, on balance, it would be better to have libel actions, like other civil actions, decided by a judge rather than a jury. Although some argue that a jury is still the best means of deciding something as subjective as the damage caused by loss of reputation, a judge would be able to build up experience on what the 'tariff' for defamation should be, ending the sometimes capricious amounts awarded by juries.

Most of the pressures on the media flow from an insufficient respect for freedom of speech in English law. The UK is bound by Article 19 of the International Covenant on Civil and Political Rights, which includes the right to seek, receive and impart information of all kinds in any form and subject only to restrictions provided for by law, such as the rights and reputations of others, national security, public order and health. Article 10 of the European Convention on Human Rights limits the powers of the British government and other public authorities to interfere with free speech unless this is necessary to a democratic society. Such principles are recognized in the constitutional and legal systems of democracies as diverse as Canada and India, yet successive British governments have refused to enshrine them in national law, whether in a general statute incorporating the European Convention into domestic law or in the form of a range of individual statutes.

'The best available means of striking and maintaining a proper balance between free speech and other public interests is by making Article 10 of the Convention and Article 19 of the Covenant directly effective in our courts. That is what everyone who cares about free speech should now demand,' Anthony Lester argued, at the Bar Association Conference in 1990.

The battle to preserve self-regulation of the British press should not be conducted in a hangdog, defensive way as an isolated issue. It should be accompanied by a vigorous campaign to extend press freedoms and access to information. There is even a chance that a press encouraged and given the opportunity to expose matters of genuine importance might have less interest in and space and time to devote to the routine exposure of itself in mindless pursuit of the merely scandalous.

11

'A delinquent press diminishes, and diminishes logarithmically, freedom and democracy'
The way ahead

THREE characteristics seem to mark the behaviour of British newspapers: an almost pathological reluctance to admit errors and say sorry, a deep sensitivity to criticism and a marked distaste for thinking about the consequences of what they do.

Ironically, newspapers which feel entitled to hold every institution in society accountable and to criticize incompetence and folly in the most vigorous and often personally wounding terms have very little taste for being held accountable themselves. With a few honourable exceptions – the editorial policy at the *Financial Times* is to correct errors as a matter of routine – getting newspapers to admit they have got something wrong is like pulling teeth. It's almost as if the press has taken to heart John Wayne's dictum 'Never apologize. It's a sign of weakness.'

The techniques used to avoid having to confess to error range from ignoring complaints and prevarication, in the hope that the problem will go away, to offers to write a new story in which the essence of a correction will be deeply embedded in the text in the hope that no one will notice it.

Reporters loathe corrections because they are a very public admission of failure. Newspaper owners and editors don't care much for corrections either, because most newspapers are sold on the assumption that the stories in them have some semblance of truth, however racily the facts are presented. It would be bad for business, so the argument goes, to dent too often the myth of newspaper omniscience and invincibility, even though everyone in the industry will admit when pressed that, even with the best of intentions, mistakes are an inevitable by-product of producing a daily paper.

Almost as strong as the dislike on many newspapers of having to say sorry is the even more acute dislike of being criticized, particularly when that criticism comes from other sections of the media.

The launching in 1989 of *Hard News*, the Channel-4 programme on the press, was an opportunity to open a public debate about standards at a time when there was growing concern about the excesses of some newspapers. The intention was to give a right of reply to those who thought they had been unfairly treated by the press, and also to cast a cool eye over the activities of some of the more unscrupulous reporters and some of the wilder stories. The result was astonishing. The programme's editor, Paul Woolwich, spent much of his time fielding telephone calls from enraged newspaper editors, almost beside themselves with fury that one of their stories had been questioned. There were also abusive faxes, references to the Broadcasting Complaints Commission (the statutory body that deals with complaints against broadcasters), threats of injunctions and a libel action against the programme by the *Sunday Mirror*, which by late 1991 had still not come to court.

With a few exceptions, such as Martin Dunn, former deputy editor of the *Sun* and since 1991 editor of *Today*, editors or senior journalists hid behind their fax machines and were rarely prepared to come to the studio or to give interviews to discuss or justify their actions. Some editors even issued formal instructions forbidding reporters from cooperating even when they were prepared to justify their stories. The former editor of the *People*, Wendy Henry, told one *Hard News* researcher making an innocuous inquiry, 'I wouldn't spit on you lot if you were on fire.'

The broadsheet papers – 'the unpopulars', as *Sun* editor Kelvin MacKenzie likes to call them – are no more popular than television when they start raising issues of newspaper ethics and standards. They are usually dismissed as being sanctimonious or 'holier than though' but another line of attack, perfected by Patsy Chapman, the *News of the World's* editor, involves deflecting the criticism and turning the argument against the critics. 'There is a veritable growth industry of so-called quality newspapers regurgitating sensational stories by reporting what the tabloids did with them. "In-depth recycling" I call it,' Miss Chapman wrote in the *Independent*. 'Some TV journalists play the same game. They make their living writing about the deficiencies of the press while repeating to millions the same intrusive material.'

The *Independent on Sunday* does appear to be guilty of 'in-depth recycling' when it retells tabloid tales for the entertainment of its readers in Lynn Barber's weekly 'Base Thoughts' column, and it is certainly true that reporting with a tone of high moral outrage the 'scandalous' way the tabloids have behaved on a particular story is a vicarious way of making the sensational details available on the more sedate pages of a broadsheet. It is difficult to see, however, how a newspaper or a television programme can raise the issues involved in a questionable story without saying what the story is about. And, anyway, attacks on the 'in-depth recyclers' by editors such as Patsy Chapman do not begin to address the question of why the tabloids were running such dubious stories in the first place.

The degree of complacency and defensiveness involved is a small symptom of a much greater malaise – the lack of self-criticism in the newspaper industry, a characteristic noted by the first Royal Commission on the press as long ago as 1947. The newspaper industry is almost unique in its low level of research into the quality of its product and into the effects of the lack of sustained quality control, even though this concerns the most important factor affecting the reputation and credibility of a newspaper – its accuracy. Newsdesks, which decide which stories will be followed up, and sub-editors, who prepare text for publication and write headlines, do their best on the night to ensure that stories are accurate and articles are read carefully by senior executives and editors. The early editions of the opposition are compared. The following morning, the editor may hold a post-mortem about how a particular story was handled, but then – unless there is a serious complaint or a threatened libel action – it's on to the next day's paper.

The issue of quality and credibility will become increasingly important over the coming years as competition intensifies not just between newspapers themselves but between newspapers and radio and television. During the last decade, across a wide front, consumers became less supine, more ready to complain, more demanding in the quality of the products they buy. Just as they are now more interested in the quality of the air they breathe, the water they drink and the food they eat, so will they increasingly be interested in the quality of information that newspapers provide. In a society that overall is becoming more sophisticated, and that can certainly draw on a wider range of sources of information than ever before, there is a danger of some newspapers falling out of step with their readers if they continue with an unchanging formula of gossip, trivia and sex.

John Birt, now director-general designate of the BBC, was so convinced of the trend towards an increasingly sophisticated citizenry that in 1988 he deliberately took BBC news and current affairs up market and made sure that editors took time to provide some of the background to the great events of world news, to help viewers and listeners to understand their significance. It was a controversial policy, and not least with some of Birt's own staff, who complained that the news was becoming boring. The result was surprising, however. The audience for BBC television news did not decline, as predicted, but increased. And among the 8 to 10 million viewers such news programmes can often attract, the majority are almost certainly tabloid readers.

Throughout the 1990s, newspapers are going to face an unprecedented degree of competition from new television channels and radio stations: competition not just for advertising revenues but for something that is in even shorter supply, the finite leisure time of readers. A new national fifth television channel is due to be launched in 1994, and if, as forecast, up to 50 per cent of UK homes have access to as many as thirty channels through cable and satellite by the turn of the century, the present dominance of television as an information-provider will be further enhanced. In addition, between now and the year 2000, the Radio Authority, the new regulatory body for commercial radio, plans to launch three new national commercial radio stations and several hundred new local stations – if the market can support them. Thus, in the medium term, newspapers will have to face competition the like of which they have never seen before.

The traditional recipe of scandal, titillation, invasion of privacy, invention and enormous bingo prizes will probably continue to retain readers in the short term – to the extent that it is now possible given the tighter regulatory environment. But unless a new formula is found, and one based more on quality and credibility, much of the press will face a miserable future of declining sales and reduced influence.

In the second half of the 1980s it looked as if a new age had dawned for UK newspapers. In the space of two or three years, some of Europe's least efficient newspapers in terms of manning levels and technology became among the most modern as union barriers to the introduction of computerized typesetting were swept aside and the change was made irreversible when Rupert Murdoch moved his four national newspapers to Wapping. Between 1985 and 1990, the national newspaper industry invested more than £1,000 million in modernization. It included the installation of computerized newsrooms, new colour printing presses, new headquarters and redundancy payments to the more than 10,000 printing workers who lost their jobs. The transformation of newspapers was paid for not just by reduced costs but also by the profits made from the sale, for redevelopment, of their old headquarters in and around Fleet Street. For a time anything was possible as new titles were launched and readers were given better value in the form of colour supplements and new sections. After years of gloom, it seemed that newspapers could look forward to an era of expansion.

The euphoria did not last, and by 1990 the new mood of confidence was seeping away. Newspapers started to run into what turned out to be, at least for the broadsheets, the worst advertising recession this century and faced both declining circulations and the threat of legislation if they could not prove that the 'last chance' for self-regulation could be made to work.

Official figures from the Audit Bureau of Circulations show that between 1984 and 1990 the popular newspapers together, despite the launch of a new title, *Today*, lost 10.2 per cent of their circulation – from 13.077 million to 11.741 million. The *Daily Express*, down 21.4 per cent, and the *Star*, down 44 per cent, were the worst performers in this period. In the same period with the help of the launch of the *Independent*, the circulation of the broadsheets rose by 8.6 per cent, from 2.33 million to 2.53 million. But without the *Independent* there would have been a decline of over 9 per cent between 1984 and 1990.

During the same time, the popular Sundays lost no less than 20.8 per cent of their circulation, with the *Sunday Express* dropping 33 per cent, the *People* 20.8 per cent and the *Sunday Mirror* 16.8 per cent. The success stories in the circulation battle were the *Mail on Sunday*, which put on 18 per cent, from 1.6 million to 1.89 million, and the *News of the World*, which increased its sales by 7.4 per cent to 5.046 million. Overall, the broadsheet Sunday papers fell by only 1.5 per cent, but without the launch of the *Independent on Sunday* the decline would have been much worse. The *Observer*, for instance, lost nearly 25 per cent of its sales, dropping to 559,000.

Although many newspapers were still profitable – and some were highly profitable, like those in the *Daily Telegraph* group, making around £40 million a year in 1991 – for the six months from January to June 1991 newspaper circulations showed further significant falls compared with the same period in 1990. The *Sun* and the *Daily Mirror* were both down by 6 per cent, to 3.69 million and 2.95 million respectively. *Today* lost 16 per cent of its circulation – down from 581,240 to 490,049. At the popular end of the market, the only paper to increase circulation was the *Daily Mail*, which increased sales by 3 per cent to 1.7 million, although the *Daily Express* held on to its 1.56 million sales. In the first half of 1991 there was little to cheer about in the daily broadsheet market either. The *Guardian* and the *Financial Times* held their own, and the *Daily Telegraph* was only marginally down. But *The Times* lost 6 per cent to 406,123, and the *Independent* fell by 5 per cent to 394,438.

On Sunday, only the *Observer* – up by 2 per cent to 579,045 – and the *Mail on Sunday* – marginally up at 1.94 million – increased circulation. The biggest losers were the *Sunday Sport*, down 18 per cent to 394,439, and the *People*, down 10 per cent to 2.33 million, although the decline of the *Sunday Express* continued, down 6 per cent to 1.62 million, and the *News of the World* was down 5 per cent to 4.8 million.

It is difficult to discern any unambiguous patterns in such figures other than to say that, with very few exceptions, the national newspaper industry is doing badly and there is real cause for concern. There is clearly no simple single cause for the serious decline in sales, although recession is almost certainly an important cause of the accelerating circulation losses of 1990–1 as families either cancelled their daily paper or took one instead of two.

The figures do not prove that the decline in tabloid sales has been caused by a revulsion against tabloid sleaze. They likewise do not prove the reverse, as some have argued – that the lack of sleaze and intrusion is to blame for falling sales as editors have become more cautious following the publication of the Calcutt Report and the setting up of the Press Complaints Commission. The decline in tabloid circulations preceded all of that and continued throughout the period when some editors, such as David Montgomery, concede that some tabloid editors went too far.

Large social changes are obviously involved. Apart from growing competition from television, newspapers are having to compete with a wider range of leisure activities, particularly at the weekend. And there is, in the end, no inevitability about the British retaining the habit of high newspaper readership. According to *World Press Trends*, produced by the International Federation of Newspaper Publishers, the UK was sixth in the world league-table of daily newspaper sales in 1990, with 393 copies sold for each 1,000 inhabitants, but a long way behind the Norwegians, with 615, and the Japanese, with 591. (The figure for the USA was 253.)

But there is some evidence that producing higher-quality newspapers is good business. The sharpest decline in circulation has, after all, been at the sleaziest end of the market – the *Sunday Sport*. In contrast, the broadsheet newspapers have, overall, been holding on to their circulations better, despite the effects of recession.

Eventually, shoddy products don't survive in the market-place. Whether it is the performance of car manufacturers or of Marks & Spencer, the public tends to seek out quality. It is therefore in the long-term interests of all newspapers, whatever the sector of the market they are addressing, to improve their standards of accuracy, decency and knowledge, and for the tabloids, in particular, to intrude less into private lives. This does not mean that tabloids should become simply broadsheets with smaller-size pages and start carrying ponderous articles about the ERM or the United Nations. They should be fun and entertaining and, as Andrew Knight put it, 'naughty, but not nasty'. They should simply do their job better and with more thought for the consequences of what they write, realizing as Harry Procter admitted more than forty years ago, what a terrible weapon of publicity they have at their command.

The Calcutt Committee quickly realized it is impossible to prove in any objective way whether or not press standards have declined over the years. Viewed against the background of nearly 400 years of press history there has been no decline – indeed, there has been a considerable improvement, with the end of corruption and total mendacity. But that is not the point – there used to be public executions, burning of witches and general tolerance of cruel sports such as bear-baiting too. The test is how fair and how accurate newspapers are in relation to social standards now and in the future.

Many veteran journalists believe that, at least on some papers, the record shows that in recent years there has been less respect for accuracy and less restraint in prying into people's private lives than in the recent past. There is certainly no doubt that the British press is not serving the citizens of a mature democracy as well as it could or should. Instead of any attempt to explain the serious issues and uncertainties facing society – everything from pollution and threats to the environment to the way in which scarce resources should be allocated between conflicting demands for health, education and social services – Britain's newspaper readers are too often served up a diet of trivia, often spiced with political bias.

It may be superficially amusing for the *Sun* to offer its more than 11 million readers routine prejudice of the 'Up Yours Delors' and 'Hop Off You Frogs' variety. But is it wise of the paper to stir up such ancient prejudices and encourage a know-nothing isolationism? The livelihoods of many of the paper's readers will in the end greatly depend on how well the UK copes competitively in a Europe that is increasingly economically interdependent and how Britons manage to cooperate with all those 'Frogs' and 'Krauts' – not to mention 'Nips'. Of course such tabloid campaigns involve great flair and skill, and they can strike a genuine chord in the consciousness of the nation, but the serious questions have to be asked. Is it ultimately wise for the national debate about the future – whether it involves European integration or what to do about AIDS – to be conducted in the language of saloon-bar philosophers – language that can often stray into the realms of racism and homophobia?

You don't have to be an obsessive reader of Britain's national newspapers to come across regular examples of articles based on personal malevolence, the almost daily elevation of supposition and rumour into fact, and the royal family reduced to the role of minor players in a never-ending soap opera.

There is, of course, nothing new about hand-wringing over journalistic standards and excesses or about doubt whether anything can ever be done about it. Before the most recent expressions of concern about press standards, Henry Porter, a journalist who has written for the *Sunday Times*, the *Independent on Sunday* and the *Daily Telegraph*, looked at the 1983 vintage of newspaper fantasies and outrageous errors. In *Lies, Damned Lies and Some Exclusives* he saw only one possible chance for improvement – and that at best a slim one.

> Ultimately we must hope for some benign intervention from the proprietors, who are still the strongest influence on the national press. Cynics will suggest this is a vain hope; in the past they have displayed a greater concern for the commercial viability of their products than their integrity. However, they may be able to recognize something which their editors have conspicuously failed to do; that unless newspapers improve their standards they will at some time indubitably become the subject of legislation which will permanently injure the freedom of the press.

The point was right then and it is right now. A small number of men have the power to improve the standards of the press almost overnight if they chose to do so. They include Conrad Black, Rupert Murdoch, Lord Rothermere and Lord Stevens, who, together with Mirror Group Newspapers, control 90 per cent of the British national press and close to 100 per cent of the problem.

In most cases the freedom of editors to edit is largely a myth: they have as much freedom as their proprietors are prepared to allow them, and editors who turn out not to be in general harmony with their proprietor's view of the world tend not to last long. In turn, journalists on a paper have little choice but to follow the lead given by editors on what standards of accuracy are expected, how far stories should be pushed and what degree of 'corner-cutting' will be tolerated.

Since Henry Porter issued his warning in 1984, both the challenge and the threat have become more pressing, because of the grand scale of some of the excesses and the prospect of legislation that lies just beyond David Mellor's Last Chance Saloon. But surely there have already been too many last chances with little result? Why not bring in legislation to give a right of reply to correct factual errors, as proposed by Tony Worthington, or a Privacy Bill with a less compromised name behind it than John Browne's? Opposition to such self-evidently sensible measures on the grounds that they would pose fundamental threats to press freedom seems like self-serving humbug.

There has, after all, been a legal right of reply in France since 1881. If a French newspaper writes anything about you, even by implication, that you disagree with, you can write to the publication to ask for it to be corrected or at least to put your point of view. An aggrieved person can demand up to 200 lines in reply, and that reply has to be printed, as long as it is not libellous or an incitement to racial hatred. If the statement is not printed within three days of receipt by the editor, there are tribunals which can require it to be published and impose fines. If you want an apology and damages, you go to the Cours Correctionel.

In France there is also strong protection for what is called the intimate parts of privacy – which can cover everything from unauthorized disclosure of sexual details to earnings and even political affiliation. In one case, a photographer from *Le Matin* took a picture of the actress Isabel Adjani clearly showing she was pregnant. She sued and the photographer was fined, even though the photograph had been taken in a restaurant. The court ruled that pregnancy, like religious or political belief, was part of the personality and that privacy could not be violated without consent. It also ruled that the actress was entitled to conduct business, or even private conversations, in a public place like a restaurant without having her privacy violated.

In Germany there has since 1874 been a right of reply to correct factually incorrect information published about an individual, and the civil courts recognize violation of a 'right of human personality' when a newspaper publishes previous convictions of an ex-offender when there is no public interest involved.

As the French and German examples show, such legislation is not incompatible with living in a democracy and might yet be necessary in the UK. But there are strong – mainly practical – arguments against both rights of reply and rights to privacy.

Nothing would seem more obvious or fair than to give the aggrieved a statutory right of reply in our newspapers, but the reality could be very different – newspapers clogged up by statute with the outpourings of cranks, eccentrics or merely those obsessed with a particular cause or interest. To take an extreme example, if a newspaper said that the world was round, would the Flat Earth Society have an automatic right of reply? It sometimes happens in France that there is exercised a right of reply to the right of reply, and a reply to that, and so on until one party to the dispute gets too bored to continue. Even if such legislation were limited to factual matters directly affecting an individual, it would not always be easy to decide what actually were the facts in each case. And what if the complaint involved even more subjective matters, such as omission, distortion, or bias?

The case for a right of privacy – the right to be let alone – looks stronger than that for a statutory right of reply, because the need is greater. There can be few more devastating experiences for anyone, unknown or famous, than having their most intimate personal experiences turned into public property over millions of breakfast tables. The problems here arise in trying to define privacy and in deciding which aspects of it should be protected. Any legal definition would have to cope with exceptions to the law where privacy could be breached by a newspaper acting in the public interest. Legislation, however carefully drafted, would be an inflexible tool to deal with the problem, and the involvement of lawyers would probably lead to both delay and expense, as happens routinely in libel cases.

A system of self-regulation, if it can be made to work, is a much more flexible and less expensive way of dealing with disputes between readers and newspapers. But, as the industry involved pays for the regulatory body and provides some of the regulators, there is a danger of cosy relationships developing between the regulated and the regulators, so making radical reform less likely. Despite such a theoretical disadvantage, however, the members of the Press Complaints Commission, with their wide range of experience, are more suitable than a single judge for taking highly subjective decisions on, for example, when intrusion by a newspaper is justified in the public interest.

The early indications in 1991, particularly after the Clare Short ruling, were that the Press Complaints Commission, and with it the last chance for self-regulation in the UK, was not yet a lost cause. Certainly its chairman, Lord McGregor, is a man of independent mind who is determined to make the Commission work, if given half a chance. 'If I owned a tabloid like the *Sun* and if it were true that tabloid circulations depend on a degree of scurrility then the last thing I would want would be a body like this,' he argues. In short, voluntarily accepting self-restraint, albeit because of fear of something worse from legislation, could actually cost papers like the *Sun* money, at least in the short term.

The Commission's first steps in trying to avoid legislation included rapidly endorsing the code of practice drawn up by the industry itself, so that there is now at least a minimum benchmark against which journalists' behaviour can be measured.

Such codes tend to be denounced as public-relations exercises – a criticism apparently supported by the content of this one, which often reads like a cub-scout oath: 'Newspapers should take care not to publish inaccurate, misleading or distorted material.' Others see them as a more sinister phenomenon and believe that, by volunteering adherence to a plethora of codes and self-regulatory bodies, newspapers are in fact gradually sacrificing press freedom by the back door.

The famous American journalist H. L. Mencken was not a great fan of codes of ethics for newspapers. Even if they were signed in blood, he believed, they became 'as much a dead letter the day afterwards as the Seventh Commandment [forbidding adultery] or the Eighteenth Amendment [which brought in Prohibition]'. If the day ever came that newspapers started honouring codes of ethics, Mencken said, he would be prepared 'to hear that the governors of the New York Stock Exchange have passed a resolution requiring stockbrokers to observe the Beatitudes'.

In fact, however modest the immediate effect, codes of practice do have a useful function for everyone from double-glazing salesmen to journalists: they provide a public statement of minimum requirements against which behaviour can be judged.

There never has been a lack of codes, merely an unwillingness or lack of ability to enforce them.

The National Union of Journalists, the trade union representing most British journalists, has long had a code of professional conduct. Its provisions include requiring journalists to strive to ensure that the information they disseminate is fair and accurate and does not pass off conjecture as fact, and to rectify harmful inaccuracies promptly. There is also a requirement that a journalist shall 'only mention a person's race, colour, creed, illegitimacy, marital status or the lack of it, gender or sexual orientation if this information is strictly relevant'.

Attempts to implement the NUJ code have not been very successful, although the union has the power to fine or suspend members for serious breaches. In practice, most attempts to impose discipline have involved the anti-discrimination clause of the code, and members who have been fined have simply left the union rather than pay. 'It's not been a happy experience. Journalists say they want a union to represent them, not to tell them how to do their jobs,' says Alan Pike, a member of the NUJ executive.

The lack of an agreed code until it was too late can, in retrospect, be seen as one of the reasons why the Press Council failed. The future of the new system of self-regulation under the Press Complaints Commission now depends to a considerable extent on whether newspapers respect the code they have agreed to. Any backsliding by the press will make it almost inevitable that the government will move on to the next stage of the Calcutt regime – a statutory Commission, possibly backed by legislation on privacy or the right of reply – and Lord McGregor has asked the government to keep up the political pressure and retain this threat, to keep the newspapers in order. He is acutely aware that he cannot keep crying wolf. A formal statement from the Commission that self-regulation is not working would almost certainly lead to the body being replaced by one with more powers.

Yet press standards involve a much broader range of issues than what sort of body deals with complaints from the public, particularly if newspapers are ever, in the words of Andreas Whittam Smith, going to have the sort of relationship with their readers that Marks & Spencer has with its customers. The possible package of 'solutions' would include a wider role for ombudsmen, more generous use of corrections, better training of journalists, reform of libel law and the continued rigorous monitoring of newspaper standards by television.

The appointment of ombudsmen on virtually all of Britain's national newspapers is an important step forward in relations between readers and newspapers. The men appointed are a strange mixture of former senior journalists – at *The Times* the ombudsman is John Grant, formerly managing editor, now the crossword editor – and external figures such as academics and politicians. Whatever their previous experience, the ombudsmen are able to offer one obvious advantage: an agreed place for the reader to go in order to lodge a complaint. In the past, complainants have often been shuffled around the paper. One of the first things that Sir Gordon Downey, the readers' representative at the *Independent*, did was to set up a more orderly system for the sending and processing of reader's complaints, which run at around 1,000 a year.

Sir Gordon, a former Comptroller and Auditor General, produces a quarterly report which is published in the paper. One of the issues he has looked into was the *Independent's* news coverage of the 1990 leadership battle in the Conservative party that swept Margaret Thatcher from power. Had articles been distorted to justify the paper's editorial position? Sir Gordon concluded that there was no evidence to justify such allegations. 'I had only one reservation to this conclusion relating to a report headed "Thatcher to be back-seat driver." On this I was satisfied that the quote was an accurate one, but I thought its significance was overstated. However I saw this as a misjudgment of tone not a manipulation of news,' Sir Gordon told *Independent* readers.

Vyvyan Harmsworth is a cousin of Lord Rothermere. He is also the ombudsman at the *Evening Standard*. He looked into, and rejected, a complaint that a feature in the paper on the victims of the Marchioness pleasure-boat disaster on the Thames had implied they were all well-off young yuppies and that this had hindered fund-raising. But he found in favour of Lord Sainsbury when the latter complained about an article suggesting that the top six supermarket chains in Britain were operating a cartel to prevent Continental European rivals entering the market. 'On investigation the article was found not to be researched carefully or indeed very much at all,' said the *Standard's* ombudsman.

Ombudsmen give the disgruntled reader a potentially powerful voice inside a paper and can sensibly be a first filter for complaints, so that only disputes that cannot be satisfactorily resolved go to the Press Complaints Commission. Their role, particularly if they are external appointments rather than existing or past employees of the paper concerned, could develop into an important part of the self-regulation process.

This did not happen at Mirror Group Newspapers. In April 1991 Robert Maxwell decided to dispense with the services of his ombudsman, Peter Archer, the Solicitor-General in the last Labour government, well before the end of his two-year contract. The reason given was that complaints could be left to the PCC. The timing was unfortunate. Archer's job disappeared before he was able to complete his adjudication on a complaint about a series of articles run by the *Daily Mirror* on Arthur Scargill, the president of the National Union of Mineworkers, and Libyan and Russian funds. 'I don't think I was going to come out with any damning indictment of the *Mirror*, but they did get one or two things wrong,' Peter Archer said.

Without going quite as far as the full ethical audit suggested by American academics, the ombudsmen might be able to carry out some modest research to see how accurate and fair coverage of a particular issue had been, whether there had been complaints or not. The role of the ombudsmen could, in fact, usefully be extended along *Washington Post* lines: he would not only investigate complaints but also review the performance of the paper in a regular column. The long-term reputation of the press might also be improved if there were a routine daily box in all papers for 'corrections and elaborations' – something that is relatively common in the USA. If something is wrong, as long as the error is not ridiculously trivial, why not correct it in the corrections box? Serious matters of ethics or potential libel could still be dealt with elsewhere, but it would be a simple way of reducing tension between newspapers and those who deal with them, and also take some of the drama out of printing corrections. A full corrections box every day might also turn out to be an incentive to do something to improve accuracy.

But, if standards are to be raised, much more attention has got to be given to the education and training of journalists.

There was for a long time a tradition in British newspapers of young trainees making the tea for their betters and gradually absorbing not just how to cover news stories but also the news values of the organization. That has to a considerable extent changed. Journalism is increasingly a graduate occupation in the developed world. There are postgraduate courses in journalism at both the City University, London, and at the University of Wales at Cardiff, as well as at a number of polytechnics, and around 700 every year take courses organized by the National Council for the Training of Journalists.

But, in a study for the European Commission, Professor Hugh Stevenson, professor of journalism at the City University, found that the British media are less committed to training and education than their equivalents in most other EC countries. 'In other countries crime reporters go on seminar courses in penology, financial journalists to courses on accounting, environment correspondents to scientific discussions about the ozone layer – usually as additional paid leave,' says Professor Stevenson (who was once appointed economics correspondent of *The Times*, even though he had never read economics).

While general reporters will not die out, there will be a growing need for specialists with the professional knowledge to deal with the most complex and technical subjects on the same level as those they interview and then turn them into readable stories for their papers. 'Environmental correspondents who understand what they are talking about are few and far between. How many on national or regional newspapers have the capacity to reach an independent judgement as to what Greenpeace is saying and what British

Nuclear Fuels is saying at Sellafield? They are just arbitrating between PR operations,' Professor Stevenson argues.

Despite this, Lord Rothermere, for one, is not about to change his recruitment policy and start employing a host of journalists with physics doctorates. 'Certainly you can't say there is any benefit in having uneducated journalists, but one of the dangers of highly educated journalists is that they can get out of touch with ordinary people,' he believes.

Clearly, journalists who have learned their trade from office boy up – and even editors of *The Times* did it that way – often have more of a feel for the grass roots than the more formally educated, but those who have, or acquire, specialized knowledge are now becoming more common.

A foreign-correspondent about to be sent abroad may be sent on a crash language course, but other specialists are expected to read the cuttings quickly and hit the ground writing. Why, apart from the cost, are newspapers so unwilling to invest in their staff? Why don't more newspapers send journalists about to tackle a new assignment on a quick course to learn something about the background of the subject on which they will soon be pontificating? There is an obvious need for continuing training for journalists throughout their career, to augment the skills learned in initial training courses which understandably concentrate on techniques of reporting and writing articles and on basic subjects such as law, government and shorthand.

One hopeful sign of a step in the right direction came in autumn 1991 when Southern Newspapers, the regional newspaper publishers based in Southampton, announced the creation of a postgraduate diploma course in journalism which can lead to a three-year Master of Arts degree in journalism. The part-time course, which means that journalists can remain at their posts, has been developed jointly with Bournemouth Polytechnic and is believed to be the first of its kind in the country. *Southampton Echo* editor Pat Fleming emphasized that the course would include fundamental principles of journalism, such as truth and objectivity. 'Accuracy is imperative, and journalists have to understand their credibility is critical in a world where there is a threat of legislation,' he argued.

In the past, newspaper ethics do not seem to have had a high priority in the training of journalists, although on City University courses lecturers do confront issues ranging from payola and freebies to bias, unnecessary racial identification and the need for sensitivity when dealing with people in the news, particularly when that news is tragic. Better training is not a panacea for the problems of credibility that newspapers face, but it is an integral part of any campaign to raise standards of honesty, knowledge and accuracy.

One form of legal intervention that could ultimately help both press and public would be early changes to the libel law. At the moment only the rich can protect their reputation at law, and the process is both risky and costly for both newspapers and litigants. In many cases in recent years, newspapers have backed down in cases where they thought they were right because they could not take the risk and the accompanying expense of losing.

There is an urgent need for the creation of the libel equivalent of a small-claims court, along the lines suggested by the High Court judge Mr Justice Hoffmann. A county-court judge would be able to hear defamation cases, but there would be a limit to the amount of damages that could be awarded – say £5,000 – and the decision would be binding on both sides. Those alleging more serious libels could still go to the High Court, if they had the money and the determination, but for the average citizen there has to be a cheaper way of protecting reputation, and for newspapers a more sensible and cheaper way of finding out they were wrong, than in the past.

Television has a valuable role to play in monitoring the standards of the press, through a programme like *Hard News* or its successors turning a spotlight on questionable behaviour or obvious transgressions.

The idea that television should monitor press standards received powerful backing from Harold Evans in a speech denouncing the standards of some newspapers at the Freedom of Information awards in April 1989. He told his audience, 'Every time the freedom you have is deployed in political distortion, intrusion, competitive malice, innuendo, exploitation of grief and sheer invention you erode the public trust.' The former *Sunday Times* editor went on, 'A delinquent press diminishes, and diminishes logarithmically, freedom and democracy.' Television, he suggested, should regularly monitor the performance of the press and 'hold it to standards of integrity that advance the cause of liberty'.

Apart from the formal influence of the adjudications of the Press Complaints Commission, how are any of these changes going to take place?

Real progress can be made by individual proprietors, through their editors, giving a lead in the newspapers they control. The internal culture and methods of working in newspapers such as the *Daily Star* and the *Financial Times* are so different that each must seek salvation in its own way. But, in each newspaper house, senior management should set aside some time away from the hurly-burly of deadlines and consider how the accuracy and fairness of each individual title can be improved without destroying its self-image or its reason for existence.

But that would only be a modest first step. Much more importantly, the newspaper industry as a whole has got to find a forum where issues of ethics, press freedom, standards and the serious competitive threats from other media can be tackled.

Journalism is not and never should be a profession. There is no central body of agreed factual knowledge to be examined on, and freedom of speech dictates that people should not be totally excluded from expressing themselves in print to a wider audience just because they are not members of a particular professional body or trade union. Journalism is not medicine, and there cannot be the journalistic equivalent of the British Medical Association's removing the right to practise; nor can it have an equivalent to the Church of England's power to unfrock clergy who have transgressed. Journalism does, however, throw up many of the ethical issues of a profession without possessing any mechanism for discussing them in an ordered way.

The debate on issues of press freedom, free access to courts and the ability to print what is said there, and freedom of information is even more fragmented than that on press standards. The abolition of the Press Council has made matters considerably worse. However ineffectually it tackled the role, the Press Council had a responsibility to defend press freedom as well as to rule on complaints. The Press Complaints Commission has no such dual role: it is concerned only with complaints against the press.

There are many self-interest groups representing sections of the press or those employed within the industry. The national proprietors are represented by the Newspaper Publishers Association, and the regional owners by the Newspaper Society. Then there are the Guild of Newspaper Editors, the NUJ (increasingly riven by factions and weakened by the push towards individual contracts and the ending of collective bargaining) and the much smaller Institute of Journalists. There are also organizations such as the British section of the Geneva-based International Press Institute, which does monitor and speak out about press freedom – usually its erosion – around the world. But there is no one place in the UK where a coherent view can emerge on the most important issues of the future of the press and its freedoms.

There is an urgent need for the creation of a new campaigning organization bringing together newspaper proprietors and all journalists – editors as well as reporters; national, regional and local to encourage higher standards and to push for greater freedom of information and freedom of the press. Perhaps the new body might be called the Council of the Press, reviving an echo of that first self-regulatory body imposed on an unwilling press after the 1947–9 Royal Commission. This Council would not, of course, have anything to do with complaints: it would have everything to do with fighting for high standards throughout the newspaper industry, arguing the case for newspapers as a uniquely practical and useful medium to both readers and advertisers, and being in the vanguard not only of defending freedom of expression but of extending it.

Because of the enormous egos, intense competition and petty rivalries in newspapers, establishing such an organization will not be easy. But the national newspaper editors have shown once, when they all met for the first time in living memory to draw up their own code, that when the threat is large enough they can see where self-interest lies.

Newspapers are very much at the crossroads. A historic leap forward has been made in terms of modernization, cost-cutting and even profitability. A second, less dramatic but equally important, newspaper revolution is needed – a revolution in quality, accuracy, fairness, responsibility and sophistication. Can the industry really look the future and powerful electronic competitors in the eye when, as Gallup found in 1991, confidence in the press in Britain during the 1980s fell from 29 per cent to 14 per cent, at the same time as confidence in the press in Continental Europe rose on average from 32 to 35 per cent?

In the end, talking about and encouraging high standards and ethics in newspapers – tabloids as well as broadsheets – is not some sort of self-indulgence for amateur moral philosophers or journalists with sensitive psyches: it is a very practical matter, involving customer relations, product improvement and profit. It is a debate that has scarcely begun in the UK. Unless such issues are taken more seriously, future generations could be reading about many of today's newspapers in the history books, rather than actually reading the papers themselves.

Select Bibliography

J. Herbert Altschull, *From Milton to McLuhan* (Longman, 1990)

Linton Andrews and H. A. Taylor, *Lords and Labourers of the Press* (Southern Illinois University Press, 1970)

Tom Baistow, *Fourth Rate Estate* (Comedia Publishing, 1985)

Susie Barson and Andrew Saint, *A Farewell to Fleet Street* (English Heritage, 1988)

Jeremy Black, *The English Press in the Eighteenth Century* (Croom Helm, 1987)

Richard Boston, ed., *The Press We Deserve* (Routledge and Kegan Paul, 1970)

Thomas Boyle, *Black Swine in the Sewers of Hampstead* (Hodder and Stoughton, 1989)

Piers Brendon, *The Life and Death of the Press Barons* (Secker and Warburg, 1982)

E. J. Burford, *Wits, Wenchers and Wantons* (Robert Hale, 1986)

Bus Found Buried at South Pole: The Best of the Sunday Sport (Sphere Books, 1989)

Caroline Chapman, *Russell of the Times* (Bell and Hyman, 1984)

Peter Chippindale and Chris Horris, *Stick It Up Your Punter* (Heinemann, 1990)

Tom Clark, *My Northfield Diary* (Gollancz, 1931)

Wensley Clarkson, *Dog Eat Dog: Confessions of a Tabloid Journalist* (Fourth Estate, 1990)

G. A. Cranfield, *The Press and Society* (Longman, 1978)

Hugh Cudlipp, *Publish and Be Damned* (Andrew Dakers, 1953)

James Curran and Jean Seaton, *Power without Responsibility* (Routledge, 1981)

Everette Dennis, *Reshaping the Media: Mass Communication in an Information Age* (Sage Publications, 1989)

Alfred Draper, *Scoops and Swindles: Memoirs of a Fleet Street Journalist* (Buchan and Enright, 1988)

Maurice Edelman, *The Mirror: A Political History* (Hamilton, 1966)

Robert Edwards, *Goodbye Fleet Street* (Jonathan Cape, 1988)

T. H. S. Escott, *Masters of English Journalism* (T. Fisher Unwin, 1911)

Harold Evans, *Good Times, Bad Times* (Weidenfeld and Nicolson, 1983)

Frank Giles, *Sundry Times* (John Murray, 1986)

Tony Gray, *Fleet Street Remembered* (Heinemann, 1990)

Duff Hart-Davis, *The House the Berrys Built* (Hodder and Stoughton, 1990)

Select Bibliography

Alastair Hetherington, *Guardian Years* (Chatto and Windus, 1981)

History of the Times (3 vols.; 1939, 1947)

Derek Hudson, *Thomas Barnes of the Times* (Cambridge University Press, 1943)

Information, Freedom and Censorship: World Report 1991, Article 19 (Library Association Publishing, 1991)

Derek Jameson, *Last of the Hot Metal Men* (Ebury Press, 1990)

Dimity Kingsford-Smith and Dawn Oliver, eds., *Economical with the Truth: The Law and the Media in a Democratic Society* (ESC Publishers, 1990)

Stephen Koss, *The Rise and Fall of the Political Press in Britain* (Hamish Hamilton, 1981 and 1984)

David Kynaston, *The Financial Times: A Centenary History* (Viking, 1988)

Larry Lamb, *Sunrise* (Macmillan, 1989)

Brian MacArthur, *Eddy Shah: 'Today' and the Newspaper Revolution* (David and Charles, 1988)

James Margach, *The Abuse of Power* (W. H. Allen, 1978)

Kingsley Martin, *The Crown and the Establishment* (Hutchinson, 1962)

Philip Meyer, *Ethical Journalism* (Longman, 1987)

Philip Pinkus, *Grub Street Stripped Bare* (Archon Books, 1968)

Henry Porter, *Lies, Damned Lies and Some Exclusives* (Chatto and Windus, 1984)

Harry Procter, *Street of Disillusion* (Allan Wingate, 1958)

Geoffrey Robertson, *People against the Press* (Quartet Books, 1983)

Anthony Smith, *The Newspaper: An International History* (Thames and Hudson, 1979)

H. A. Taylor, *The British Press* (Arthur Barker, 1961)

S. J. Taylor, *Shock! Horror! The Tabloids in Action* (Bantam Press, 1991)

Francis Williams, *Dangerous Estate* (Longman, 1957)

Index